THE COMPLETE
CARP ANGLER

THE COMPLETE
CARP ANGLER

ANDY LITTLE

The Crowood Press

First published in 1992 by
The Crowood Press Ltd
Ramsbury, Marlborough
Wiltshire, SN8 2HR

British Library Cataloguing in Publication Data

A catalogue record for this book is available from the
British Library.

ISBN 1 85223 690 6

Edited and designed by:
D & N Publishing
DTP & Editorial Services
The Old Surgery
Lambourn
Berkshire RG16 7NR

All photographs by the author.
Line drawings by Keith Linsell.

Cover photograph: the author happy with a good catch.

Phototypeset by FIDO Imagesetting, Witney, Oxon.

Printed in Great Britain at The Bath Press.

CONTENTS

1 HISTORY AND DISTRIBUTION

The carp (*Cyprinus carpio*) is undoubtedly the cult fish of present-day angling. And why not? It is the largest, best-looking, most intelligent and hardest-fighting of all our popular coarse fish. Just the sheer size of a carp sparks wonder in most people's eyes, for even a ten-pounder is huge in comparison with other species. And when you consider that the current record held by Chris Yates is a fantastic 51lb mirror carp caught from Redmire Pool, a ten-pounder might be classed as something of a mediocre fish.

ORIGINS

The carp was introduced into this country some five hundred years or so ago as a source of food for the monks on their meatless days. These fish looked completely different from the king carp of the present day. The original stock of fish, whose direct descendants still survive as 'wildies', rarely grew to double figures, were quite long and lean and were fully scaled, like today's common carp. Over the years, intensive selective breeding has produced strains of varying scale patterns and a much faster growth rate. The common carp has regular scales covering its entire body. They run in long lines from behind the gill cover to the root of the tail. The body is much rounder in shape and more solid-looking than that of the original wildie. The largest common known at the moment is a fabulous 45lb 12oz monster caught from the Snake Pit by Damian Clarke. It is one of the best-looking large carp in this country.

The leather, or nude, carp has no scales whatsoever. Genuine leathers are fairly rare. One of the largest around is a fish known as 'Heather The Leather' which was captured from the Yateley Car Park Lake in June 1985 at 41lb 8oz by Robin Dix.

Mirror carp have scales of various shapes haphazardly scattered all over the body. They are probably the most frequently caught variety of the king carp and are among the largest that exist in our waters today. Two of the best are a fish known as Basil, which resides in Yateley's North Lake, caught recently by Don Orriss at 46lb 1oz, and a newcomer to the big-fish list captured for the first time ever in its life at 45lb 6oz by Pete Springate at Wraysbury Number One Pit, where he has specialised in tracking down the carp over the last decade.

Within the mirror carp variety there are one or two special scale patterns. The linear carp has two perfect rows of scales on each side of its body, one running along the back just below the dorsal fin and the other running the entire length of the lateral line.

The fully scaled mirror is another rare scale pattern of the king carp and perfect specimens are a prize catch. As the name implies, the fully scaled mirror has scales covering its entire body, but they are not so uniform in size and shape as in the common carp. Occasional specimens of more than 30lb are to be found in the United Kingdom.

INDIVIDUAL FISH

Of course, the lovely thing about carp is that they are all so easily identifiable, with no two carp being the same. Even common carp with their rows of scales all over their bodies have the odd irregularity which always makes individual identification possible.

A stunning example of a small common carp. The captor is the author's son, Mark Little.
Hopefully it won't be too many years before this fish goes on to be 20 lbs plus.

This easy identification allows us to study and follow the life and history of individual specimens throughout their years, looking at growth rate and condition, as well as the number of captures compared with pressure and angling trends. Many of the regularly caught large fish in this country are now more than 30 years old. Just how long they will survive under angling pressure is difficult to assess.

When I first started carp fishing over thirty years ago a lot less was known about carp and their habits. So much has changed in the last three decades. All those years ago there were very few carp anglers; in fact, it was rare to bump into another fisherman who was specialising in a species. Waters that contained carp also seemed to be few and far between. Today this specialist branch of angling boasts over fifty thousand regular carp anglers, making it the largest single-species participant branch of angling.

DISTRIBUTION

One of the reasons for this dramatic increase in a relatively short space of time is that the carp is now so well distributed throughout virtually the entire length and breadth of the country. Even in the far north, where carp fishing is still in its infancy compared with the Midlands and the south, carp and carp waters are increasing in numbers every year. Carp are very adaptable fish and are just at home in running water as in still, which is strange since until recently the carp has always been given the label of a stillwater fish. The reason for its success and the wonderful way it has established itself in so many waters is that it can withstand a great range not only of temperatures but also of acidity and alkalinity.

They are hardy creatures able to withstand many repetitive captures. Some well-known fish have found themselves on the bank more than twenty times during the course of one season's fishing. Because carp anglers are very particular when it comes to handling and the conservation of their favourite species the future and the life expectancy of these known individuals looks very rosy indeed.

For some time it was thought that carp reached maximum weight and length at about fifteen years of age. Modern studies have proved this incorrect, for even carp that had thought to be freewheeling – in other words, to have levelled out in both length and weight – have suddenly started to grow again, even though in many cases these fish are more than thirty years old. We obviously still have much to learn.

Even with my thirty years' experience in the sport, as each season turns yet another corner I reflect on that term's achievement and just what I have learned. It is often full of contradictions and changes of direction – one of the things that makes this such an interesting sport and maintains my enthusiasm. Carp fishing is not a defined science, there are no definite rules. Theories and beliefs will often be shattered and broken in our never-ending quest for knowledge of our favourite species. So dare I predict just how large carp will grow in this country? Well, I will give you my two pennyworth on how I see the present situation regarding some of our big carp.

BIG FISH

At present the record has been held since June 1980 by Chris Yates's linear mirror from Redmire Pool weighing in at 51lb 8oz. When Chris banked that magnificent beast many of us thought that the record had been put completely out of sight for ever. But with at least six known fish in excess of 45lb being caught recently opinions have once again changed and the speculation is really not if but when it will fall again. I certainly wouldn't be surprised if one of those aforementioned 45lb-plus fish or an unknown biggie (Pete Springate's recent 45lb 6oz fish from Wraysbury was an unknown) was gracing the top of the record lists within the next twelve months.

Just what the ceiling is for carp in this country is almost impossible to ascertain. When we look in on a European or world basis and try to draw a comparison almost anything could happen in the future. Carp on the continent have already been captured at more than 75lb and it is known that fish over 100lb certainly exist in places farther away. With our ever-changing climate and as the carp become more adaptable perhaps we could also see true home-grown fish of this size being caught one day.

But for the time being all this talk of large carp should in no way belittle lesser-sized specimens. It is all relative, for not everyone can or indeed would want to fish for massive record breakers. Ten-, twenty- or thirty-pound carp are still very much sought after and with anglers entering the sport at varying levels of experience and ability there is always something to cater for everyone's needs.

I had a somewhat lengthy apprenticeship in my thirty years of carping, much of which was dictated by the fact that there was not the abundance of large carp and the many varied carp waters that we are fortunate to have today. However, I think a gradual building up of ability, knowledge and size of fish is no bad thing. We are already seeing far too many instant big-fish carp anglers. On one water I know there are two or three lads fishing there for a known forty who have yet to catch their first twenty. I find this situation sad. Those lads will never know how much that first double, twenty and thirty mean. To go in at the very top end of the sport with relatively few carp under your belt will usually mean a speedy exit from carping altogether, either in frustration at not catching a fish at all or as a result of instant success without starting at the bottom of the ladder and with relatively few steps left at the top.

There are also many anglers who have been in the sport as long as I have who have not even caught a twenty and probably have no desire to catch one. They are more than happy fishing on their own terms for singles and doubles and enjoying themselves – size does not always mean a harder fight and greater difficulty in landing.

HABITATS

With so many waters available which vary in population, the size of their carp, the degree of their catchability and places to fish, there will be a water out there somewhere to suit everyone. With our vast network of motorways, huge and extensive gravel extraction has left us with marvellous chains of gravel pits throughout the country, and especially in the south. Anyone flying into or out of Heathrow cannot fail to notice the huge chain of gravel pits that runs the length of the Colne and Kennet valleys.

These vary greatly in size from less than an acre to more than 200 acres and virtually all contain carp. King carp seem to thrive in the open rich waters of the gravel pits and weight gain is tremendous with the massive food chain that very quickly builds up. Carp, unlike many other species, will capitalise on just about any food source available to them. They are certainly not picky eaters. Bloodworm, snails, shrimp, all manner of water larvae, crustaceans and weed itself will be consumed. Other small fish, tadpoles and newts will all be devoured at varying times of the year and even their own spawn will not get overlooked.

Stocking levels very often dictate growth rate, but not always. Left to their own devices, a light stocking in large gravel pits with an abundance of natural food will thrive on neglect and grow fat and long over the years. More heavily stocked waters where there is greater competition for food may also see the growth of large carp but this is usually an artificial of baiting by anglers.

Of course, there is everything in between. On my local patch I have both extremes – large gravel pits nearly 200 acres in size in which less than fifty carp live a very quiet life, nomadically roaming the vast acreage cherry-picking the best food. However, a few miles down the road is a 10-acre park lake where the stocking is so dense that catches of up to fifty fish in a day are by no means uncommon. Small ponds, artificially created lakes and reservoirs all contain carp. Remember that the last three record carp have all come from that very famous tiny insignificant 3-acre lake, Redmire Pool, on the Herefordshire border, which demonstrates just how adaptable the old carp really is.

Our vast network of rivers and canals have been vastly overlooked from the carp angler's point of view in recent years. I was surprised to find just the other day that a fish of over 30lb had recently been caught in my local canal, a stretch of water that I have driven over probably two or three times every week. But it is the rivers that are probably almost the final frontier for any of the would-be pioneering carp anglers left out there. It is known and even well documented that major rivers such as the Thames, the Trent and the Hampshire Avon all have a good head of fish in them and I am sure it is only a matter of time before the Thames and Trent both produce forty-pound carp.

And what of all the other smaller rivers? The carp have spread their wings here too and they have found their way into the smallest tributaries and again capitalised on food items that have been overlooked by other resident species. So that insignificant little stream that you pass over on your way to work may well be worth stopping off and looking at. Don't be too surprised as you peer over the bridge into the murky waters if the ghostly shape of a magnificent carp does emerge. Even the good old Grand Union Canal – where many of us started our fishing career with a bamboo cane, bent pin and worm for gudgeon and stickleback – has shared in the carp explosion. I must admit I never thought that I would see the day when anglers would be bivvied up on the towpath of the local canal.

A well-known fish, "Split Tail Mirror' weighing over 40 lbs, from the South of France's St Cassein.

STOCKED WATERS

How have these carp managed to get into so many and such a variety of waters? Angling clubs and water authorities have not been slow to see that the carp is an extremely good sporting fish and, whether they are fished for at match level or by individuals camping out for weeks on end, they make a very attractive proposition for the paying angling customer.

With literally hundreds of fish farms specialising in carp there is no shortage of fish to stock into club waters and the others. The fact that there are so many carp waters available to us means that the individual can choose his level of water much more precisely. Whether it comes down to the size of the fish, the money invested or the hours available, there will be a water to suit. Large clubs and gravel companies offer very reasonably priced tickets and it is in some of these types of waters that the largest carp exist, so it is not a matter of paying for the right to fish for forty-pounders.

Leisure Sport Angling, for example controls the fishing at places like Wraysbury, Horton and Yateley. All these systems boast forty-pounders and fishing can be obtained on some of them for as little as £24. Of course at this sort of price you will not be alone. For more exclusive waters you will have to dig a little deeper into your pocket.

Syndicate and club waters can cost anything up to £300 and on some really exclusive waters you will pay even more. This will not necessarily buy you big fish but it will ensure you peace and quiet and tranquil surroundings in which to pursue your favourite species. With so many carp anglers it is not surprising that specialist groups have been formed and organisations such as The Carp Society, with with its 5,000 members, will be helping safeguard the future of carp angling. Because this is a thriving business, some fishery owners can be unscrupulous if they see a quick way of making a good buck or two. The illegal importation of large carp into the country has been a big problem in recent years and The Carp Society along with the National Rivers Authority (NRA) are trying to stamp out these illegal importations.

The problem is that these imported fish bring disease into the country. We have already seen many major carp waters wiped out as a direct result of illegal stockings. So whereas on the one hand things look rosy, with the carp settling down and expanding within our own watery network, we must not get complacent and allow our heritage to be destroyed by a few greedy beings.

With this in mind The Carp Society has already secured three of its own waters: the very famous Redmire Pool, yes the one that is still the holder of the record carp, Yewtree Lake in Norfolk, and Horseshoe Lake at Lechlade. This at least gives a chance of some marvellous fishing to Carp Society members.

DOING BATTLE

So choosing a carp water should not be a problem, whether it is a day-ticket, a club or a syndicate water. It only remains then to do battle with the carp. What is needed to be successful now that you have found your venue?

Location
Location is obviously top of the list. On heavily stocked waters this is really not a great obstacle, but to be confronted with twenty fish in a hundred acres is another matter. Observation is naturally the greatest key to location. We are very fortunate that carp show themselves so well, often throwing themselves completely out of the water. When they are not jumping they can often be seen bow-waving just below the surface. If not on the surface they may be bubbling and rooting about on the bottom. Even when lying in thick weed carp can be easily observed with a keen eye.

Watercraft
This is something that is almost impossible to teach. We have to look to our own evolution and call on our natural hunting instincts and use them accordingly. The ability to sneak up on a fish without its being aware of your presence, especially on hard, lightly stocked waters, is of vital importance. There of course will always be leaders of the pack as well as the also-rans but no one should despair as carp are a very catchable species.

Presentation
Having located your carp and crept up on them without spooking or alerting them to your presence, what sort of rig should you use? In fact, what sort of hookbait should you use? The permutations are endless. So how do you make the right decision?

As you make your way through the pages of this book, I will relate many of my own experiences and knowledge that I have built up in my angling career and pass them on to you. When you add to this your own input and observations, I am sure you will soon be making the right decisions.

Once you have mastered location, watercraft and presentation, the remaining requirement, and perhaps the most important, is confidence. Without confidence and a conviction in what you are doing you may as well pack up and go home, for there you have little chance of catching on a consistent basis. When all these elements come together and you have chosen the right tackle to do battle with your quarry on the day, only then will you become the complete carp angler.

2 BEHAVIOUR PATTERNS AND FEEDING

Before we get down to looking at specific feeding areas and the way that carp actually take food items, let us take a look at a year in the life of a carp to get a clear picture of how our quarry occupies itself as the seasons change. Naturally, the timetable will differ from year to year and geographically, because most of the carp's behaviour patterns are influenced by temperature, day length and weather conditions. Generally speaking, the further north and the colder the climate the later the following events will occur.

SPAWNING

We will start with spawning. Supposedly the close season, which runs from 15 March to 15 June inclusive is intended to accommodate the spawning ritual of our coarse fish, leaving them in peace and quiet to carry out their annual act. But, of course, in reality, with our colder springs, spawning rarely takes place until the end of June or the beginning of July. Although the close season was designed with the best will in the world it is completely impossible for all of our coarse fish to spawn during the three months of its duration.

Mind you, I would hate to see the close season abolished, as it has been in some parts of the country. I love there to be a beginning and an end. There is always something to look forward to and somehow or other coarse fishing would not be the same without the great build-up and air of anticipation towards the glorious 16 June. Likewise after 14 March we have time to take stock of the situation and make plans for the forthcoming season, investigate new waters and repair tackle ready for the off.

And the three-month close-down also gives us a great excuse for travelling to the Continent in search of foreign carp.

Anyway, back to the spawning. It is only when the water temperature starts to rise after the cold spring that the carp start to show interest in spawning. The shallow areas of the lake will quickly warm up in the warm summer sun. If there is good weed cover, trailing branches, overgrown brambles hanging into the water, reeds, or even submerged tree roots, the carp will be attracted to these places and utilise them for their spawning ritual. This is an intriguing time of the year as it is the only period when carp can be positively sexed externally.

For many weeks before spawning and several weeks afterwards the males will develop tiny tubercles around their heads, gill covers and pectoral fins. They are very easy to miss so one must look hard. They resemble thousands of tiny whitish-grey spots which feel slightly rough to the touch. A carp caught during this period which displays these tubercles is definitely a male fish; and more often than not it will be smaller than the females on any given water.

Females are far more difficult to sex, but a fish caught during this period which does not display spawning tubercles is likely to be a female. Other indications are a reasonably plump stomach and a reddish abdomen.

It is not uncommon for as many as eight or ten males to be serving one female. If the whole spawning ritual can be viewed – and it can often last for several days – the scene is a fascinating one. At first the fish will start to gather together, their movements becoming faster, erratic and unpredictable. The males aggressively head the females into shallow water. Any thoughts of feeding will by now have completely gone out of the window and from the angler's point of view it is far better just to stand, watch, learn and be spellbound by what is about to occur. Towards the peak of spawning the water will often explode in a frenzy of activity with weed and branches being scattered up the bank by the thrashing fish. Amongst all this flurry of water the males will induce the female to expel her eggs. Eventually, in a most disorganised fashion, or so it would seem to the onlooker, her eggs will be laid and the milt from the males will fertilise them. They will be sticky and adhere to any aquatic vegetation or submerged roots or branches. The eggs are almost transparent and are about 1 – 1.5mm in diameter. The fecundity is unbelievably enormous as a 15lb carp can produce several million eggs at a time. Of course very few will get through the next few days and actually hatch out as fry. The spawn is most vulnerable to birds and the fish themselves. Anyone who has witnessed this magical event for the first time cannot fail to be impressed – and to some extent embarrassed, as it almost seems an intrusion into their private life.

SUMMER

From after spawning until middle or late summer is when the carp start to regain a lot of their lost body weight, and of course in the angler's eye this is a great time to capitalise on a feeding frenzy. However, do not be surprised if a carp caught immediately after spawning looks in very bad condition, with split fins, missing scales and body scratches. All these are a direct result of the very intense and uncontrollable act of spawning. As they start to regain their body weight their injuries will also begin to heal.

After the initial feeding frenzy after spawning many of the warmer days will see the carp cruising in the upper layers of the water or basking in the sun. A marvellous time for stalking or surface fishing! On big open waters, which are greatly affected by the weather fishing will be frustrating at times as the carp will find the most

comfortable position to be in. Generally speaking this is the warmer water which is not always the easiest to spot.

AUTUMN

As we slip into autumn, days get shorter and the nights get longer and temperatures will even out. The carp will now start to feed for much longer periods and weight gain will be at its highest. It almost seems as if the carp have an inbuilt clock which tells them that autumn is just around the corner, closely followed by winter, when food will be scarce. So it would appear that they are building up their larder to see them through the colder months.

WINTER

As autumn turns into winter the carp are in tip-top condition, positively bristling. All the colours are enhanced and they look fresh from the mould. Carp caught at this time of the year in the now drab surroundings will seem almost to glow in their winter colours. Temperature drops as the winter starts and so too will the carp's movements slow down. They will now be at their highest weight of the year. As the winter wearily drags on the carp will feed less each day and it was not so many years ago that fishing for carp after November was considered to be something of a lunatic act as folklore said that the carp actually hibernated and sank into the mud until the spring.

Of course this myth has been totally dispelled in recent years and in fact with the right attitude of mind carp are no more difficult to catch during the winter months than they are in the summer. On most waters with a well-balanced stock it is not unusual for the carp to feed only for an hour or two each day and on some waters they may even go for several days between feeds. On more heavily stocked hungry waters this is not so apparent as the carp rely more on the anglers' feed than the food that is naturally available. The constant competition for food changes their feeding pattern and they will always be hungry. On well-balanced waters, however, the body movement of the carp has slowed down dramatically, and obviously less food is needed to maintain body weight. But provided that food is available the carp will carry on feeding right throughout the winter, even in very cold conditions. The angler can play a great part in this process by continually introducing his baits. The carp then become accustomed to finding this artificial food larder. By the end of winter there is a noticeable weight loss in individual fish but, more than this, their body appearance will have changed dramatically. They now look dull and drab, almost grey and an extra layer of mucus or slime seems to have built up. I am sure this is a protection system against any would-be passengers on this very attractive host.

EARLY SPRING

As the water temperature starts to rise once again as the countryside starts to shrug off its winter coat so too will the carp's movements increase. We are now into early spring and the carp will be at their lowest weight for the year.

Because of their increasing movement they will also start to look a little better in colour and any parasites that have found their way on to the carp will now find life a little harder as the carp actively try to rid themselves of the freeloaders. It almost seems that there is not enough food to go round in relation to their activities at this time of the year and, oddly enough, this usually coincides with our close season. So perhaps the timing isn't quite so bad after all.

As the days get longer and spring turns to summer the natural food larder starts to increase and so the carp are on the rampage again. Their body weight starts to increase as they now tuck in to the natural abundance of natural food. The females especially will show a marked increase in weight as their eggs are now starting to mature. So it's back into the summer and once again the spawning time for the carp.

FEEDING

The imagination of anglers has endowed carp with almost magical feeding powers. You could be excused for thinking that they actually have hands when you read some of the extraordinary explanations of how carp pick up baits. The fact of the matter is that they are voracious feeders and will take anything from tiny pinhead snails to massive swan mussels. They have a huge set of pharyngeal teeth in their throat which they use to crush up hard food items. The way they actually extract their food from the surroundings depends on the environment they are in. On silty lakes where bloodworm are found several inches into the bottom layers, the carp root around, sometimes with their heads completely buried in the mud. They suck in great mouthfuls of mud along with all the food items suspended in it. This is all passed through into the gut and once there food items are broken down with the aid of enzymes.

These enzymes occur naturally in the carp's gut and break down food into four broad categories: protein, carbohydrate, fats (oils) and cellulose. The protein is converted into protoplasms, which are absorbed in the carp's gut and aid the growth of the fish. Carbohydrates are the carp's energy source and provide power for movement, breathing and heartbeat. The fats and oils also act as a back-up energy source but generally they are plentiful and mainly responsible for weight gain. The cellulose extracted from the food, along with all the other indigestible matter, acts as roughage and is eventually excreted.

Bubbling

When carp are foraging in silty areas for bloodworm, fishing can often be frustrating. The carp can easily be located by the tell-tale signs of bubbles rising to the surface. Natural gases escaping from the silt also cause bubbles, so to be sure that carp are responsible for the bubbling concentrate on one set of bubbles and see if it moves. If it does and it's on a fairly constant and predictable route, then it is sure to be a carp. If the bubbles remain stationary and appear in the same place hour after hour they are best ignored as they are unlikely to be caused by the activity of the carp.

A carp can soon become preoccupied with this type of feeding and are often oblivious to any other food in its surroundings. Unless a bait can be placed accurately in the path of the carp and at the depth it is feeding at the angler is unlikely to be successful. However, from time to time the carp will rise up from the bottom, sometimes going to the surface, head-and-shouldering or leaping out completely. I am sure this is a way of cleaning out blocked-up gill covers.

It is at this moment between feeds that the angler stands the best chance of catching one of these preoccupied bubblers. A pop-up boilie or similar suspended several inches above the bottom will often be taken just before the carp gets its head down and starts feeding once again. A shrewd angler who has a baited rod at the ready can quickly cast at a leaping fish and will often get an instant take. Otherwise, the best that one can do is to intercept the path of the bubbling carp with a tightly grouped patch of bait hoping that it will stop in its tracks and investigate.

These silt feeders most commonly found on natural lakes and ponds often have extremely soft mouths, sometimes with a flabby inner skin. You should bear this in mind when confronted with this type of fish, and adjust hook pattern and hook-link lengths accordingly to ensure success.

GRAVEL PIT LARDER

Gravel pits, which generally have a solid bottom and sometimes gravel bars and plateaux with small, shallow silt pockets in between, are a completely different prospect. Here the carp's natural larder will more likely consist of shrimp, small snails, mussels and other crustaceans. Carp in this environment will generally be sucking in and blowing out food items suspended within mouthfuls of water they engulf. This natural feeding action loosens and sorts out the small edible crustaceans from the surrounding gravel and stones. As you can imagine, these will be very hard-mouthed fish and the set-up should be chosen

accordingly. Here it is much easier to intercept a feeding fish. Similar tell-tale signs will be evident. With the movement of gravel caused by the feeding carp, small pockets of natural gas which have been locked between the stones will escape, rise and form bubbles on the surface. These will be much more irregular in shape and size than those of the silt feeders of soft-bottomed lakes, but the same applies – watch out for the bubbles that move.

Try to predict the path of the carp and bait an area accordingly. Particle baits can often score better over boilies in such situations, especially small grains such as hemp, dari seed, mini-maples and the like. Of course, much will depend on how far from the bank the carp are feeding. Small boilies often score over particles in this situation as they can be catapulted further and far more accurately than the more irregular-shaped seeds.

Wherever possible I personally like to fish bottom baits on waters of this type, with a reasonably long hook link – a minimum of about 12 inches – to allow the free passage of the bait as the carp sucks in and blows out. If you can see fish feeding in this manner you will be quite astounded just how far a bait can be sucked in from. From 6 to 9 inches is by no means unusual and when they reject it it seems to go even farther. I am sure it is this act of powerfully blowing out a bait that was responsible for many of the twitch bites we used to get in the days before hair and bolt rigs.

On gravel pits with multiple bars the carp use them like motorways, often following the same route backwards and forwards from one part of the pit to another time after time. If the water is clear and shallow they can easily be observed. If not, the angler is sometimes lucky enough to witness a carp rolling several times on its route. A mental note should be made of all this activity and spots baited up accordingly. Although the tops of bars and flat, clean plateaux will see very little in the way of natural food, they are often good spots to intercept patrolling fish. But it's in the silt pockets in between that they will normally feed naturally and, unless the carp are in a

The wide open expanses of an Oxfordshire gravel pit. This is a typical venue where monsters grow.

ravenous mood, I would far rather present a bait in these small depressions between bars than on the tops of the bars in the hope of stopping those patrolling fish.

Margin Feeders

The nice thing about carp is that they are nice social animals and are natural shoal fish. So find one and there is a very good chance that there are more close at hand. Carp are natural margin patrollers and for some reason or other this is an area of the lake that is often overlooked by new-comers to the sport. After all, most of the food is going to be in the margins, where there will be a natural build-up of silt and debris – perfect conditions for the food chain to thrive in. Anywhere

where there is food the carp will never be far away. Once the carp have been caught from the angler's own margin several times they will be wary of these particular places. But there will be other margins which the angler can fish. These may be distant private banks which scarcely see anyone at all or around islands, which are plentiful on many gravel pits. These will be the next stopping place once the carp have been pushed from beneath the angler's rod tip.

Weeds

Carp love to forage in densely weeded areas, especially in warm weather. Gently manoeuvring their way through the underwater entanglement, they suck off tasty morsels from the underside of

Remove the water for a unique look at what is beneath the surface: bars, gulleys and plateaux abound. The troughs in between are full of life – the carp's natural larder.

lily pads and broad leaved floating plants. Carp will often give themselves away by slurping and sucking noises as their lips come into contact with the surface. When feeding just below the surface on subsurface stems and roots, carp will be observed 'tenting' amongst the weeds. As the body lifts towards the surface, the great back will push up tent-shaped pieces of leaves above the surface. Then the angler has only to decide which is the head and which is the tail and place the bait accordingly. Here surface baits can come into their own; Chum Mixer catapulted between the gaps in the weed could soon have the carp's attention drawn away from its natural foraging and homing in on the angler's baits.

Those that cannot be enticed to rise to the surface may well be fooled into taking a freelined bait draped over the edge of a lily pad. This might be a natural, such as a large lobworm wriggling away just below the surface or an exotic boilie, perhaps even one the carp has rejected in a different part of the lake but whose flavour and smell proves too irresistible for the carp to ignore.

In these densely weeded areas carp will also forage near the bottom. Bubbles rising to the surface in the midst of weedbeds are again the telltale sign of a feeding carp. A float-fished boilie or particle dropped in a small gap in the weed may be all that is required for the angler to be successful. Stalking fish in this manner can be entertaining, to say the least.

There are rich gravel pits as well as lakes which will see an abundance of weed growth over vast areas. Even in lakes where there is 8 or 10 feet of water weed can often be floor to ceiling and at first glance look impenetrable. This is naturally off-putting to anyone not confronted with this situation before. Do not despair, there will always be somewhere to put a bait. Close observation will reveal small clear patches in the weeds, often caused by feeding carp. In the height of summer these can change from day to day as the avidly feeding carp clear them out. As they vacate one spot the weed reappears as if by magic only for another small clear area to become apparent a few yards away. An accurately placed bait on this spot will generally get instant results.

When fishing these very weedy waters always remember that the view from the surface is very different from the one underneath. These water plants start off with a small stem at the bottom spreading out at the top as they reach towards the sunlight.

So what from the surface is a seemingly impenetrable jungle will undoubtedly have clear, almost motorway lanes between the plant stems close to the bottom. Even when you can't find a suitable hole in the weed a bait blasted through the dense vegetation will often land in a clear area on the bottom amongst the much more sparsely growing stems.

COVER

Carp love cover over their heads – overhanging trees, bushes, staging and virtually anything else where there is water deep enough for the carp to swim under will be visited on a regular basis. In clear water where the bottom can be seen keep a close eye out for patches that have been cleared of small twigs, leaves and other fallen debris. These may not necessarily be feeding spots but resting-up safe houses where the carp's movement and the vortexing of the water have completely cleared an area of debris. Because these are generally safe havens away from the more popular and open swims of the lake, baits placed

in them will be treated with less caution than those lying in more normal spots. Areas of this type, especially ones that are extremely difficult to place a bait in, will often be the scene of good catches of fish when other known hot spots on the lake appear to have dried up.

Another type of cover that surprisingly doesn't automatically spring into most anglers' minds is wind on the surface. Anyone who has done any underwater diving will tell you what a marked difference there is between a windy surface and flat calm. On calm days everything will be distinctly silhouetted against the surface when viewed from below by the carp. Floating lines viewed from below are like great lumps of black rope suspended on the surface.

No wonder the carp are spooky in such conditions! It's another reason why many anglers fail the first time they try surface fishing.

The carp can be easily seen cruising often with their backs out of the water on hot, flat, calm days. Because they are not responding to a bottom bait, the frustrated angler then resorts to chucking out surface baits and floating lines and wonders why the carp show no interest. A slight ripple on the water and this will change dramatically. The carp cannot easily identify surface items so they are less cautious. Introduce free offerings and the curiosity factor will bring them into feeding mode almost as if someone has thrown a switch. This is just as well as carp are not naturally good surface feeders. The position of their eyes in relationship to their mouth means they can feed only clumsily on floating items; their co-ordination is diabolical. But, given a rippled surface, at least they will try several times once they have picked up the scent.

WEATHER

Weather conditions undoubtedly are a great contributing factor to the carp's feeding habits and their location within a water. Prevailing winds will drive food items into the same bank year in and year out. Generally speaking, we are blessed with south to south-west winds for many months of the year, so whenever in doubt the north and eastern banks of a lake are well worth a look in unfavourable spotting conditions. A change of wind will often throw lethargic carp into a feeding frenzy, especially if the strong winds have sprung up after a period of calm, sultry weather. The oxygen level will immediately rise and this spurs the whole food chain as well as the carp into life. Even a complete change of wind direction can have the same sort of effect. Weeks on end of moderate south westerlies will have seen the carp getting more lethargic in the way they feed as time goes on and the wind persists.

Should a strong northerly suddenly spring up the carp could well be thrown back into that intensive feeding mode again. It's almost as if they have become bored with too consistent weather conditions and the change is like a breath of fresh air.

Of course, you must be prepared to move quickly if this happens, as the change of wind direction will not only spur them into feeding but will often have them disappearing to the other end of the lake which the wind is now blowing into. It's not a bad theory to hang your hat on to say that it is always best to fish into the wind. Probably eight out of ten times this is true but of course carp, being the contrary creatures they are, will often throw a spanner in the works and whilst all the anglers are battling to put bivvies up at the windward end of the lake the carp are merrily feeding away in flat calm conditions at the other end. But if you play the percentage game you will eventually be rewarded.

There appears to be one kiss of death in all this and that is the dreaded easterly wind. I am grateful that we don't experience too many of these since, for whatever reason, they undoubtedly consistently put the fish off the feed. I really have no idea why this should be. In the winter I suppose I could understand it to some degree inasmuch as easterlies and north-easterlies are generally extremely cold winds and the chill factor could send the water temperature plummeting. But I have a sneaky feeling that it is more to do with atmospheric pressure than anything else. Much more research must be done before we can get a clear picture of exactly how the carp are affected by varying atmospheric pressure levels.

Another old wives' tale is that the carp don't feed in the rain. Really, I suppose it's more the case that the anglers don't go out in the rain to see if the carp feed! I know there have been one or two occasions when I have thought I wished that they didn't feed in the rain, having had my third or fourth soaking of the day, fishing amidst a torrential downpour. It's rather like the myth that carp feed better at night. I don't think that carp actually feed better at night (in fact, looking back through my records I have caught far more carp during the daylight hours than in the hours of darkness but then again I do more daytime fishing). What I think actually happens is that generally speaking the carp anglers themselves are less active at night, being fast asleep in their bivvies, and so have less chance of spooking the carp by crashing around the bank or casting over their heads.

OBSERVATION

Of course location is one of the keys to consistent carp catches and, once you have located them, understanding the carp's feeding patterns will help you decide what bait to use and how it should be presented. This chapter should have given you a little insight into just what the fish can and do get up to. But please bear in mind that it is only a guideline and it should be used to give you some basis on which to build your knowledge of a given water. Hours spent watching fish will never go wasted and the old adage that five hours watching and one hour fishing is better than one hour watching and five hours fishing still holds very true. Use your eyes, observe the carp in their surroundings and make your own decisions about where the carp are and just how they are feeding. And, for that matter, what they are feeding on. Build up this mental picture and a whole new world will open up for you. Suddenly you will be able to see the wood from the trees and the path will be open and you can take your first step to consistent carp catches.

3 TACKLE: THE MAJOR ITEMS

The carp-fishing scene has changed so much in the last couple of decades that anyone comparing the tackle that we used twenty years ago with that of today could be forgiven for thinking that we were in pursuit of two entirely different species. The terminology that surrounds modern-day tackle must be extremely confusing to the beginner. Just look at the rod industry alone – IM6, IM7, IMX, high modulus carbon, Kevlar, woven graphite, and so on, and that is just the materials the blanks are made from. What I will attempt to do is to cut out a lot of this mumbo-jumbo and address myself simply to the facts of the matter and tell you what I believe are the advantages or disadvantages of any items of our kit. I shall discard all that I consider to be not a genuine aid to angling as the industry seems to be fraught with lots of Mickey Mouse gimmicks aimed to catch the carp angler rather than the carp itself. All that follows will be based on pure fact that has been gleaned from my own personal experience and that of close friends, and not from common folk-lore.

Much of this may seem very fundamental – not over-elaborated and backed up with extraordinary explanations. There is a good reason for this. I honestly believe that far too many so-called experts attribute to the carp much greater intelligence than the fish actually possesses. There is a phenomenon that I call bedchair theory, which bears little resemblance to what is actually happening.

There is tackle that will certainly help you catch fish, and make the catching of them a little more pleasurable and life on the bank more comfortable.

When I first started carp fishing some thirty-odd years ago there was little or no specialist tackle available. If you wanted anything to do a particular job that was out of the ordinary you either had to make it yourself or get someone else to do so for you. This certainly cannot be said of today's industry, and some may say sadly so. The purist and most traditionalist amongst us had to work very hard to catch carp in the early days, and to land them successfully on tackle that you had made yourself only added to that triumph. Maybe the edge has been taken away from that early pioneering – life is a little easier but the thrill every time another carp slides over the rim of the landing net hasn't changed one iota.

It is now possible for a newcomer to the carp scene to go to his local tackle shop and purchase every single item of tackle that he needs for the sport. That is, of course, once he has fought his way through the jargon that is currently so prominent within the sport.

RODS

Before you go out and spend your hard cash you must bear one thing in mind: there is no such thing as one rod that will proficiently cover all aspects of carp fishing. As with most things in life, there has to be compromises. Since the rods will probably be financially your biggest investment, please take your time to look at what is on offer and do not fall for the extraordinary claims made in a lot of the glossy ads.

Action
First let's look at the rod's action. Rods range from stiff, fast-taper models to a very soft progressive taper. Generally speaking, the stiffer and faster-tapered the rod, the farther it will cast.

Note the very tippy action of a fast taper rod, ideal for picking up line at long range and for distance casting.

Such a rod, however, will be less forgiving when it comes to playing fish.

Controversially, there are some very soft models around that resemble little more than elastic bands, giving no backbone to control the fish, leaving the carp to do pretty well as it pleases.

Length

Traditionally carp rods always used to be 10 feet in length, but the modern-day carp rod has settled around the 12-foot mark. Having said this, of course length is a matter of personal preference. For small waters an angler may well prefer models of 11 feet, especially where bankside foliage is restrictive. On the other hand, on open waters long-range casting may well be the name

of the game and here in the right hands 13-footers can be a distinct advantage.

Materials

I believe that mixed fibres are the best compromise for a fishing rod. Two that are currently being used with great success are carbon and graphite. Carbon is a light, stiff, steely material, which responds very quickly and produces a rod of extremely low diameter. Graphite woven into a cloth acts as a cushion, giving a softening effect which makes the rod easy to handle and reduces the chance of breakage in casting. High-modulus carbon comes in many grades. There has been much talk about IM7 but I am happier with IM6, for this has already stood the test of time very

The very progressive action of a slow taper rod is very safe when playing a large fish at close range. This type of action absorbs the heavy lunges of a hooked fish.

well. To my mind a base of high-modulus carbon overwrapped with woven graphite provides the perfect combination and, although I am sure that with modern-day technology this too will be improved, for the time being I am happy to stick with something that I have absolute faith in.

Rod Joints

Spigoted, put-in and put-over are the three modern methods of joining sections of rods together. The selection again can be a personal choice. My preference is for a put-over, although I can say I have had few bad reports of any of the others Modern rod building is a reliable technology, so you really shouldn't have any problems.

Test Curves

Now here is something really difficult to hang your hat on. Back when carp rods were first made commercially they were virtually all of compound or progressive action, which meant that by pulling a rod through an arc to a right angle against a balance you could get an accurate reading of the test curve. Modern rods are not quite the same as there are very few genuine, compound-tapered rods. This is because middle-to-tip-action rods have a greater advantage in fishing terms over the compound designs, but generally speaking they are pro rata a much beefier tool. In actual fishing compound rods will bend right down through the butt when a fish is

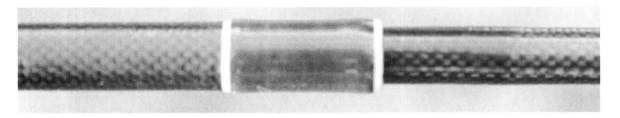

There are many types of rod joints available. This overfit design is one of my favourites.

played but the middle-to-tip-action rods rarely bend much below the joint of the rod – all the action being in the tip.

Therefore relative test curves of the two designs are no longer compatible. As an example, an average 12-foot rod of middle-to-tip-action rated at 2lb test curve could well have the stated 2lb test curve in the top three-quarters of the rod. To measure the test curve from the butt by pulling the tip at right angles could give a rating of 2¾lb. Bear this in mind when purchasing a rod. Ideally, try someone else's beforehand to see just how well it suits you.

It is claimed in the trade that test curve is related to casting weight. A rod of 1½lb test curve is said to be capable of casting 1½oz; one of 2lb, 2oz; 2½lb 2½oz and so on. This is OK as a rough rule of thumb, but do not place too much reliance on it. So much depends on the rod's action.

Rod Rings

I will not bother going all through the hundred and one different types of rings or line guides that are available. Suffice it to say that my own preference, along with ninety per cent of the angling fraternity, is for silicon-carbide-lined rod rings. Whether they are Fujis, Seymos or one of the Far East equivalents I really don't mind: they are all of superb quality, very hard and will rarely groove. For the butt ring I prefer a three-legged variety, the butt ring takes a lot of punishment and this robust design wears extremely well. For the rest of the intermediates I prefer single-legged varieties. As for diameters, these can be anything from a 30mm diameter bore on a long-range rod

to a 24mm butt on a close to middle distance rod, tapering down to 10 or 8mm respectively. Most modern rods will be equipped with seven, eight nine – a radical change from the eleven plus or even 10-foot rods of yesteryear.

Reel Fittings

Again I will not go into the many that are available. The most popular and reliable and my own personal choice is a Fuji FPS-type screw fitting. Much debate has taken place regarding which way round these reel fittings should be fitted to the rod, although in actual fishing terms it makes very little difference. If there is a preference on a carp rod it should be for the non-adjustable end towards the tip of the rod. It is far more comfortable in the hand this way round, which is enough consideration in itself but it also allows a line clip to be fitted on the handle in the correct position over the spool.

Handles

The actual material from which they are made is a personal preference. The more traditional amongst us prefer cork whilst the majority appear to prefer Duplon or EVA. Full handles or abbreviated, again it's personal preference, but the majority appear to go for the abbreviated, with a couple of inches above and below the reel fitting and about 6 inches as a hand grip right at the butt of the rod. How far the reel fitting should be fitted from the butt varies from manufacturer to manufacturer and from person to person. But between 24 inches and 28 inches from the butt to the top of the reel fitting will cover every requirement unless you are a midget or a giant.

Custom-Made or Commercial

Up until fairly recently there were very few pro-duction-made carp rods which a serious special-ist would consider using. There are now quite a few but there will still be those who want to make their own or have them custom-built to their requirements. Quality blanks can be purchased from companies such as Tricast, Sportex and North Western. If you don't fancy making them up yourself go to one of the good rod builders like Vic Gibson or Bruce Ashby. However, if you are choosing one of the production-made rods, Daiwa, Shimano, Ryobi and of course DAM all make good competitive rods.

My Own Choice

Naturally I am biased but my preference is for rods I have specifically designed for DAM with a middle-to-tip action in 12- and 13-foot lengths. For close to middle range work my 12-foot 1¾lb or 2¼lb work well. The 2¼lb are preferable for heavier lines and fishing in snags.

For long range my choice is for the 2½lb 13-footers.

Extreme range

For ninety-five per cent of general carp fishing rods between 1¾ and 2½lb will be more than ade-quate. These can cope with distances from the margins up to about 140 yards in favourable con-ditions. Beyond that we are getting into the realms of something very special. There is a small band of anglers who can fish proficiently at ridiculously long range, and by that I mean up to about 170 yards. As you can imagine, the sort of rod for this distance is a different animal alto-gether. This could well be a 13-foot 4lb-test-curve power-casting tool capable of throwing out leads up to 5oz in weight. This game is not for the faint-hearted and quite honestly not for me. I have the greatest respect for these extreme-range specialists but personally it takes some of the edge and pleasure away from my carping. But if that is what these lads have to do on their

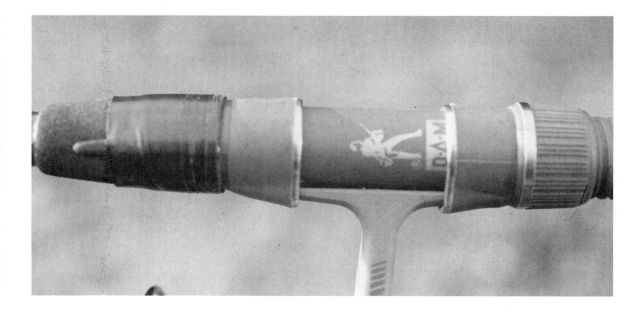

A Fuji F.P.S. type screw fitting is superb for holding the reel securely to the rod. Note the position of the line clip – it should always be directly above the spool. This clip is made out of carbon fibre and is taped to the handle in an appropriate position.

particular waters to catch carp then so be it. But I do stress that it is very specialised and there are few that will be able to cast that sort of range consistently.

My only worry with this sort of equipment, which resembles a beachcaster more than a carp rod, is that it may be used in the wrong hands. These rods are powerful and could exert unnecessary pressure on the carp, especially at close quarters. If you are tempted to have a go at this horizon bashing please spare a little thought for the carp when dragging them back to the bank.

Stalking Rods

This is just about at the opposite end of extreme-range fishing and is practised by just as few. Elsewhere in this book my good friend and angling companion Jan Wenczka has written a specialist chapter about stalking, which may well convert many of you into this exciting branch of carping. So I will not dwell too much on the subject here except to say that there is a place for a stalking rod in my armoury against the carp. My preference is for a two-piece 8-foot model which has a test curve of around 2¼lb.

This is equipped with a very short 17-inch handle which can easily be manoeuvred around the body in a tight swim. The eyes are three-legged Fujis throughout as there will be great demand made on this piece of equipment. In the tightest swims, which are among the best for stalking I

could possibly end up landing the hooked carp on the top section alone.

Telescopic Rods

Until very recently telescopic rods had never caught on in the United Kingdom. Telescopic rods have been used with great success throughout Europe for many years but have never been taken seriously here and have often been labelled Mickey Mouse. I have to admit that I shared that view for quite some time. I just could not see how it would be possible to make a rod with seven or eight sections that could come anywhere near matching the action of any of our traditional two-piece models. But like so many other anglers I have had to eat my words.

It has only really been in the last couple of years whilst I have been travelling throughout Europe, that I have looked towards telescopic rods. With stringent baggage allowances on most European flights, somehow or other the weight of tackle had to be cut down. Two-piece 12- and 13-foot rods are very problematic to take on aircraft – they are a vulnerable and expensive piece of kit that needs adequate protection. This used to be done by the way of a 6-inch-diameter heavy-duty drainpipe tube. Not only were these very restrictive on weight (the tube itself could weigh as much as 4 kilos) but they would also have to be left in the hands of airport baggage handlers. You should see the mess that a heavy-

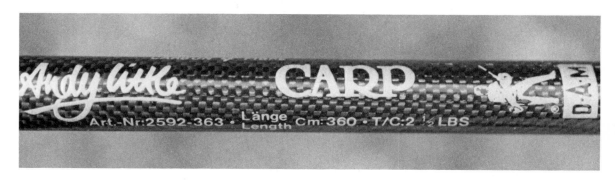

Over eighteen months of design work went into this range of rods that carry my name.
They are not just off the shelf blanks but ones that I have designed to do a specific job.

duty baggage conveyor can make of even one of the heavy-duty tubes, let alone the valuable rods housed inside. After one disaster enough was enough. If I was going to take rods with me they were coming on as hand baggage.

So started my serious look at telescopic rods and I am pleased to report that all my original scepticism has been laid to rest. I am now happy to use one of the modern band of specialist Tele Carp rods. Mine are 12 feet in length, of 2½lb test curves, and fold down to under 34 inches in length, so my new-found friends travel in comfort with me, tucked down the side of the seat.

Final Compromise

For my own fishing my stalking rod, a set of Tele Carps, and set of 12- and 13-footers cover all my carping needs. But what of the newcomer or the guy who just cannot afford such a range? Where does this leave him? I guess that most of the newcomer's sport is going to take place somewhere between the margins and 100 yards out and on lines ranging from 8 to15 lb. This being the case, I would strongly recommend purchasing a pair of 12-footers with a middle-to-tip action and a test curve of 2¼lb. These need not be at the top end of the range. Many manufacturers now offer quality rods from £50 to £150, so there is a price that should be affordable to everyone.

Traditionally, the carp set-up consists of a matched pair of rods and reels. This looks extremely nice and I'm sure it makes the owner quite proud. This is fine but something that always niggles at the back of my mind is that if

This is my ideal stalking rod: two piece with a short, full Duplon handle. It is only 8 ft in length, ideal for extracting carp from tight spots.

A telescopic carp rod, something I thought I would never, ever use. However, for the globe-trotting angler its space-saving qualities, together with a superb action, make it the ideal candidate

finances are short surely it would be a good idea to purchase two rods of slightly different design so that the water concerned could be more proficiently and more adequately covered.

REELS

Fixed-Spool Reels

For so many years the Mitchell 300 dominated the market, and then the Abu 55 ran a close second in the popularity stakes for a carp reel. Both of these now look completely old hat and it's a shame that these companies did not respond as well as others to the changing needs of the carp angler. We are now in the age of two-speed oscillating tapered long conical spool reels. Many of these also have free-spool and bait-runner facilities.

Instead of fishing for reel churners (where the reel is turned backwards by the taking carp) or an open-bail-arm system, where line control can often be problematical, today's carp angler uses the new method of disengaging the spool's drive mechanism, allowing it to rotate freely and give line to a taking fish while the bail arm is still closed. This offers the ultimate in line management. Re-engaging the spool's drive is a simple matter of turning the reel handle. The long conical tapered spools offer perfect line lay, with little line drop-off relative to distance, which aids longer and smoother casting. Where it is not desirable to use a free-spool system, these long tapered spools are still a plus for easy casting.

The size of reels has also improved; in fact the old Mitchell 300 looks positively miniature by today's standards, with manufacturers striving to offer a competitive and practical reel for the carper of the nineties.

Many companies are in fierce competition for this market and amongst the leaders are Shimano, Daiwa, Ryobi and DAM. As far as fixed-spool reels are concerned – and they are the most popular for carp fishing and include all the aforementioned – my own choice is as follows: for my standard reel which I use for methods including

The quick 250 CDi reel is now my bulk standard carp reel. It has a superb smooth clutch and the long conical tapered spool offers smooth and free casting.

stalking, float fishing and surface fishing, I prefer the DAM Quick 250 CDi; for free-spool work I use the 350 FS; and for real long range I favour the BC 65, with its massive spool for greater distance. I like to carry a couple of spare spools for each reel so that I have to hand a comprehensive selection of lines of different breaking strain. Generally speaking most of the reels will be loaded with 8, 10 and 12lb BS. For heavy work I will go up to 15lb. For the main reel line this is as high as I consider it practical to use.

Centrepins
The only other reel that I carry is a special centrepin, made for me by Dave Swallow. It is a reel I use for very special circumstances when I am

stalking. The method of line retrieve with a fixed spool reel is pumping the hooked fish back to the bank. The rod is lifted under pressure and then the angler winds down to gain line before lifting the rod again and repeating.

In tight situations where a couple of inches of lost line can mean a lost fish the centrepin comes into its own, for the line can be retrieved under full pressure. In the same situation a fixed-spool reel could easily lock up, causing a stalemate, or, even worse, allowing the fish to gain sanctuary in nearby snags. I will describe this method in more detail in Chapter 10.

If you are choosing a centrepin reel for this type of use it is essential that it is constructed on a very robust centre spindle and heavy-duty

The quick 350 FS – made from a similar design to the 250 but it has a unique free spool system giving perfect line management, allowing the angler to fish for runs with the bail arm closed.

bearings. Small, lightweight centrepins designed for trotting on a flowing river have no place in this type of fishing.

Multipliers

Although multipliers have yet not become part of the carp angler's equipment I can honestly see a time when some of the lads who fish at extreme range get round to using them. You have only to look at the phenomenal distance that the top beachcasters achieve to realise that there could well be a place in carp angling for such a reel. As I said before, not my cup of tea but surely an attraction to those big-pit lads where carp have been pushed way out from the margins.

LINE

In my opinion line is the second most important part of the carp angler's equipment – the first being the hook. (I will go into greater detail about hooks when I discuss rigs in Chapters 5 and 7.) Generally speaking, ninety-nine per cent of carp-angling needs concerning a main reel line are filled by monofilament. Like many other items of tackle, this has really come on in leaps and bounds in recent years.

The carp angler's requirements of his main line are many and often seemingly contradictory. A standard reel line for general carping applications must be supple, have a reasonable amount of

The B.C.65. This is a huge reel with a large long tapered conical spool. If you are to hit the 140 yards mark this is the sort of beast you need to do it.

elasticity but not stretch too much, have high abrasion resistance, superb knot strength, a good breaking strain for the diameter and be as unobtrusive as possible when lying in the swim. On top of all this it should be available on bulk spools and at a relatively low price to enable the angler to change his line regularly.

All that may well sound nigh on impossible, but the truth of the matter is that at the top end of the line market all these requirements are achievable. In fact, tests conducted by many anglers over a long period of time show that there is little to choose between one brand and another at this end of the market. What tends to happen is that anglers have their own individual favourite brand and will swear that that brand outfishes all

the others, but this is rarely the case. As with most mass-produced items, things do go wrong from time to time – the odd bad batch will spring up; spools could well be mislabelled; and very occasionally, although this tends not to happen with modern monofilaments, line is stored in strong light or heat and deteriorates before the angler even sets eyes on it.

Carp anglers like to buy bulk spools when filling their reels. Most modern reels will take somewhere between 250 and 350 yards of 15lb to 8lb respectively. It is important that there are no knots joining the main line together and that it is one continual length from start to finish. This makes bulk spools of 300, 600 and 1,000 yards very attractive to the carp angler.

This is my Centre Pin Reel that was made for me by Dave Swallow.
This gets used a lot for my heavy stalking and close-range work.

Which are the top makes? In the country as a whole, the most popular in current use are Maxima, Sylcast, Brent, DAM, Drennan and Berkley. These account for over ninety-five per cent of lines purchased by specialist carp anglers.

BITE INDICATORS

Electronic Indicators

These bite alarms or buzzers are an extremely useful item of the angler's kit. Rather than having to stare at a visual indicator for hours on end, the angler can busy himself with other important things such as looking for fish, tying up rigs, making bait or even having something to eat. I must stress, however, that the angler must not be tempted to wander away from his rods whilst the electronic alarm is turned up to full volume.

Buzzers have been around for many years. The early models consisted of a piece of bent wire which acted as an antenna, round which the line was passed. When a carp moved off a switch was pulled, sounding the alarm. We have come a long way from those early models. The two most popular and by far the best are the Optonics and the Daiwa Sensitrons.

The Optonic was the first to break away from the antenna design and incorporated a vane

We are now lucky that we have such a comprehensive range of monofilament lines to choose from, most of which are of superb quality.

wheel over which the line was fed. On the central axis of this vane wheel is a two- or four-blade propeller. When rotated forwards or backwards the line breaks through a photocell beam which activates the alarm. This really was a revolution, for there was now no resistance at all on the line. Optonics detect runs as well as dropbacks (when a fish moves towards the angler) and by the pitch of the alarm even tell how fast the take is going.

This design has stood the test of time very well. The principle has not changed, but the latest models are louder, with volume and tone control and latching LEDs (light-emitting diodes). The latching lights, which stay on for several seconds after every movement of the vane wheel, allow the angler to identify a small movement of line

which has stopped which could be a line bite or a carp investigating the bait. This is very useful when fishing with multiple rods.

Hot on the heels of the Optonic is the Sensitron. This detects movement of line via two vertical rollers as opposed to the horizontal vane wheel of the Optonic. As the line is pulled through the Sensitron rollers, they rotate and a disc breaks the electronic circuit giving an audible and visual alarm. The unique feature of the Sensitron is that it can be adjusted to detect varying movements of line. At its finest point it will register line movement of about a quarter of an inch or so, and at the most coarse setting a couple of inches of line. This is very useful to help combat heavy weather conditions when the

The Optonic Bite Indicator. It has to be said this is probably the most popular of all electronic indicators currently being used by the carp angler.

The Daiwa Sensitron is now hard on the heels of the Optonic in the popularity stakes.

indicators can give false bleeps caused by wind or undertow.

Both the Optonic and the Sensitron are compact. Everything is housed in one head, including the power source, which is a 9-volt PP3 type of battery. Although both models are equipped with volume control it's not always desirable to have the buzzers turned up at full volume when you are bivvying up during night sessions. Many anglers prefer an extension box which can be run back into the bivvy via a set of long leads. These are connected to the heads of the bite indicators via a jack plug. These remote boxes now mean that the bite indicator head volume can be turned down and the audible and visual sounder box can be positioned close to the angler's head. This gives him an immediate alarm even in the middle of the night without disturbing or alerting other anglers in adjacent swims.

One of the best remote boxes I have seen is manufactured by JA Electronics and can take up to four heads with latching LEDs and a volume control. These sounder boxes also have to have their own power source, which again is driven by a 9-volt PP3 battery.

Visual Indication

It is advisable as well as having an audible alarm to have some sort of mechanical back-up visual indicator. This immediately allows the angler to see just how much and how quickly any line is moved in either direction. Also, these visual indicators double up as a secondary line management system, ensuring that no loose line is left lying

Although there are many extension boxes available, this J.A. Electronics system is my favourite. Four separate heads can be fed into one box, making it ideal for anglers doubling up in the same swim.

around to get tangled up in undergrowth. In years gone by we used to use Fairy Liquid bottle tops, silver paper and cylinders of white plastic. These were hung on the line between the first two rod rings and would rise and fall under their own weight as line was taken. This was OK on calm, windless days – a very good, reliable system – but enter the wind and the whole thing could be turned into a nightmare. Swinging backwards and forwards in the breeze, they would inevitably end up getting tangled, usually just at the moment when the carp were about to take, often ending with disastrous results. If that wasn't bad enough, these indicators were still attached to the line once you had struck into the fish and on the odd occasion while striking could actually spin completely round the rod – again with the inevitable result.

From then on we progressed to using long needles pushed into the ground on which the indicators were housed. This prevented any problems with the wind but still the indicator remained on the line. But the ever-inventive carp angler was not to be beaten and so was born the monkey-climb system.

Monkey Climbs

These were the brainchild Ricky Gibbinson. He started a whole new industry, for there are now literally dozens of different monkey-climb sys-

tems on the market. This in some respects gave us the ultimate in line-management control. The monkey body runs up and down on a stainless steel needle which is positioned in a vertical position directly below the rod. The monkey body always remains on the needle. At the top end of the body is some sort of line-retaining mechanism – this could be a hinged piece of bent wire, an eye on flexible tubing, or just part of a purpose-made moulding. Whatever line-retaining system is used, it pulls clear of the top of the needle, ensuring that the trapped line is given clear passage from the system. Provided that the top of the needle either touches the rod itself or is positioned so that the needle is above the rod in the fishing position, the monkey-climb system will always automatically reset itself, thereby keeping line always under constant tension. Anglers have their own favourite position in which to site the monkey climb. Those who fish free-spool or baitrunner reels usually position the monkey a couple of inches in front of the electronic indicator. Anglers who still use the open-bail-arm system will position the monkey a couple of inches in front of the open spool. In fact this really is the situation that the monkey was originally designed for. With this unique set-up the line coming off the open spool goes under the line retainer and then on to the rod rings. As a take develops, the monkey body rises up the needle till it is in front

An open day for monkey climbs. As you can see we are blessed with so many good set ups –
the choice is yours.

of the spool. In this position the line flows freely from the open spool. If the run stops or slows down the monkey body automatically falls back down the needle, once again trapping the line and keeping it under tension all the time and free from the risk of tangling. At any time, regardless of position, the angler can now strike and the line will automatically pull free of the system. Some of the better monkey systems around come from companies like Fox International, Gardener Tackle, Ultracult, Solar Tackle and Magnum.

Swingers

Just when you thought that the visual indication systems couldn't be improved, another innovative design jumps out of the woodwork. The reason for the improvement is that, good as these monkey systems are, there is always some resistance between the monkey body and the needle. The swinger bite indicator eliminates this completely. Under normal circumstances the resistance created on the monkey system is not a problem; in fact, sometimes it can actually be an advantage, helping the carp to hook itself. But on some waters where the fish have really wised up we are often looking for the minutest indication signalling a taking fish and this is really where the swingers come into their own.

Basically, the construction consists of a line-retaining clip held on the end of a thin stainless steel wire arm which pivots at the rear end, allowing it to swing in an arc to indicate a bite. Along

The Fox International Monkey Climb Set Up features here with the standard open bail arm arrangement.

The alternative to the monkey climb system — The Fox International swingers now being adopted by many of the top carp anglers.

this arm runs a sliding counterbalance weight which can be adjusted between zero and 25 grams, allowing just the right amount of weight to be applied to the line to combat any drift or drag without forfeiting sensitivity. As the arm is held in parallel with the rods and the arc of movement is either upwards or downwards, depending on the bite detected, it is a very stable set-up and operates proficiently even in very windy conditions. The line-retaining clip consists of two moulded balls held under tension with an O-ring. The line is clipped between the two balls and is free to run in the orifice below. When a strike is made the line automatically pulls through.

Although the swinger system is very sensitive and offers good line management, it can only be realistically used with a closed bail arm or free-spool and baitrunner systems. It cannot be used with an open bail arm. All of these modern production-made visual indicators have facilities for housing an isotope which will make them glow at night so that the same fine degree of sensitivity is available during the hours of darkness as in the daytime.

That is a look at the major items of fishing tackle with which the carp angler should familiarise himself. Whether he is using one rod or three, he should be comfortable with the set-up and it should almost become an extension of himself. Uncomfortable and clumsy tackle inevitably leads to bad fishing. Take the time to look at what is available and choose accordingly.

4 TACKLE: SUNDRIES

Having had a look at the major items of tackle I will now address myself to the more sundry items of carp gear, excluding everything concerned with rig-end tackle, which is covered in depth in the next chapter and Chapter 7. Although most of these sundry items are not necessarily absolutely essential, nonetheless they are an important part of the carper's gear be it for stable rod set-ups, personal comfort, or luggage.

ROD-SUPPORTING SYSTEMS

Having selected your electronic indicators you obviously need something to house them on. This also becomes part of a rod-support system.

Bank Sticks

The most basic are bank sticks and rod rests. You will find that a standard thread is used throughout the angling industry. This thread is used for attaching all manner of things together and is ⅜ inch BSF (British Standard Fine). Bank sticks are equipped with a female thread into which rear rod-rest heads and electronic bite indicators can be screwed. You will need two bank sticks to every rod, the rear one will support the butt end of the rod. This will be placed somewhere along the handle just behind the reel and towards the very end of the rod.

There are very many good rod-rest tops available from companies such as Drennan, Ultracult, Gardener and John Roberts. My own preference is for the John Roberts Mini Grip. This is injection-moulded out of a soft rubbery material and will house a full cork or Duplon handle or the much slimmer abbreviated design. These grip tight and are therefore very useful on steeply

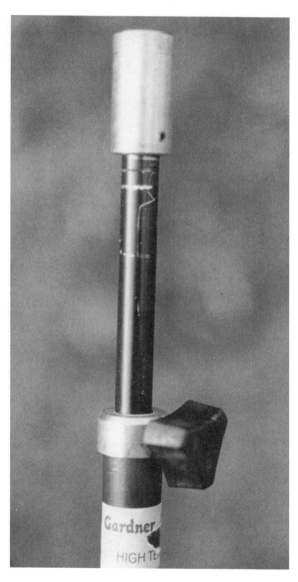

A sturdy bank stick is a must. Ensure that the threads are cleanly cut and the thumbscrew is large and easy to grip.

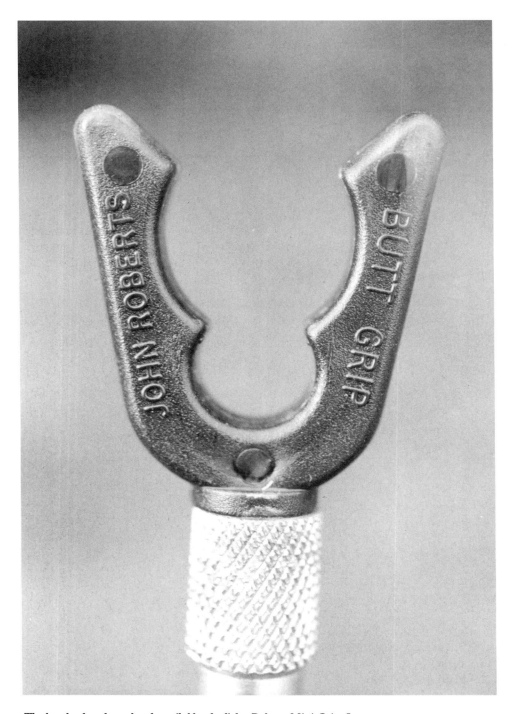

The best back rod-rest head available, the John Roberts Mini Grip. It will accommodate both full cork or Duplon handles as well as abbreviated handles.

inclining banks where the rods often have to be positioned at an acute angle. The front bank stick housing the electronic bite indicator is normally positioned somewhere between the first and second rings, or the reel and the butt ring, according to personal preference.

Bank sticks are available in varying lengths, normally between 18 inches and 3 feet. Most are adjustable, with an inner section sliding in and out of the outer section. The two sections are locked in place at a given height, either by a thumb retaining screw or a locking collar. They should be equipped with a good solid point and a clean-cut thread.

There really are only two materials of any use for this bankside equipment, as it is always in the wet and will rust and corrode very easily. Only aluminium and stainless steel are worthy of consideration. Aluminium is lighter, cheaper, but less robust than stainless steel. However, stainless steel should last a lifetime.

Bank sticks are normally available in two diameters: ½ inch and ¾ inch. There are some real cheap and nasty ones around. Avoid them at all costs as they will definitely let you down. Brands to be relied upon are Ultracult, Gardener, Solar and Magnum.

Buzzer Bars

Most carp fishers use more than one rod – sometimes three or in the extreme even four. In recent years the buzzer-bar system has become very popular. The reason for this is twofold. If you are fishing with, let's say, three rods, normally you

There is always an alternative. More affordable than stainless steel, these are good quality aluminium buzzer bars from the Gardener Tackle stable.

The best quality buzzer bars that money can buy. These are from the superb Magnum stainless steel range.

have to take six bank sticks along to support them. With the buzzer bar system all three rods can be housed on two bank sticks supporting a cross T–bar on which the three rods can be fitted.

Buzzer bars come in various shapes and sizes. They can have either fixed or adjustable centres. An angler fishing with two rods only would normally purchase a fixed-twin set-up; for anyone fishing on varying waters where he is allowed to use two or three rods an adjustable set is well worth considering.

The nice thing about buzzer bars and the second reason for their popularity is that they automatically align the rods. Generally speaking, the front buzzer bar, which houses a set of electronic indicators will be slightly wider than the rear buzzer bar, which houses the butt grips. Therefore the rods fan out at a slight angle. This is ideal, as individual baits will often be positioned quite a few yards apart and the fanning out allows the angler a more direct line from the rod tip to his hookbait, cutting down any resistance which might occur if the line left the tip ring at an acute angle.

As with bank sticks, it's a case of you get what you pay for. At the cheaper end of the market Gardener Tackle offers a comprehensive range of aluminium fixed and adjustable bars; at the top end Magnum supplies the ultimate in buzzer-bar luxury with their stainless steel fully adjustable systems.

An Ariel Bar will keep your monkey climbs clear of the ground; ideal in rainy and muddy conditions.

Ariel Bars

These are used to support the monkey-climb needles and are very useful when fishing a three-rod set-up. Working on a similar principle to the buzzer bar, a single short bank stick can be pushed into the ground and on this the ariel bar fitted. The three needles can then be positioned in exactly the right spot beneath the rods. When an ariel bar is not used the angler is forced to push the needles into the ground, which could damage or bend them. Obviously, any distortion of these needles can cause extra tension to be exerted on the monkey body. The worst scenario is that they could actually jam up completely, causing disaster.

Another plus with the ariel bars is that the system can be positioned several inches above the ground. This is a distinct advantage in rainy conditions as mud and grit could splash up on the needles if they were fitted closer to the ground. This could jam up the system in the same way as a bent needle.

Rod Pods

These are another recent innovation and are gaining popularity at a rate of knots. The system is such that no bank sticks have to be pushed into the ground at all: the rod pod is self-supporting and simply rests on the ground. The legs are splayed at an angle to give a very stable support. Holes in either end allow ½ -inch bank sticks to be fitted, to which buzzer bars are then added.

Rod Pods are now taking over from the twin bank stick set-up. They can be set up on just about any bank, including concrete or wooden staging. This is the Fox model.

The Gardener Tackle Rod Pod, one design of many this company offer.

There will also be some kind of sliding collar to which the needle ariel bar can be attached. You now have a totally independent system for housing your set of rods that will automatically be correctly positioned and support the whole set-up on virtually any bank.

On our modern gravel pits, where the banksides are often steeply sloping and extremely hard, the pods really come into their own. And as for concrete-reinforced swims, paths round park ponds and piers, these can all now be fished without difficulty; and you can imagine just how easily wooden platforms can be approached with the use of the pod.

There are two major companies in the running when it comes to rod pods, Fox International and Gardener Tackle. You should be able to find one

to suit your individual requirements from either of these firms. They all offer slightly different features but they are all well thought out and again you really get what you pay for.

PERSONAL COMFORT

We are now starting to get into the realms of comfort and it is in this sector of the market that things are really starting to open up. For so many years we used chairs that were not made for the angling, but basic garden seats which were only designed to be used on level ground – which, as we all know, is rarely the case around any of our lakes. The only chairs that were worth considering were the now defunct Lafuma, which used to

A good quality low chair with adjustable legs is ideal for short sessions.

For the angler who intends to fish at night or for long sessions a good quality bedchair is an asset.
This is the top of the range Fox model with its adjustable legs and padded sprung mattress.

be the Rolls-Royce of specialist French camping bedchairs and seats.

Recently, however, a new company, Sunnflair, has hit the market with a few nice designs of low chairs and bedchairs at a sensible price. But if it's luxury you want than you should look no further than Fox International. The company has two low chairs on the market: the Standard Adjusta-Level Chair and the Super version. These are high-backed and hammock-style, giving you full support. The legs are adjustable so that steep, uneven banks can be compensated for. For short sessions this is about all you require – they are reasonably light, easy to carry and not too cumbersome when you want to move quickly from swim to swim.

Bedchairs

There are now many anglers who seem to spend a lifetime on the bank, so naturally their creature comforts need to be looked after properly. At the Rolls-Royce end of the bedchair market, the Fox Super Deluxe Adjusta-Level Bedchair simply cannot be beaten. Although they are made largely of aluminium, and are hence nice and light, they are amazingly strong. The padded mattress is laced to the frame by heavy-duty bungee-type cords, which makes it amazingly comfortable. The back frame has a positive-locking multi-position system and naturally the legs are fully adjustable. During the daytime it can double up as an upright chair to enable you to sit beside the rods.

A good quality umbrella is essential for keeping off wind and rain. This 50 inch Wavelock model has now become the standard part of the carp angler's equipment.

Umbrellas

To keep dry, the bare essential for a short session is a good-quality umbrella. Most carp anglers have now turned to a 50-inch wave-lock design. These are a hundred per cent waterproof and offer a sturdy frame. The centre pole can be moved so that it fits in between the rear two ribs, giving the angler more room beneath. For the odd night session, especially in the summer, these will all but cover your bedchair. Most people will use an extra bedchair cover as double protection. To ensure stability of the umbrella the centre pole must be driven firmly into the ground.

Thankfully, gone are the days of those annoying rubber mallets. You always knew when someone was about to set up as there would be the methodical thump-thump in the next swim as your new neighbour tried to drive his brolly pole into the ground. There are now one or two screw-in-type poles: the Powerspike from Ultracult and the Screw In Solid Aluminium Pole from Gardener Tackle. Both of these models are fitted with a hole in the top of the pole into which a T-bar can be inserted, and then it is a matter of literally screwing them into the ground. I have found all but the very hardest of banks no problem with either of these models.

Bivvies

For the angler who is doing more than one night a bivvy can become a home from home, keeping

For angler's doing more than one night a bivvy is a plus. This is the Kevin Nash model that fits over a 50 inch umbrella.

you warm and dry as well as all your gear. There are now so many designs that I could almost fill this chapter talking about them but I will mention only a few of the more popular designs.

If you have a 50-inch umbrella it is probably a good idea to buy an overwrap. Some of the best of these come from the Kevin Nash stable. The brolly is erected at an angle of about the one o'clock and then the one-piece waterproof unit is then thrown over the top and pegged down at eight points coinciding with the eight brolly ribs. There is a zipped door on the front with a see-through panel.

This can be fastened down in arctic conditions. It's a good idea to use a couple of storm rod poles to give extra support and stability. These are fixed to the ribs by a special connector at either side of the door opening. It's surprising just how much difference these couple of poles make. In damp or wintry conditions a good-quality groundsheet will keep any rising moisture at bay, making your stay that little bit more comfortable.

Regular session angle may well invest in one of the all-in-one designs. The latest of these is the Super Bivvy from the Fox stable. This is quite a revolution in bivvy/umbrella design. The ribcage supporting system has been completely done away with and replaced with a unique centre-locking system and six solid fibreglass arms. This means that the set-up can be positioned much lower to the ground as there are no internal protrusions restricting the angler's movements. This

The latest in bivvy technology, the Fox International Super Bivvy. This is an all-in-one model with no separate umbrella.

I have found a great help in tight swims and windy conditions as the whole construction is that much smaller. Like the Nash design the Fox Bivvy benefits from extra storm rods to give extra support and stability.

Bivvy Pegs

I suppose I really ought to mention briefly these often forgotten items of kit. It's all very well having the latest all-singing, all-dancing bivvy set-up, which may well have set you back £150, but you need something reliable to hold it down. Short bent-up pieces of wire that you often see in camping shops have little or no use and at present I have seen only two models on the market

that I consider worthy of mention. These are the Ultracult Screw In Bivvy Pegs, which are fitted with a T-Bar and a spiral coil of wire which can be screwed firmly into the ground; and the Kingfisher Pegs, which have a moulded plastic large key-type top on them, again with a screw-type shaft. These hold firm in both soft and sandy conditions as well as hard gravelly ground.

Sleeping Bags

To complete the outdoor set-up, good-quality sleeping bags have become as much a part of the all-season carp angler's gear as the bivvies and bedchairs. The requirements for an angling sleeping bag are totally different from those for a

You will need something substantial to hold these bivvy systems down, especially in windy conditions. The Ultracult Screw In Bivvy Peg is ideal.

camping bag. It is essential that the angler can quickly get out of the bag in the middle of the night if a take occurs and this is only possible with a full-length quick-release zip. Someone jumping about like a giant mailbag may look quite hilarious as he struggles to free himself from a cheap half-zipped camping bag, but not only is it positively dangerous, it could well mean a lost fish.

Good-quality all-season bags are now available to the angling fraternity. These usually have a tog rating of 13.1 and have a full-length central quick-release crash zip. A built-in hood and waterproof underbag will complete a good design. The two top sellers on the angling market are the Coleman Peak One and the Fox 30. A

good-quality sleeping-bag cover, which can be thrown off before your speedy departure from the sleeping bag will complete your outdoor comfort.

A Travelling Outfit

While on the subject of our creature comforts, to spare a thought for the travelling angler, especially those who have to suffer the traumas of flying off to one of the favourite European venues. The very meagre baggage allowance just doesn't give us the opportunity of taking all the items of kit that we need for a session abroad. The best allowance you can hope for is about 20 kilos of hold baggage and 10 kilos of hand baggage, on many flights it can be half that amount. Naturally there is no chance of taking umbrella, bivvy, and bedchair – these alone would exceed your allowance. So I have come up with a format that goes a long way to making life comfortable as well as being within that allocated allowance. Instead of a bedchair I now take a good-quality inflatable lilo, not one of these cheap plastic jobs but a fabric camping design. I replace the umbrella and bivvy with an ET Bivvydome. This is a lightweight igloo-style tent which offers a twin-skin protection, keeping out rain and reducing condensation. A sewn-in groundsheet stops any of the nasty crawling things getting in and attacking you at night and a mosquito door stops those flying pneumatic drills bombarding you.

The Bivvydome is supported by four fibreglass rods and the whole construction is very lightweight. The only disadvantage is that in rainy conditions the door has to be zipped up as the rain comes in the sloping sides if it is left open – but then you can't have everything. Certainly the advantages far outweigh the disadvantages.

LUGGAGE

Long gone are the days of bunging everything in an army supplies rucksack. Many companies have now set up specialising in angling luggage. As a result, there have been some amazing developments in recent years. The first company to make a major impression on the market was

Left: to *keep you warm on cold nights a sleeping bag is an essential and not a luxury, especially in the winter.*

Below: *a shelter with a different design. This E.T. Bivvy Dome is very lightweight and igloo shaped and has proved to be ideal for the travelling angler.*

You will need something that is cavernous enough to eat up all your essential items of tackle as well as food, bait and cooking equipment. This is a good design from the very comprehensive range of specialist luggage that Kevin Nash has on offer.

Kevin Nash with his Happy Hooker products, which included rod bags that would house three rods with reels on as well as umbrellas, bank sticks and bits and pieces. They also supply large cavernous rucksacks to take all those items for a weekend's fishing. A few years on Wychwood have really hit the top end of this specialist luggage market and are at present the best in the field.

I also feel very privileged that I have been in a position to put over my own ideas about specialist luggage, so much so that DAM recently launched a Ruck-A-Bag and a Rod Caddy endorsed with my name. These two items of equipment are designed to house everything for a full weekend's fishing. The Rod Caddy will take a 50-inch brolly plus wrap-round or overwrap in the main section, and three made-up rods complete with reels fitted to the outside. Landing net and pole also have their own compartments whilst rod pods, bank sticks and the like, are stored in yet another pouch. And finally on the Rod Caddy there is a pocket for housing sacks, slings and unhooking mats.

The Ruck-A-Bag has pockets on the outside for storing camera equipment, buzzers and buzzer bars, a Stewart box with all the bits and pieces in and any other odd small tackle boxes. The main compartment will accept bait, food, cooking equipment and clothing. A sleeping bag is held in place under the large retaining flap and lastly there are four D-rings so your bedchair can be strapped on the back of the bag.

With these two items of luggage you can transport all your gear to the swim hands free. This is obviously an advantage, especially if there is a long walk and you have to negotiate fences, styles, ditches, and so on.

TACKLE BOXES

There must be literally dozens and dozens of different sizes, shapes and colours of tackle boxes. With such a variety you would have thought there would be dozens to choose from. In fact this is not the case at all. Many designs fall down because of loose-fitting lids, gaps between the compartments and lid, hinges that fall to pieces and brittle material that cracks at the first knock.

The only make that I have any faith in is the Stewart box, which has been around for years. In the largest size there are two or three different-variations offering different-sized compartments and colours. My own personal preference is for the grey non-see-through model, with its strong hinge and clip. This one box actually houses ninety per cent of my end-tackle bits and pieces, hooks, leger weights, swivels, beads, rig tubing, baiting needles, hair stops, hook-link material, scissors, knives, floats and a hundred other things that I cannot possibly do without.

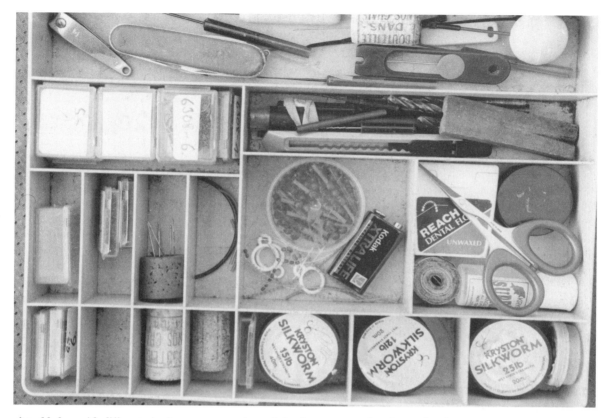

A tackle box with different-sized compartments is needed to house our various items of end tackle. This is the very popular Stewart Box design.

The only other boxes and bags that I carry are a couple of rig pouches where twenty or more pre-tied rigs can be stored and some spare spool containers. It is not unusual for me to carry nine or so spare spools of different breaking strains of line. This is quite an investment and needs storing well. I cringe when I see expensive spare spools just kicking around in the bottom of some people's tackle bags and they are always the first to complain when the spool or line gets damaged.

Opposite: this is a system I designed myself so that every item of tackle, including rods, reels, bedchair, bivvy, and the like, can be carried hands free to the bank.

FEEDING ACCESSORIES

As the baits that we use for carp fishing are so varied it stands to reason that it is impossible to use a single type of feeding device. Boilies alone vary in size and consistency and need different treatment to get the best out of them. Particles can be anything from hempseed to brazil nuts, again needing specialist individual treatment. So have a delve into my tackle bag and look at some of the feeding devices that I use.

Catapults

These are the first and most obvious method of getting baits out into the swim. Although there are many brands on the market I have settled for just two, Drennan and Keenets Milo brand. All of these are fitted with modern latex elastics,

*Spare spools can be very expensive so it makes sense to house them with adequate
protection. Here is shown the Terry Eustace Spool Bag which has been well thought out.*

which vary in strength and can be altered to suit
distance and application. Pouches are also
widely varied – the tiniest one will just accommodate a single 14mm boilie while the largest
will eat up a good handful of tiger nuts. Both the
Drennan and Milo models are made from injection-moulded frames with nice handgrips and
easy-change latex systems.

I have about four different-sized pouches and
all are interchangeable, which gives me a great
many permutations so that I can bait from
literally a few rod lengths out up to about 80
yards with an 18mm-diameter boilie.

Wrist Rockets

For large, hard boilies which need to be catapulted at ranges beyond 80 and up to about 110

yards in favourable conditions, these powerful
hunting catapults are extremely useful. They are
constructed from a heavy-duty sturdy steel frame
with a vital wrist support to ensure accuracy. The
moulded plastic grip gives a powerful hold while
the strong, thick, latex elastics make it possible to
fire a single bait towards the horizon. The thin
leather strap in which the boilie is encapsulated
is cut down to the minimum size so that it offers
as little air resistance as possible.

Throwing Sticks

These really are only any use for firing boilies out
into the swim. The most basic of them consists of
a 1-inch-diameter plastic tube, the top cut off at
about forty-five degrees with a handlebar grip on
the other end. There is quite a knack in using a

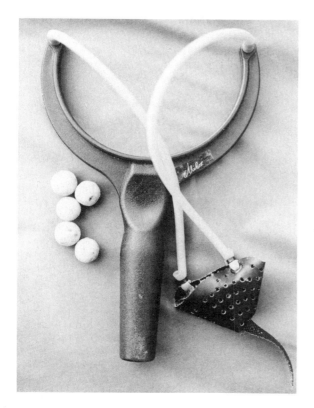

There are a vast range of catapults available to us – I always seem to end up with a bagful of them. This is the Milo design from Italy with a small pouch for firing single boilies.

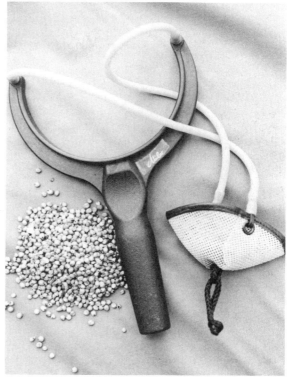

Another Milo design but with a much larger pouch for putting out particles or large balls of ground bait.

throwing stick – some people are naturals while others have to practise for some while before they get the timing just right. Generally speaking, it is a short, sharp movement on an extended arm with the starting point at about nine o'clock and the release point being at about one o'clock. The basic plastic models are capable of putting out hard round boilies up to about 80 yards or so.

The most popular design of throwing stick is the strange-looking swan-necked Cobra. These come in varying lengths and diameters and are much easier to use then the more standard parallel models, so much so that the Cobra has become a standard part of the carper's equipment. The King Cobra which is a slightly different shape from the ordinary Cobra, can put a

hard round boilie out to about 120 yards in favourable conditions with relative ease.

The beauty of throwing sticks is that there is nothing to go wrong – no elastics to break and no pouches to replace. But as I have said, they are restricted virtually to boilies.

To achieve the best accuracy from any of the aforementioned feeding devices baits should be as round and as aerodynamic as possible. The smallest flaw in a boilie will be magnified as it flies through the air and it will stray off of the intended target and lose distance. This will definitely be more apparent with the Cobra throwing sticks as the boilies will leave the end of the tube at great velocity whilst rapidly spinning at the same time. Boilies for Cobra use should also be

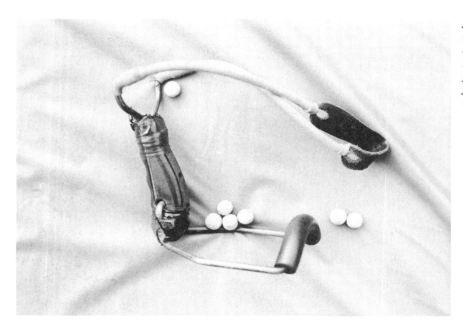

A very powerful wrist rocket. This is an American design, originally used for killing vermin. Extremely powerful, it is one that I use for putting out hard boilies at long range.

made from a good hard mix that binds together well – soft baits will merely explode in mid-air as they are thrown from this powerful tool.

Bait Rocket
This is a very useful device for baiting up accurately with very small light particles or mini-boilies at reasonable range. The Bait Rocket is actually used on a spare rod, which should be of a beefy design as a loaded rocket can weigh up to 5oz, depending on the type of bait. For the best performance I like to use a shock leader of about

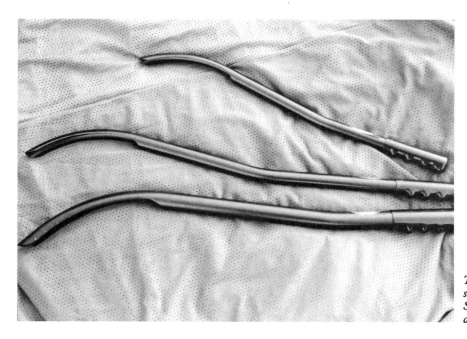

Throwing sticks come in all shapes and sizes but the Swan Necked Cobras are definitely the best.

Some people are naturals at using a throwing stick, with others it can take many weeks to become proficient, but it's worth the effort.

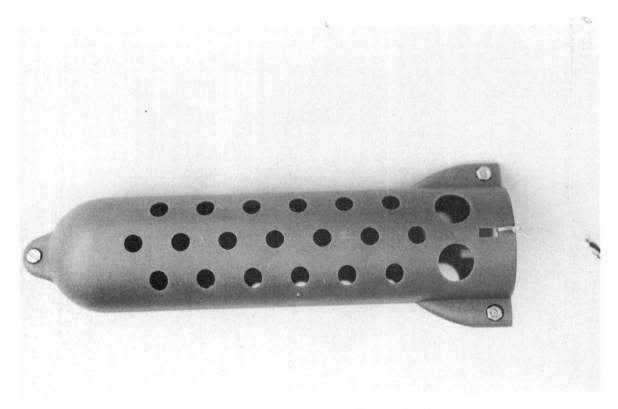

For putting out small boilies and particles beyond catapult range, the Gardener Tackle Bait Rocket is ideal.

20lb and a main line of 7 or 8lb BS for casting out the Rocket. If you don't use a shock leader there is a very good chance that you will crack off during a powerful cast.

The Bait Rocket is about three-quarters filled with your chosen particle and then cast out into the swim. It's a good idea to line up with some sort of marker on the far bank. On massive waters a semi-permanent visual marker can be left in the swim. As the Bait Rocket hits the water it will turn turtle because of the polystyrene ball in one end and automatically jettison its load of bait in the swim.

Naturally, splashdown with such a device can make a great disturbance in the swim. Depending on the type of water this can be either an advantage or a disadvantage. On easy, hungry waters the carp get to know that it's feeding time as there is a splash followed by a shower of bait, giving them a quick meal. On hard waters the reverse is true and the angler may well have to wait many hours or even days for the carp to re-enter the area. This is always worth bearing in mind.

Something else to give a little thought to when using a Bait Rocket is that, because they do disturb the swim, you might annoy an adjacent angler, so out of politeness it's worth just having a word first. With beachcaster-type equipment a Bait Rocket can be thrown out into the swim some 80 yards or so, way beyond normal catapulting range for light particles.

Model Boats

I had to do much mind wrestling concerning this prickly subject and decided that I should expose

Although controversial this has to be the ultimate baiting system – the Alpha 1 Radio Controlled Boat. This will dispense 8 lbs of bait at distances in excess of 300 yds.

all the cards, wrinkles and all. There has been much controversy over the use of model boats for putting baits out and really this is not the time or the place to discuss the ethics surrounding the subject. Suffice it to say that on occasions I have to hold my hand up and say that I do use model boats. I must stress, however, that in this country it is a rare occurrence and only on waters where I have first gained permission and also tried all other methods of catching the carp. I can hear the cries now – that has to be cheating!

Well, I can only justify it by telling you that I fish the odd massive gravel pit with very low numbers of fish which are considered to be some of the hardest venues in the land. For whatever reason, the carp in a couple of these particular venues never seem to feed within casting range of the bank. This probably sounds unbelievable,

but I can tell you we have really tried. On one such water the carp will occasionally pick baits up in the margins of an island some 250 yards from the nearest fishable bank and this is where the remote-controlled boat comes into its own.

The other times I have used this quite unique baiting method is when fishing on the Continent – not at long range, I hasten to add, usually only 50 yds or so. With the boat it is far easier and much quicker to put out freebies to ravenous shoals of heavily feeding fish.

I have discovered only a couple of good purpose-made model boats designed for the angler – the Broadlands and the Alpha 1. I am currently using the Alpha 1 with great success. It is constructed on a sturdy fibreglass hull and has two unique sloping bait compartments with flip-up doors. The combined capacity of these two compartments is about 7lbs of boilies, which is a great deal of bait that can be distributed into the swim in one go.

It will probably take me about an hour to introduce that number of boilies with a throwing stick from the bank, and that's assuming that I could achieve the distance. As well as putting out the free offerings, the rig and hookbait can also be transported out to the desired spot. In fact, two hookbaits can be put out in one trip with a little practice, one in either compartment. The method is to run the boat out with the rods on the rests and the bail arms open. First the door on one side is opened up and out come freebies, hookbaits and rig. The boat then can be driven to the second spot, possibly only a few yards away, with a repeat performance for the second set-up.

The nice thing about the Alpha 1 is that it is not of normal propeller and rudder design; instead it is equipped with a large above-the-water fan mounted on the rear of the boat. This swivels, giving forward movement as well as direction. I have used this model successfully up to nearly 300 yards with the aid of a pair of binoculars for spot-on accuracy. I don't profess to understand all the electronics and mechanics of the thing; all I can say is that it has caught me an extra fish or two when the going has got really tough.

But please, if you are tempted to use one, putting aside the ethics for one moment, do ensure that you gain permission to use it first. One little thought I will pass on to you, however, which will perhaps go some way to justifying the use of the boat is that I am a little concerned first about the trend of using 5oz leads to cast to extreme range. The guys who do this are obviously trying to achieve the same ends as myself so there is no argument on that score. But 5oz of lead whistling through the air at 100 m.p.h. is a pretty lethal weapon, especially in the event of a crack-off. I won't dwell on the outcome of such an incident.

Secondly, sadly we have already experienced at least one death of an angler rowing his baits out on the famous Queensford Lagoon. Perhaps if he had used a model boat he would still be in pursuit of those magnificent fish. So I will just leave you with that thought before you condemn the use of model boats out of hand.

5 BOTTOM RIGS

Before I turn to any of these rigs I would like to remind you that all that follows is based on fact that has come to light from the experiences of myself and a few close friends. You will see that I have not included some of the so-called most up-to-date rigs. This is for two reasons. First, I believe that a lot of them are simply bedchair theorising and I am personally not prepared to write about rigs that have not been successful for me. Second, there are others, such as the use of long-shanked fly hooks that are bent at an angle, and huge patterns of sea hooks, that I believe can be detrimental to the carp's well-being. So I am sorry but you will not find any of these types of set-up endorsed in the pages of this book.

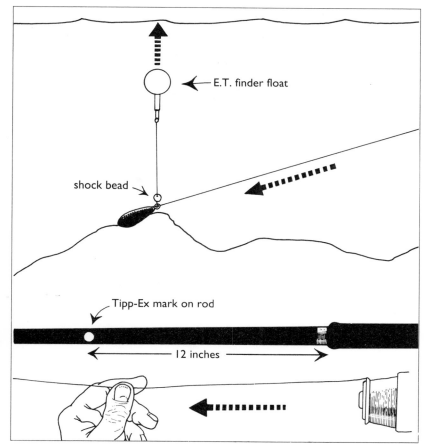

The feature finder.

FEATURE FINDER

Although this is not strictly a fishing rig in the true sense of the word it is nevertheless one of the most important set-ups that I use. I am always quite staggered that even supposedly top-flight carp anglers have really no idea of the topography of a particular swim. Rash assumptions are made into why fish should be in a certain area at a given time. I believe it is of great importance to get to know any lake in intimate detail. It is only then that you can unlock the key that leads to consistent catches.

A feature finder will enable you to look beneath the surface layers and build up a mental picture of just how the undulating bottom is made up. Small variations in depth, changes from gravel to mud or to silt are all useful notes to make. Bars, plateaux and sunken islands are more obvious but it is often a small feature in an open sheet of water that produces the goods. So the hours spent with such a set-up will undoubtedly pay dividends for future catches.

Really the set-up couldn't be simpler: a leger weight of 2 to 3oz is slid onto the main line and left free running.

A shock bead is then put on the line before you tie on the feature finder. The shock bead will protect the knot that you have just tied as well as helping the set-up to be tangle-free.

The method of practice is as follows. The feature finder is cast to the extremities of the swim.

One of my most useful pieces of kit – the E.T. Feature Finder. Just the job for pin-pointing hot spots.

The line is sunk between rod tip and leger weight and then pulled tight so that the feature finder is pulled down hard against the leger weight. It is then a matter of gently paying out the line until the feature finder appears on the surface. The amount of line that is payed out is measured, giving you the depth of water. The easiest way to do this is as shown, by Tippexing a mark on the rod itself about 12 inches in front of the reel. The line is then pulled out in front of the spool and the number of times counted. The rest is obviously simple arithmetic.

The feature finder is then pulled a few yards back to the angler and the procedure repeated. Carry on doing this until the whole swim has been covered and you have accurately mapped out all the different depths in the swim. From this you will be able to establish bars, plateaux, sharp drop-offs, and the like.

While you are carrying out this exercise you will also be able to tell how the bottom is made up. This is done by feeling how the lead travels across the bottom itself. Shingle, fine gravel and the like will give a juddery, bouncy type of retrieve which almost feels quite hard. Larger flints, gravels and boulders will be given away by jerky movements of the rod tip, with the leger weight occasionally locking into position. Mud and fine silt will be felt through the rod by a fine, steady, easy retrieve, almost like pulling the lead

back across the living-room carpet. Deeper silt will reveal itself in similar fashion but feel heavier than the actual weight attached to the end of the line.

Heavily weeded swims are difficult to explore so it's worth taking time out in the winter months to do the mapping out even if you are not going to fish until the following summer.

The best feature finder that I have found is the illustrated ET model, which consists of a large very buoyant polystyrene ball which has been dipped in Day Glo fluorescent paint. Inserted into the polyball is an injection-moulded plastic stem which terminates in a small neat eye. It's well worth having two or three of these in the bottom of your tackle box.

KNOTS

The weakest part of any set-up is the knot. There are good knots and some that are not quite so good, but rarely any bad knots. But badly tied knots are blatantly in abundance when you listen to anglers talking. I am often asked which is the most reliable knot to use in any given situation and in reality the answer is always that it is far better for the angler to tie a good simple knot rather than a bad complicated knot. The best that you can do is keep practising until you

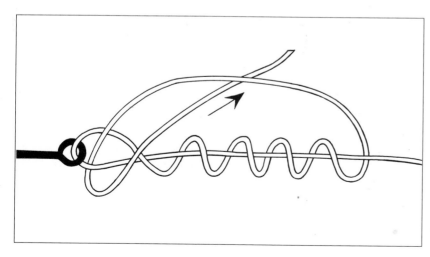

Half blood knot.

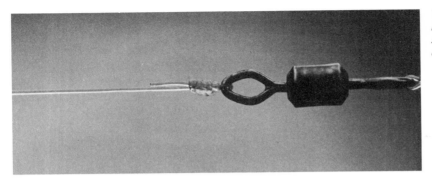

This is a close-up of a Grinner knot showing just how each coil should lie behind each other to obtain ultimate strength.

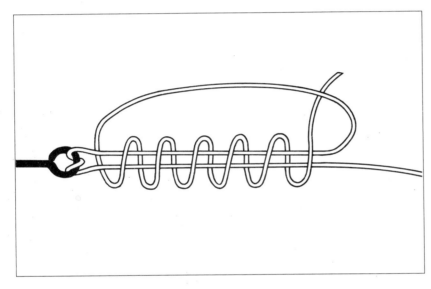

Grinner knot.

become proficient at three or four different knots, which will cover you for most of your angling requirements. Here are a few of the knots that I use myself with some of the features of them.

Blood Knot

Undoubtedly this is the simplest of all knots to tie and quite reliable. Its performance can be improved by passing the line twice through the eye before commencing the knot and tucking the end back through the first loop after tying the barrel. The blood knot is ideal for joining all monofilament and attaching eyed hooks, leger weights and swivels. As with all knots, all the turns should lie neatly behind one another and the knot should be moistened before finally being pulled tight.

Grinner Knot

If I had to choose one knot to rely on for attaching any eyed accessories this would be the one for me. It is equally at home with monofilament, Dacron-type braids and the new breed of HPPE hook links.

When attaching main lines or hook links to an eyed piece of tackle the knot strength will always be improved when the line is passed more than once through the eye. Twice will be a great improvement, but three times is ideal for most situations. This is more apparent with new multi-fibred HPPE (high-performance polyethylene) materials. These super-soft braids have now become a standard part of every angler's kit.

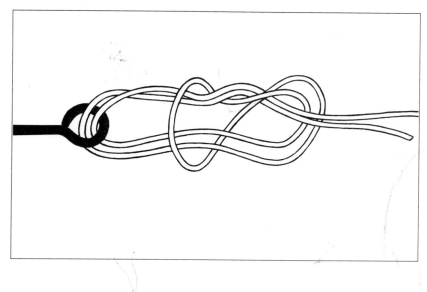

Palomar knot.

Two-turn slip knot.

Palomar Knot

Following hard on the heels of the grinner knot in terms of reliability is the palomar. Care must be taken when tying this knot as you are dealing with two thicknesses of line throughout. It is important not to get them crossed over as this will weaken the knot.

The palomar has the advantage of having very little barrel to it, and so it does not have the same stiffening effect as some knots do immediately up against the eye.

Two-Turn Slip Knot

This is one of the most reliable knots for monofilaments, especially with heavy, thick, stiff lines. But I do not like using it with HPPE's as there is a tendency for the second overhand knot to come unwrapped when the pressure has eased off with

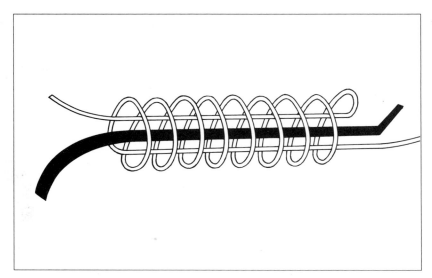

Multi-turned whipping knot.

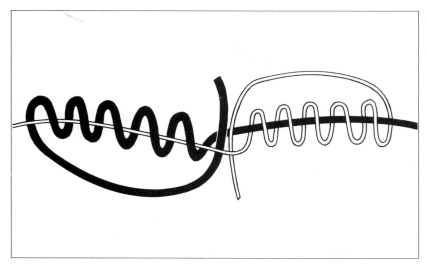

Full blood knot.

the rig lying on the bottom. But it is great with monofilaments.

Multi-Turned Whipping Knot
Many anglers prefer some of the heavy-duty short-shanked spade-end hooks for carping, and there is only really one knot that I am happy in using with them and that is the multi-turned whipping knot. Generally speaking, the greater number of turns the better the knot performs, but realistically, with breaking strain lines that anglers use, between eight and twelve turns is sufficient.

When using the multi-turned whipping knot it is of the utmost importance that the hook link leaves the shank on the underside of the spade as illustrated. The other way round and the pressure on the line as it runs over the spade could easily sever it. Once this knot has been tied and pulled tightly together I like to smear a small drop of Superglue over the barrel for extra security.

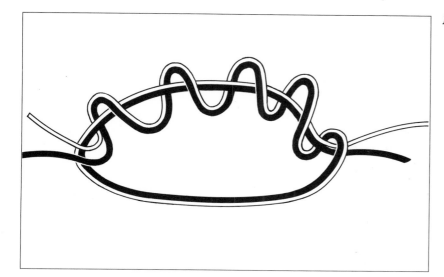

Four-turned water knot.

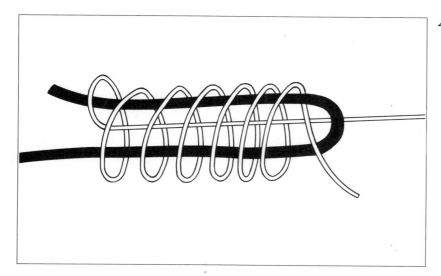

Albright knot.

Joining Line

There will be the odd occasion when you will need to tie two lengths of line together. This may well be when attaching a new batch of line onto the spool, tying up a paternoster rig, or something similar.

There are only three knots that you should ever consider for this purpose: the full blood knot, the four-turn water knot and the Albright knot.

For lines of similar diameter the full blood knot is best. It will tie lines of different diameters but the smaller the difference the better. The four-turn water knot is good for lines of varying diameter but should not be used with diameters of greater than fifty per cent difference. This is where the Albright knot comes into its own. It's ideal for using with different diameters of line but the thicker must always be the looped end, with the thinner wound around the outside.

This is occasionally used for shock leader knots, which I shall be covering a bit later in the chapter.

HOOKS

Having said that any set-up is only as good as the knots tied in it, the second most important item is undoubtedly the hook. I often smile to myself when such an important part of kit merits no more than a passing glance in most people's eyes.

Realistically, we have never ever had it so good, for it wasn't so many years ago that we had little in the way of hooks to choose from. The fact of the matter is that we now have so many that it is almost impossible for the angler to use every pattern available to him and pick out the best. Most anglers will have their own favourites and stick with them until they get let down. There have been trends in hooks but I get a feeling that the whole thing has come full circle and some of the patterns that started off in the early days of carp fishing have been rediscovered.

I haven't got the space available to document every pattern and list good and bad points in detail. So instead I will simply describe the hooks that I have used and have the utmost faith in, and I apologise in advance if your favourite is not amongst them. So here is a selection of some that I am currently using or have used in the last few seasons:

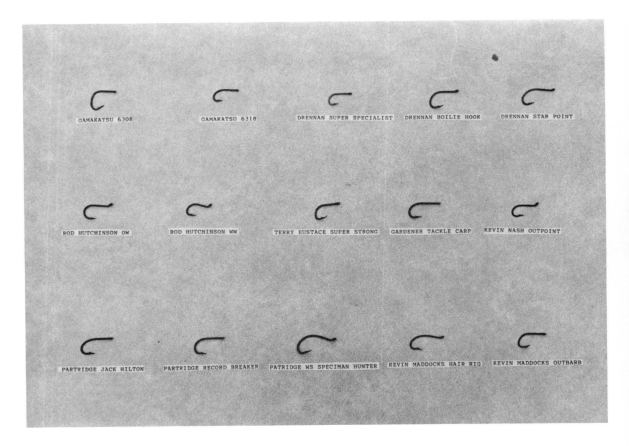

With such a comprehensive range of carp hooks, we are now spoilt for choice.

1 – Drennan Super Specialist
2 – Drennan Boilie Hook
3 – Drennan Starpoint
4 – Gamakatsu 6316
5 – Gamakatsu 6318
6 – Gamakatsu 6308
7 – Partridge Jack Hilton (Black)
8 – Partridge Jack Hilton (Niflor coated)
9 – Partridge Rod Hutchinson VW Hook
10 Partridge Rod Hutchinson OW Hook

These are my top ten favourites. They vary in wire gauge, forging, shape, weight and strength and I find that they are more than enough for me to carry and service my current carping needs very adequately. A thing to remember is that these are mass-produced and will occasionally vary in quality. Things do go wrong from time to time; it is almost inevitable that a rogue batch of hooks will occasionally find its way onto the market – perhaps over-tempered (too soft and bend out easily) or under-tempered (brittle and break

easily). Other faults are eyes that have not been finished a hundred per cent and cut-through hook links, or even barbs that have been cut too deeply so that the points break off easily.

We are now in the era of chemically sharpened hooks, which only a decade ago were ridiculed as being not safe to use. Chris Ball and I used the first Japanese models of these when they first came into the country and we have stuck with this type of hook ever since. I remember only too well in those early days of chemically sharpened hooks just how much stick we took for condoning their use. Ten years on it's almost impossible to find a pattern that hasn't been treated in this way. I'm glad we occasionally get things right.

HOOK-LINK MATERIAL

Third in the priority stakes has to be the hook link. There are some waters where straightforward monofilaments still regularly catch fish, and

Dacron offers us a much more subtle hooklink than standard monofilament.

Kryston Silkworm, one of the new high-tech H.P.P.E. hooklink materials.

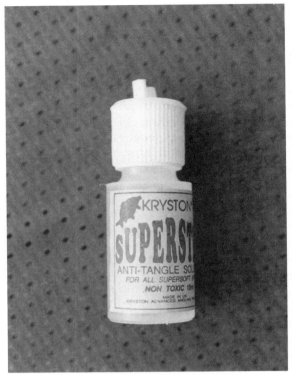

Kryston Super Stiff Gel. This makes any of the super soft hooklinks more easy to manage.

Kryston Multistrand, an unbraided version of Silkworm. Some say this is the ultimate in hooklink technology available – it certainly catches a lot of fish.

if this is so there is no point in changing. But with increased pressure things start to change and it's worth considering an alternative material for the hook link.

Terylene and Dacron braids are the first move towards a softer hook link. Leeda, Berkley, Drennan, DAM and Masterbraid are all very good makes. These are much softer than standard monofilaments but generally speaking they will absorb on water and mirror the contours of the bottom – which in some respects can be a good thing. But at the same time it is possible for them to create extra resistance to the taking fish. The next move is towards braided HPPE (high-performance polyethylene). A whole new industry has sprung up almost overnight concerning these hook links. Kryston have an extremely comprehensive range braided on this material. Silkworm, Merlin and Super Silk are the three current favourites. Gamma Braid from the Nash stable, Hi-Tenacity braid from the Drennan stable and Multitech line from the DAM stable are also excellent. When the carp have sussed that little lot out the last resort at the moment is multistrand hook links.

This is the same HPPE material but instead of being braided the strands lie parallel with each other. If you are attempting to use this stuff as hook-link material I really suggest that you apply the Kryston Stiffening Gel before you attempt to knot it up. Its very fine filaments are hard to handle and you can get in a real mess if you don't use the water-soluble gel.

Both Kevin Nash and Kryston supply this multistrand hook-link material.

SWIVELS

The hook link has to be joined to the main line in some fashion. By far the best way is to use a swivel. There are basically two good types of swivels to consider: the Berkley round-eyed variety and the DAM crosslink type. Similar patterns are available under different brand names but as I only use these two makes I cannot really speak for the reliability of the others.

Sizes 7–10 will cover most of our carp angling needs, and I shall discuss later in this chapter which type to use with which set-up.

Swivels – the best two designs available. The round-eyed Berkley design and the cross-linked diamond-eye type, the most popular designs with the carp angler.

HOW DO CARP FEED?

The answer to this question dictates the way we design our set-ups. Some of the extraordinary explanations are given for using some very complicated and unnecessary set-ups but – except for the really ultra-difficult highly pressurised big-fish waters where the carp have seen just about every conceivable set-up – I think you only need concern yourself with two basic types.

When you spend a lot of time observing carp, as a lot of us do, it is noticeable that individual carp feed in an individual way. If we could guarantee that a particular fish would definitely pick up our hookbaits we could fine-tune our rig to suit that individual carp. In realistic terms, this is virtually impossible. Let us therefore consider the two basic ways in which carp feed on bottom bait.

Sucking and Blowing

The first and most common method of feeding is what I call sucking and blowing. The carp inverts internal muscles in its mouth to cause a vacuum, which draws in water. Food items suspended in the waters are carried into the cavities of the mouth itself. The reverse then happens: the water is expelled and any food items that haven't been passed back to the pharyngeal teeth are blown out.

Carp can be observed feeding in this manner for most of the time, not just on suspicious hookbaits. The distance from which they can draw food items into the mouth varies between about ½ inch and 4 or 5 inches, depending on the size of carp and the type of food items involved.

Up-Ending

In the second type of feeding pattern we have observed the carp almost up-ends itself, with its tail pointing towards the surface. It literally clamps its open extended mouth hard down on the bottom before drawing in the food items. At one time I thought that this second feeding behaviour had come about as a result of angling pressure, with the carp beginning to wise up to our terminal rig set-ups. But recently I was fortunate enough to observe at very close quarters

some young naive carp which had never been fished for. They displayed exactly the same feeding pattern, which disproves my earlier theory. But a thought has just crossed my mind. Could this feeding behaviour have been passed on through the genes of the parent fish? Now there's a thought!

First let's have a look at by far the commonest feeding method, sucking and blowing. Before the days of the hair rig, when we used to think that the hook should be completely buried in the baits, we experienced lots of twitch bites. The indicator would make a sharp upward movement of a couple of inches at the most. We would hover over the rods in anticipation of these twitches, trying to time the strike just right.

I now realise with the benefit of hindsight that most of these twitches were actually caused by the carp blowing out the bait, which is more vicious than when they suck it in. No wonder we only ever converted a small percentage of these twitch-like bites! Slowly it was realised that we could actually show more of the hook outside the bait than we originally thought. This came about only because of a change in the bait format. We had moved on from specialist paste baits, which were soft and moulded round the hook to skinned baits.

These were lightly boiled, which gave them a tough skin round the outside. They later became known as boilies. These obviously couldn't be moulded round the hook and when drawn onto the hook with the baiting needle were very difficult to strike through. So, in the evolution of things, we started to just nick the hook through the skin of the boilie, exposing seventy-five per cent of the hook outside the bait. What a difference this made to takes! As the carp were sucking and blowing the baits, occasionally they would be pricked by the now exposed hook, which caused them to panic and resulted in a screaming take. This was the first step towards self-hooking bolt rigs.

As time went on and as we headed towards the late seventies, hooks became larger in relation to the size of bait, hook links shorter and leger weights heavier. The carp now had restricted movements of bait on the hook link; the area of hook exposed with a larger pattern was now quite huge in comparison with the earlier set-up; and a carp lightly pricking itself would be exposed to the full brunt of a 3oz leger weight. And so the bolt rig was born.

If that wasn't enough for the carp to cope with, the year 1979 should go down in history as the origin of the greatest leveller in carp fishing – the hair rig.

The Hair Rig

This was the brainchild of Lennie Middleton and was to change the face of carp angling as we know it today. Lennie's forward thinking had now completely detached the bait from the hook, save a very fine filament of line called the hair. As you can see, the boilie, particles, or whatever were attached to the hook at the point of the bend by this fine strand – at first a human hair and later light monofilament of 1lb BS.

Although Lennie's original theory was brilliant, if you look closely at how the bait is sucked in and blown out of the carp's mouth it did not provide the complete answer. A great move forward with a high degree of self-pricking, but not the ultimate. The bait, by its nature, and aided by the drag of the line, would enter the mouth first;

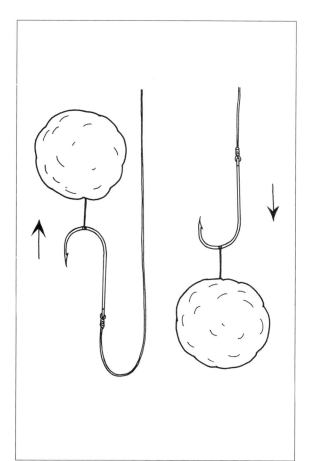

Original hair rig.

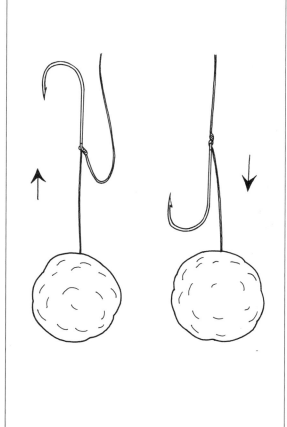

'Off' the eye hair rig.

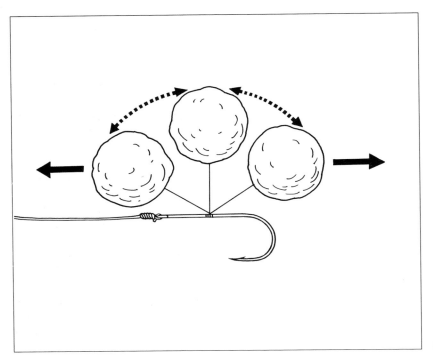

Mid-shank pivoting hair rig.

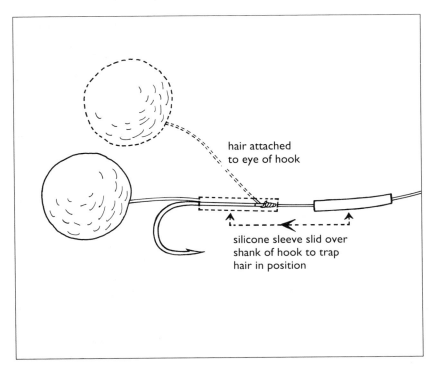

hair attached
to eye of hook

silicone sleeve slid over
shank of hook to trap
hair in position

Mid-shank hair rig.

it would also be expelled first dragging the hook out behind it by the bend, which did not give the point of the hook much of the target area of the carp's mouth to come into contact with.

Of course this revolution inspired lots of other thinking anglers and the hair was now being attached to different points on the hook in the search for better presentation. The next easiest place to attach the hair was at the eye, but again all was not perfect. Look at the drawing and you will see that there is an immediate problem. As the bait is drawn into the mouth there is a chance of the hook pivoting round and going in eye first. This hit the target area bang on but usually from the outside of the mouth, which is not really desirable, because it gives a light hookhold and fish tend to fall off during the fight. Also, there was an ethical question about hooking fish on the outside of the mouth. However, it wasn't long before the ideal position for the hair attachment became apparent.

Mid-Shank Pivoting Hair Rig

You can see what an effective set-up this mid-shank position offers. The bait will draw the hook into the mouth bend first; on ejection the bait will pivot round on a perfect hinge and be blown out eye first and at a slightly downward angle. Bingo! We now have what I believe is the best chance of pricking the inside of the carp's mouth. This mid-shank position is quite critical and should always be as near as possible opposite the point of the hook. If it is to be at all off-centre slightly, but only very slightly, towards the eye.

Tying the hair mid-shank can be a bit of a bind. By far the easiest way is to tie it to the eye of the hook and then slide a silicone sleeve down over the hook link onto the hook, trapping the hair along the back of the shank. This allows you to dictate the take-off position precisely.

Hair Materials

We have come a long way since the original hair-rig. Lennie always used to think that the hair itself should be as fine as possible, but has now realised that the finest is not always the best. Monofilament does not like bending back on

itself and if we are to create a living hinge for ulti-mate hair-rig presentation the pivot point where the hair leaves the hook must be as flexible as possible.

Fine filamented stranded materials like dental floss and multistrand have proved to make an excellent hinge. They have the added advantage that a higher breaking strain than with monofila-ment can be used, which avoids the hair breaking on a very hard cast. Also, there is no need for the hair to be re-tied every time the bait is changed as with the original set-up. A small loop is tied in the end of the hair into which a boilie stop is placed, which holds the bait firmly in position.

A baiting needle is pushed through the boilie and hooked into the loop, and the boilie is trans-ferred from the needle onto the hair, as shown in the drawing. The length of the hair is almost as critical as the pivot point, and with this type of set-up I like the bait to be in such a position that the bottom of the bend of the hook lies in exactly the same plane as the top edge of the bait.

To get the best from this set-up, the size of the boilie must be matched to the size of the hook. My rule of thumb is that a size 10 hook is mar-ried nicely with a 12mm diameter boilie, a size 8 hook with a 14mm, a size 6 with a 16mm and a size 4 with an 18mm diameter boilie. This gives you a very good starting-point and can be finely tuned to suit the individual requirement.

Pop-Up Rig Hook

This is the type of set-up I use when confronted with carp 'up-ending' as described earlier, with their lips extended and pinned to the bottom of the lake over the food item they are trying to take. If you use the standard pivoting hair in this situ-ation the hook link would be trapped under the carp's lips and the rig would not enter the mouth. With this set-up, the hook actually sits above the bait so that it is already well inside the mouth as the carp's lips are lowered over the boilie. What I am sure happens is that, as the carp inverts and the water and suspended bait are drawn upwards, the set-up rattles about, giving the hook an opportunity to prick lightly on the inside of the mouth. As the carp straightens up again before

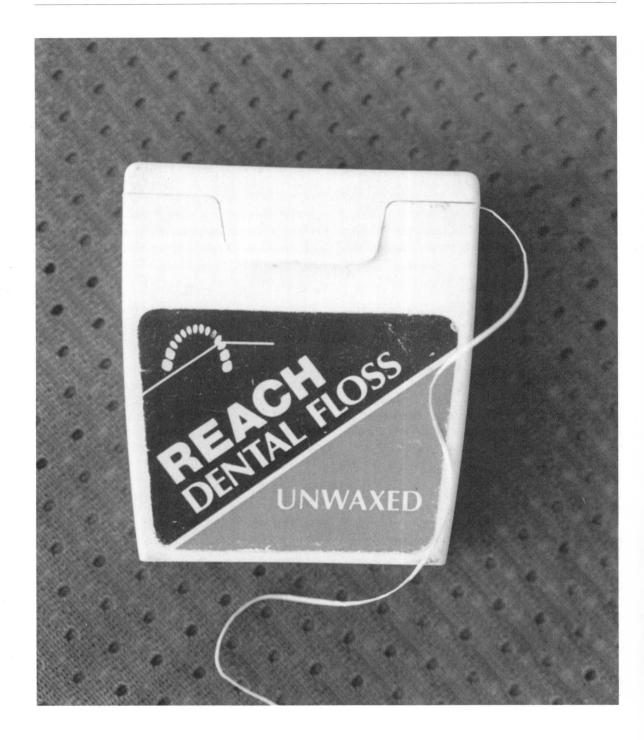

Dental Floss. One of the best materials from which to make the Hair itself, always use the unwaxed variety. The fine filaments can be split down to give the chosen diameter.

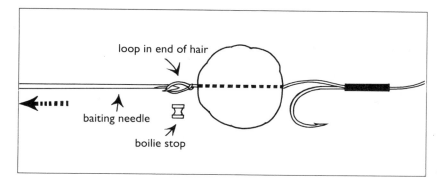

The Easiest way to mount a boilie on a hair rig.

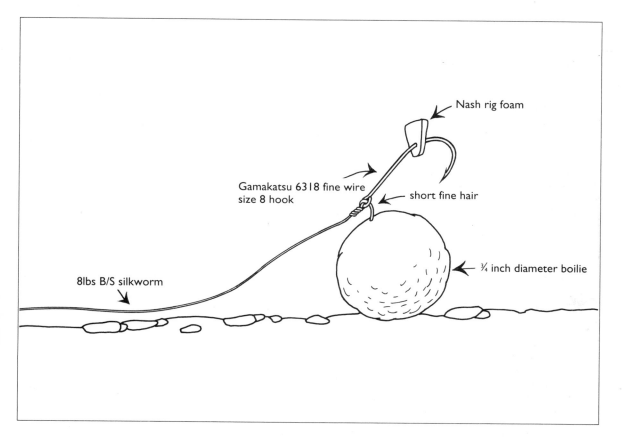

'Pop-up' hook rig.

moving off, the hook is pulled in even further by the weight of the lead and a take develops.

There are two hooks ideal for this set up: the Gamakatsu 6318 and the Drennan Starpoint. A piece of rig foam is mounted on the back of the bend as shown so that the hook is suspended above the bait. The hair must be very short and come off of the inside of the eye. This is easily achieved, as the drawing shows. If you use a soft hook-link material such as Silkworm you can use

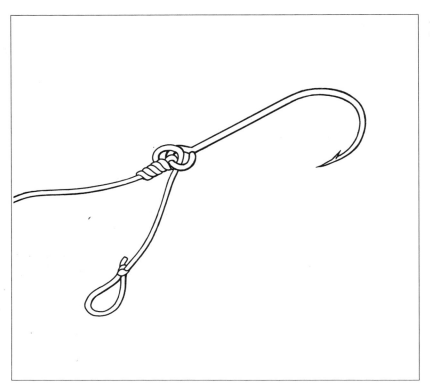

Hair set-up for 'Pop-up' hook rig.

the same for the hair itself. When the hook is knotted onto the hook link, leave an extra-long tail, pass it back through the eye and make a small loop in the end of it. If you think a finer diameter hair would be better, a separate material can be laid under the turns of the knot and again passed back through the eye so that the hair comes out on the inside of the hook.

With hard distance casting it is possible for the point of the hook to stick in the boilie. If this is experienced, the hook should be PVA'd back against the hook link, leaving the boilie hanging below out of harm's way.

Pop-Up Set-Ups

Both of the feeding methods described suit the use of a pop-up set-up. This is a very buoyant boilie, which unless tethered down, would float to the surface. Three successful pop-up rigs are illustrated. In the first a very tight hair is trapped against the hook in the mid-shank position with

some silicone tube. Partridge Hilton or Gamakatsu 6308 hooks are ideal for this set-up. The buoyancy of boilie should be greater than the weight of the hook, so some sort of counterbalance weight will be needed to hold it down. Either a lead substitute split shot or tungsten putty is ideal. The rig can be balanced out so that it only just sinks, allowing it to be drawn easily into the carp's mouth. I personally find the Kevin Nash Heavy Metal Putty ideal for counterbalancing.

The second pop-up illustrated is mounted tight against the upturned eye of a Partridge Rod Hutchinson VW or OW hook and again it's counterbalanced so it only just sinks.

The third example is an extension rig set-up with a stiff piece of rig tubing pushed over a straight-eyed hook – something like the Partridge Jack Hilton is ideal. The hair is then attached almost at the base of the tube, pulling the boilie very tight against it. The extension allows the hook to be pushed out even further from the bait

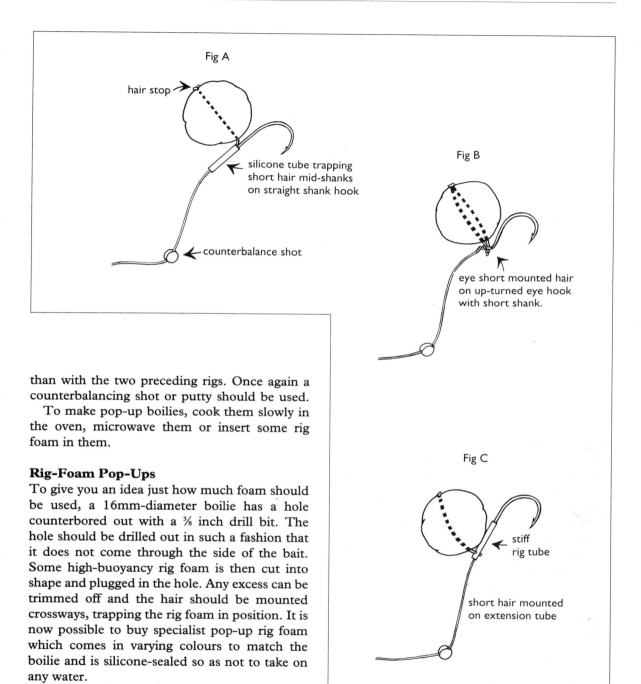

Fig A

hair stop

silicone tube trapping
short hair mid-shanks
on straight shank hook

counterbalance shot

Fig B

eye short mounted hair
on up-turned eye hook
with short shank.

Fig C

stiff
rig tube

short hair mounted
on extension tube

than with the two preceding rigs. Once again a counterbalancing shot or putty should be used.

To make pop-up boilies, cook them slowly in the oven, microwave them or insert some rig foam in them.

Rig-Foam Pop-Ups
To give you an idea just how much foam should be used, a 16mm-diameter boilie has a hole counterbored out with a ⅜ inch drill bit. The hole should be drilled out in such a fashion that it does not come through the side of the bait. Some high-buoyancy rig foam is then cut into shape and plugged in the hole. Any excess can be trimmed off and the hair should be mounted crossways, trapping the rig foam in position. It is now possible to buy specialist pop-up rig foam which comes in varying colours to match the boilie and is silicone-sealed so as not to take on any water.

With every major development there always seems to be a drawback and this is very true with the new soft hook-link materials that we are currently using. Although they give us marvellous bait presentation, they do not cast very well

Three 'pop-up' set ups.

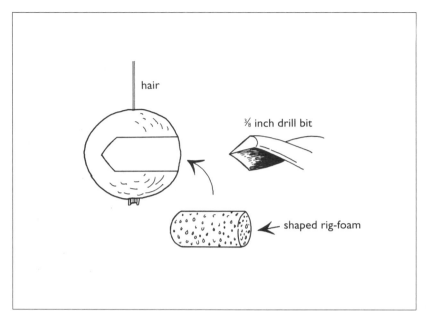

hair

⅜ inch drill bit

shaped rig-foam

Rig foam pop-ups.

without tangling. There is little point in having a super-duper set-up only to find it has landed in a tangled heap on the lake's bed. In the right hands, with careful casting, it is possible not to tangle these soft hook links with a fairly basic set-up, provided that the twist that is naturally put into the main line on the retrieve is taken out.

Taking the Twist out of the Main line

The method shown is by far the easiest way of removing the problematic twist that builds up in the main line. It is a simple matter of holding the lead up away from the hook link while the baited rig hangs immediately below. You will find that once the weight has been removed from the rig, so to speak, it will spin round of its own accord as the tension unwinds. If you don't do this you will inevitably get a tangled set-up.

Anti-Tangle Rig Tube Set-Up

For those who don't have the confidence to use the standard running lead in conjunction with soft hook links, there are a few anti-tangle set-ups which just about guarantee tangle-free casting and bait presentation. The first comprises an in-line bomb mounted on some very stiff rig tubing. The main line is passed down through the centre of the tube and tied to the stop swivel with a shock bead in between. Ideally the swivel should be a cross-link design and the shock bead should have a large enough centre bore to cover the stop swivel knot Completely, thereby giving it some protection. The hook link is then attached to the free eye of the stop swivel. The hook link must be at least 2 inches shorter than the rig tubing to guarantee tangle-free casting. The in-line bomb mounted on the stiff tubing is in the free-running mode. The second set-up utilises a length of flexible rig tubing over which the swivel of the leger weight is wedged. This should be pushed onto the rig tubing about ½ inch. The stop swivel is attached to the main line after it has been threaded through the tube and wedged back into the bore of the tube. This set-up is now in a semi-fixed mode giving the full weight of the lead to the taking carp, Which helps to hook it.

It should also be a safe set-up since the stop swivel will automatically pull out of the rig tubing should the leger weight become tethered.

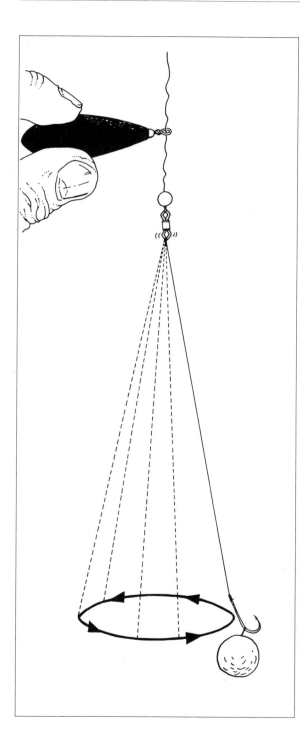

Taking the twist out of the main line.

Again the hook link must be that vital 2 inches shorter than the tubing.

The third set-up is also semi-fixed but it incorporates a Kevin Nash bolt bead. This is purpose-made for the job. Two spigots are positioned opposite each other with a hole through the centre and a third projection is positioned at right angles to them. There is a hole through this projection where a link and leger weight can be attached. To one of the spigots is fitted a length of flexible rig tubing; to the other a short length (½–¾ inch) of silicone sleeve. The rest of the set-up remains the same. The silicone sleeve that joins the stop swivel and the bolt bead together will automatically come apart should the lead become tethered. It is very important with all of these rigs not to set them up in such a way that the leger weight is firmly attached to the hook link.

Helicopter Rigs

An alternative anti-tangle set-up is the helicopter system. The lead is attached to the end of the main line while the hook link rotates round it by means of a Nash Mini Swivel Bead or a Berkley Swivel mounted on an ET Helicopter Bead. It is very important with both of these set-ups that a good shock bead with a large hole is used to protect the knot attaching the leger weight. This knot is under great stress when playing a fish because of the acute angle of the hook link against the main line.

Both systems shown are backed up with DAM Twin Float Stops. These should be positioned so that there is about ⅛ inch movement between the stops and the first bead. This allows the hook link to rotate freely round the main line. The two float stops will easily move up the main line should the lead become tethered, thus alleviating the chance of the carp being condemned to towing the lead around in the event of a breakage.

Lead-Core Fly-Line Set-Up

On some waters where the carp wise up to lines running taut through the water there is an advantage of nailing the main line down on the bottom in close proximity to the rig. The method shown

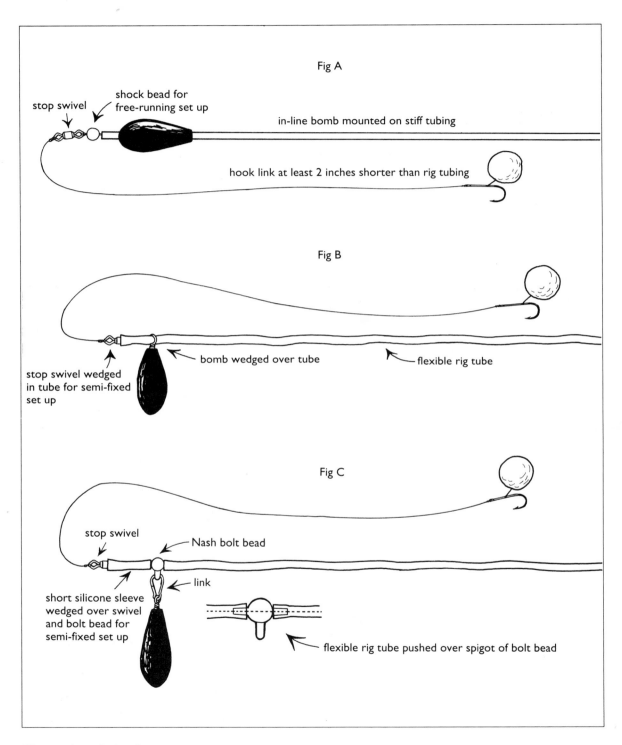

Fig A

stop swivel

shock bead for
free-running set up

in-line bomb mounted on stiff tubing

hook link at least 2 inches shorter than rig tubing

Fig B

bomb wedged over tube

flexible rig tube

stop swivel wedged
in tube for semi-fixed
set up

Fig C

stop swivel

Nash bolt bead

link

short silicone sleeve
wedged over swivel
and bolt bead for
semi-fixed set up

flexible rig tube pushed over spigot of bolt bead

Three anti-tangle rig tube set-ups.

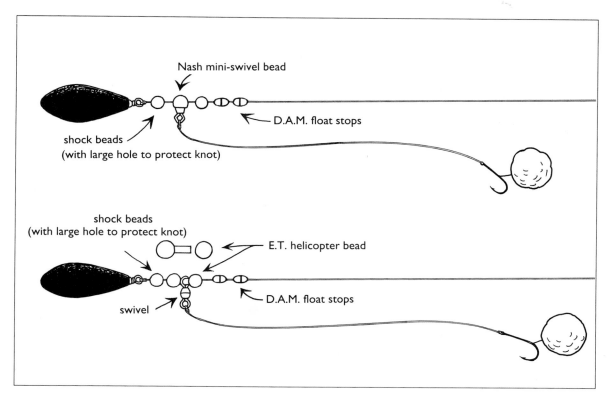

Nash mini-swivel bead

D.A.M. float stops

shock beads
(with large hole to protect knot)

shock beads
(with large hole to protect knot)

E.T. helicopter bead

D.A.M. float stops

swivel

Two helicopter rigs.

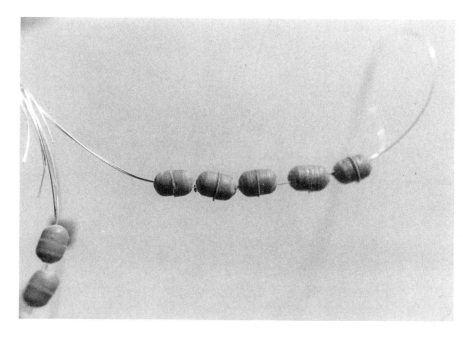

*D.A.M. Rubber Float
Stops. Although originally
designed to lock a float
securely on the mainline,
these have now gained
popularity with the carp
angler for use with
helicopter rigs and
backstops.*

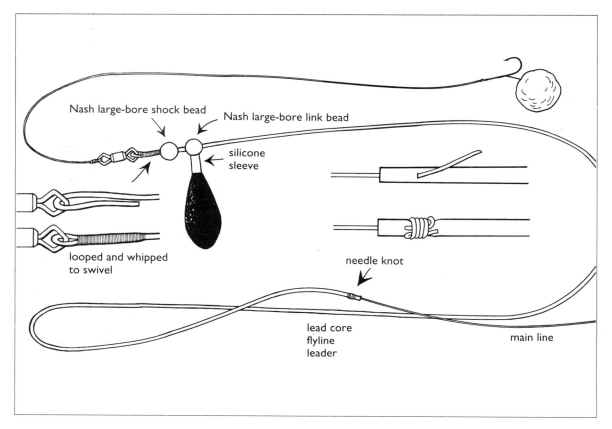

Lead core flyline set up.

Nash large-bore shock bead

Nash large-bore link bead

silicone
sleeve

looped and whipped
to swivel

needle knot

lead core
flyline
leader

main line

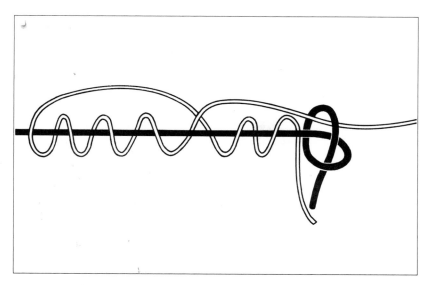

Shock leader knot.

Berkley Big Game Line. In the last few seasons this has become one of the best-selling high abraisant resistant lines.

utilises about a 3-foot length of lead-core fly-line, attached to the main line by a needle knot. A large-bore Nash Link Bead to which the leger weight is attached is allowed to run free along the lead core-leader. It is very important that the link bead passes easily over the needle knot. The other end of the lead-core fly-line is looped and whipped to the swivel as illustrated. A large-bore shock bead is fitted between the stop swivel and the link bead to protect the whipped joint. The hook link, bait, etc., are attached as usual.

When this set-up is cast out and the line has straightened and sunk a small amount of slack line should be payed out to allow all of the lead-core fly-line leader to lie tight on the lake's bed. There will now be no line running through the water within 3 feet of the hook bait.

Shock Leaders

On many waters where the angler is required to cast farther and farther from the bank, heavy leads and strong rods are used to obtain the distance. Some sort of shock leader must be used to ensure that there is no danger of the main line parting under the enormous pressure that is exerted on the tackle during a power cast. The shock leader should be a minimum of 16lb BS and possibly as much as 30lb, depending on the size of lead.

The leader itself should be three times the length of the rod. Because we are trying to achieve the ultimate range the main line may well be as low as 6lb BS.

There is only one knot that I have found ultimately successful for attaching a thick shock

leader to the main line and that is the one illustrated. Any knot that joins two lengths of line together like this is very vulnerable and it should be checked at every cast for damage and re-tied as necessary. The positioning of the knot on the spool when casting is also very important. It should always be right at the rear of the spool so that no other loops of line cross it. If it was at the front, beneath two or three coils, it could snatch during a power cast, causing all sorts of problems, let alone reducing distance.

Shock leaders can also double up as snag leaders where zebra mussels and flints perched in predominant positions on top of bars and the like can easily sever the line. The most vulnerable area is immediately adjacent to the rig itself. As the carp bolts for freedom the line could well be pulled under pressure over a bar strewn with sharp objects. This is where high-abrasion resistant snag leaders come into their own. Berkley Big Game and Damyl Steel Power are two of my favourite monofilaments, whilst Kryston's Quicksilver is one of the best new high-tech high-resistant braids.

Silt Set-Ups

On many waters soft, silty bottoms cause the angler serious problems as the lead can often drag the baits down into the stinking mire out of the sight of the carp. On a few waters that I know it seems that the whole lake bed is covered in soft silt. Here the carp do not root very deeply, generally only sifting through the top few inches. On such waters it is not unusual for the leger weight to sink a couple of feet into the silt, rendering the set-up useless. Here are a few ideas that will I hope alleviate the problem.

The two set-ups illustrated actually sit on the top of the silt itself. The first is a purpose-made

Opposite above: *D.A.M. Steel Power. A great high-resistant shock leader with a low diameter.*
Opposite below: *Kryston Quick Silver. They make army flak jackets from this material so it must be strong, whether used as a shock leader or snag leader it offers great reliability.*

leger weight that only just sinks. It is constructed from a ¾-inch drilled bullet cut in half with a pear-shaped section of balsa wood fitted to the top and held in place by a brass wire attached to the swivel. A shock bead is fitted between the stop swivel and the counterbalance leger weight. The hook link should be made of one of the lightweight HPPE materials which contain a fair amount of buoyancy, and the hookbait should be counterbalanced so that it only just sinks or is a pop-up.

The second set-up is a 2oz leger weight used in conjunction with a 2-inch-diameter plastic disc. This disc is wedged over the eye of the swivel in the leger weight as shown and when cast out it will just sit in the surface layers of the silt.

Both these set-ups are OK for short-range casting and where takes are confident, but in conditions where you have to rely on tight lines they will easily move out of position, which can be a problem in windy conditions on shallow waters. Then I use a paternoster-type set-up.

Paternosters

Illustrated are two of my favourite paternoster rigs. The first is a running rig stopped with a swivel and shock bead. The second is a fixed rig with a small Drennan ring or swivel attaching main line, hook link and bomb link together. With the fixed paternoster the leger weight is obviously in a permanently fixed position on the set-up and therefore the link attaching the leger weight to the Drennan ring or swivel should be lighter than that of the main line and hook link.

The bomb link on both of these set-ups should ideally be three times longer than the depth of silt you are encountering. In other words, if the leger weight is sinking a perceived 2 feet into the silt the link should be 6 feet long. Hook links and baits again should be similar to the other silt rigs, ensuring that the bait only just sits on top of the silt so it can be easily found by the carp.

Just about all the aforementioned rigs can be modified so that they are fished with boilies, particles or processed foods such as luncheon meat and cubed hard cheese. On some waters where there are no problems with small nuisance fish

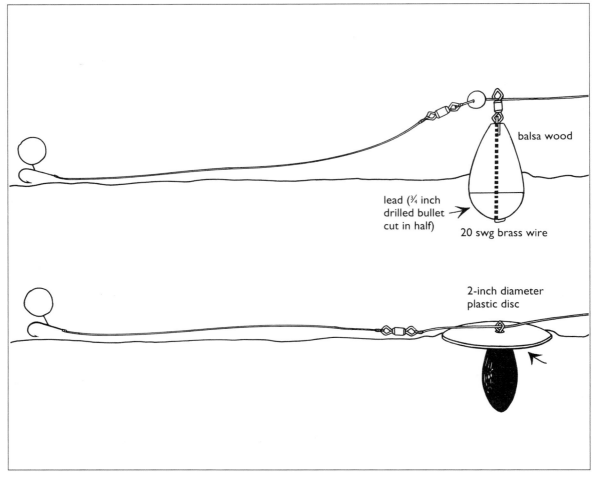

Silt set ups.

the angler may well find it desirable to use maggots as the bait. In this case a different set-up from those mentioned so far in this chapter should be used. I deal with a few specific maggot rigs in Chapter 9 but there is one that I feel should be included here.

The Madusa Rig

This is an idea of that great thinking angler, Harry Haskell. It is basically a pop-up maggot rig. A 6–10mm-diameter polyball is attached to a short hair fixed in the mid-shank position. The maggots are then threaded onto some fine nylon

of about 6–8oz BS with a small needle. As you can see from the drawing, they are literally sewn through the polyball. This is repeated several times with four or five lengths of nylon carrying up to ten or so maggots until the whole of the polyball is covered as illustrated. The pop-up maggots are counterbalanced a couple of inches off of the bottom with a non-toxic shot or tungsten putty. The squirming maggots wriggle very provocatively just off of the bottom, and continually firing in pouchloads of maggots over the hookbaits should have the carp homing in on the swim. The sight of that juicy mouthful

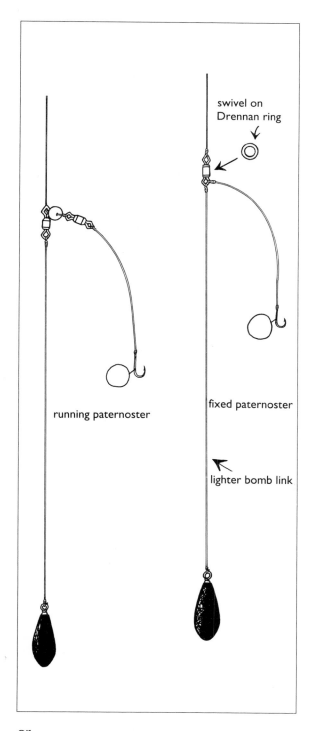

Silt set-ups.

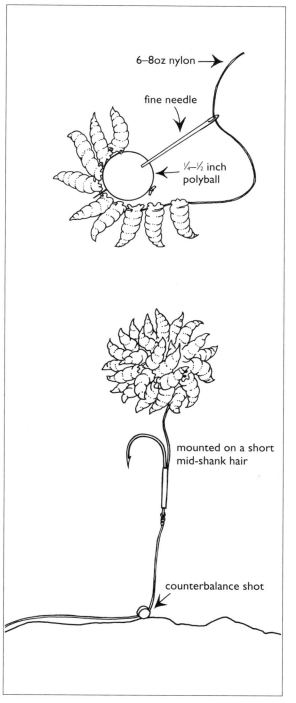

The Madusa rig.

suspended in the swim will, I'm sure, be just too much for them to resist.

FLOAT RIGS

As well as bottom rigs, used in conjunction with leger weights, with the angler sitting behind static rods, we really should have a quick look at some of the float-fishing set-ups that I use. I always keep a good selection of floats from the Milo and Drennan range, including wagglers, crystal inserts, loafers and chub-type floats.

For most of the clear-water work wagglers fixed bottom end only are my standard set-up. These are held in position by a couple of DAM float stops. Wherever possible I like to use a soft hook link. This will normally be between 9 and 12 inches in length attached to the main line by a number 7 cross-linked swivel. The float is counterbalanced with some 'Heavy Metal' lead substitute putty and the bait is attached to the hook by a mid-shank hair in the normal way. I like to adjust the float so that the counterbalance weight cocks it within about ½ inch so there is very little of the sight tip showing. Add the bait and the rig will sink out of sight if the float is adjusted under depth. If the depth is assessed correctly and the float adjusted accordingly, so that the lead substitute only just rests on the bottom, about ½ inch of the float should show. So whether the carp sucks in the bait and moves off

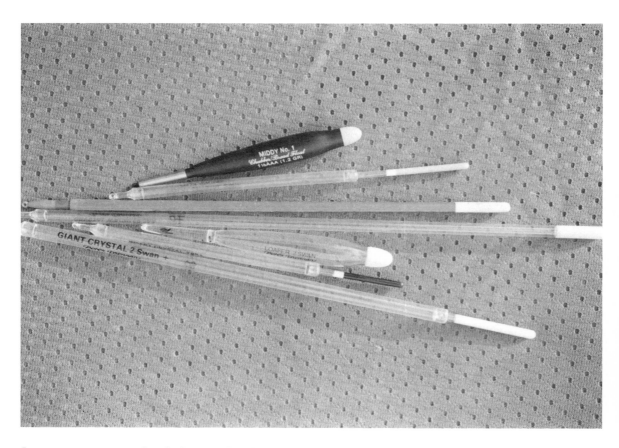

I am sure many carp anglers don't own a float, but here are just a few from the comprehensive range that I always carry.

Kevin Nash Heavy Metal: the best lead substitute putty available to us. It has loads of applications from counterbalancing pop-ups to shotting down floats.

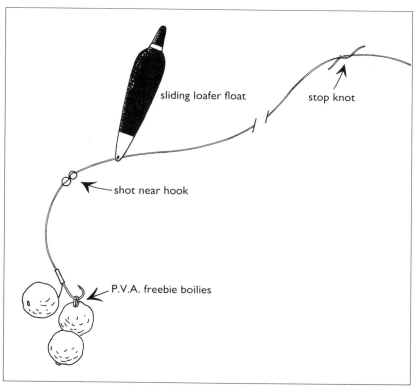

sliding loafer float

stop knot

shot near hook

P.V.A. freebie boilies

Lily pad float set-up.

or just rises in the water I will get instant bite registration.

Lily Pad Set-Ups

This is the rig that I use for dropping bait between tiny holes in the lily pads. I use a short, squat loafer-type float as a slider, with the stop knot adjusted at the correct depth. The counterbalance shots are positioned only 2 or 3 inches away from the hook. This makes for a compact set-up which can be cast easily even in very limited spaces in quite dense lily pads.

The hookbait is attached mid-shank as normal and it's useful to attach an extra bit of weight in the form of a couple of freebie boilies via a short length of PVA string. This extra weight will help with accurate casting. Once the rig has been dropped in the desired position, immediately let out some line so that the main line can run through the bottom eye of the loafer float until the stop knot rests in place. When fishing in dense lily pads I have rarely found it necessary to use a soft hook link as the carp will feed with confidence in what they consider to be a safe environment. This is great as it helps to simplify the whole rig so that you only have the one potential weak spot – the hook knot itself.

I hope that having read through this chapter you will now have a better understanding of the way I select my rigs, dispelling all the myths and fantasies and really getting down to the basic nitty-gritty. All the rigs I have covered have caught considerable numbers of carp from all manners of waters, not only for myself but for many of my many good friends. My rule is: always keep it as simple as you possibly can. Be aware that the carp can be finicky and highly unpredictable at times, but as yet I don't believe any of them have a degree in the latest rig set-ups. Let us not educate them too fast beyond their years. A slow progression through the development of rigs is far better than going in with the best set-up that's available to you.

6 SPECIALIST STALKING
Jan Wenczka

Because even the longest journey starts with but a single step I will retrace some of my early faltering steps – not for any nostalgic reasons but because fishing is an inexact science made up of conjecture and opinions based on our experience. So by recounting a couple of my more poignant early experiences and what I concluded from them I will try to build a framework on which to hang some of the principles I use in my specialist stalking approach.

The lake was California Country Park a name evocative of scantily clad nubile nymphets and musclebound bronzed surfers. But this California Country Park was in Wokingham, Berkshire. I'll be brief in describing the lake, only because it could have been any lake in any county and the experiences could have been the same. At about six acres it used to be a holiday retreat for smog-bound Londoners which fell into decline with the increase in personal transport. The chalets were still intact, a couple of concrete pillars in the middle of the lake paid homage to where the diving board used to be. The boats had long gone and the bankside vegetation which would have been manicured was now very overgrown. I hope that from the description you don't get a sullen view of the place because on the contrary, as we all do, I fell in love with it in spite of its imperfections, and maybe even because of them.

Once I had that blinding revelation which comes to most carpers, that carp spend quite a bit of their time in the margins and not shoaled up in the middle, I started to work out ways of catching them from the edge. I began with floating crust. There was an area in the lake where the carp felt safe, it being totally overgrown with a fallen tree across it. They could often be seen there, but it would be impossible to land fish in

such a place – though you would be surprised at the amount of people who tried using sea hooks and 50lb line. (I'll expand my views on that approach later.) I didn't think it was possible to catch the fish in the snags, but I did think it possible to entice the fish to the edge of them and catch them there. Casting was a problem so what I did was to wade out from the nearest swim and stand with the water to the tops of my waders trying to blend in as far as I could with the overhanging trees. The trouble with crust is that it keeps coming off the hook which meant rebaiting again and again.

Quite how long I stood in this position I don't know – long enough. Eventually standing there in the water I felt a tapping on the side of my wader, I looked down to see a carp feeding on the small pieces of bread which I had dropped. The fish was feeding so close to me that its tail was tapping against my wader. So I slowly wound my bait in, discarded the crust and replaced it with a squeezed piece of flake which I lowered into the path of the fish. It took one look at it and thundered out of the area like a bat out of hell.

I spent many a long hour thinking about that incident, not what a carp sees and whether it can or cannot see various materials, but what it concludes from what it sees, given that a pair of waders must be more obvious than a piece of mono.

The second incident involved me being out on the edge of a branch and observing some carp feeding on some sweetcorn I had introduced. I got my tackle together but I had a problem in that I usually tried to lay the line along the bottom so as to eliminate having line coming up vertically close to the bait. Unfortunately, because of the position I was in, this was impossible. So with the wader incident in mind I tried an experiment. I waited till the carp were out of the area and then put the bait in the hot spot and pushed the rod tip into the bottom of the lake no more than a few feet from the bait and waited.

To say it looked peculiar is an understatement and I didn't know what to expect. The fish returned and immediately you could see that they had noticed the rod – how could they not have done. Though aware of it, they were not startled or afraid and after a few minutes they started to feed again, soon to be feeding around the rod completely oblivious of it. Needless to say, I caught one of them.

The question I am most asked when I explain this particular method of stalking is how do you strike? Well the answer is in the question or more precisely it isn't. The word 'strike' in fishing terms immediately brings a picture of a rod being swept overhead flashing into one's mind. So what I do is exchange that word for more appropriate ones which give a more useful picture. For strike I use 'set the hook'. You then visualise a hook that travels just a few inches to get lodged in the carp's mouth. And to get the hook to travel those few inches at that short distance all you have to do is grab the line, usually between reel and first eye, and pull, which is what I do.

This method of hook setting has some other advantages. With the hookbait only travelling those few inches, should you miss – pull the bait straight our of the fish's mouth – nothing very dramatic has happened in the swim and though the carp may leave the area for a while, they will usually return and often will stay and carry on feeding. Sometimes I've had four or five chances in an area before a fish is caught, whereas, if the more typical strike were employed one mistake would be all you could afford, as the resulting commotion would have the area vacated by the carp.

A STALKING PHILOSOPHY

I'll move away from California Country Park now, not because I didn't learn anything else there but because I don't want to repeat myself. But I will just say a piece about the philosophy of my stalking. Basically there are two kinds of people who go fishing, travellers and destination people. To the traveller, stalking becomes an almost transcendental spiritual experience; the emphasis will be on surroundings, equipment usually old. The journey ends up the greatest part of the experience. I, on the other hand, am a destination person.

Though I don't pretend to be a complete philistine and am appreciative of all the various aspects of the journey, it is the destination which is paramount, so when I go stalking it's not for any fundamentalist reasons. I'm driven by pure pragmatism: having assessed the problem, stalking is the medium I use to overcome it. The first thing to do on a water is to spend time there. I look in all the likely spots, then look between the likely spots and then in the unlikely spots. If it is allowed, I swim in the lake. I'll take a boat out and climb every available tree. What you're looking for is clues.

Throughout all this I try to keep an open mind. For this piece I will dismiss anything which doesn't relate to stalking, though in reality everything is interrelated.

Stalking means margins. Just at what point stalking turns into educated fishing is debatable but in essence we are looking at situations where fish can be seen. The clues to look for are areas where the bottom has been swept clean, which can tell you half the story, because not all carp grub around when in the margins; some stay high in the water. Other clues are unnatural movement of weed, lilies or water and of course the most obvious, sighting of fish themselves. I start with only one or two areas, though I would expect more and more to come into the equation as I become more conversant with the lake.

Stalking is about the exploitation of situations which either occur naturally or are manufactured and when working a water the two run concurrently. Bait is employed as a crucial tool but at this point you still have an open mind and are still searching for more clues, so baiting is done sparingly and reactions are observed.

Jan Wenczka up a tree again! He is bent into another stalked fish. Jan is to my mind undoubtedly the best stalking angler that I have ever had the pleasure to fish with.

BAITS

Carp fishing is full of faddists, of whom bait faddists are the most prevalent. You are better off not affording that luxury. But we all have preferences and mine is boilies. They seem to be the most versatile bait and for stalking situations the criterion I use is very simple. I prefer high visibility, so I first try red or yellow if the carp don't object. I like to be tried and tested. If I'm combining stalking with a more static approach I'll use one built for both so a compromise might have to be reached.

Paste baits not only have all the advantages of boilies but you can further enhance your chances by moulding shapes, which forces the carp to eat in a certain way. I prefer to squeeze pieces of paste between forefinger and thumb to give a flat conical shape, which encourages the carp to suck them up off the bottom. Particles are another option and sometimes on waters where carp have become preoccupied on them they are a must, though I steer clear of mass particles as they create a situation difficult to control.

I prefer my particles large enough so that when presented in a swim the hookbait can be identified – sweetcorn, peanuts, tigers and the like. Alternatively, you can use a boilie as a hookbait over a particle bed, but on very hard fished waters it may be viewed with great suspicion.

Do not forget surface baits. In fact, mention stalking and some people associate it only with surface fishing, though in the manufacture of a stalking situation it's well down the list. The problems with a surface bait are that it doesn't stay in the places you want it to and it gets eaten by wild life.

TACKLE

Line

The maximum breaking strain of line I use is 15lb. It's a restriction that not only takes in the respect and care of the fish, but one that gives me the right triggers in my mind as to the worthiness of the situation. As a fish gets bigger its flesh doesn't get any tougher so anything above a 15lb pull on the hook would rip it out of the fish's mouth. Also you could be lulled into believing that by using stronger line you could physically stop a fish getting into a certain snag by what is called hooking and holding, which is a technique spawned from the mind of anglers who generally fish for carp of less than 25lb. The shock comes when you hook a fish in excess of this. Using 15lb line you have to have a plan on how to land a fish, even if it is sometimes within taxing physical restrictions.

This is an altogether more useful and productive concept. Put in simple terms, if your only plan is to hook and hold you are fishing in the wrong spot.

Having tried all the various materials on the market I have still kept to my original two – monofilament and braided terylene.

Hooks

Hooks are one of the most important pieces of equipment. Jack Hiltons are quite good but a bit too thick in the wire for me. I have seen two or three on the market at the moment which look as though they should be good, but at the present I'm using an obsolete Mustad pattern which I had given to me a few years ago and of which I still have a few left. So what I will do shortly is to get together some of these new patterns which I think will work and test them to destruction. I tie them up to some very strong line then put a softish piece of wood (pine) in a vice, put the hook point into the wood and pull hard. If the hook snaps it's too brittle; if it straightens it's too soft. What should happen is that the point should start to go in the wood and maybe begin to open out but no more.

With the patterns I have that pass this test I try sharpening them. I try to get a point which I think is lethal. With a hard stone I hone both sides of the hook towards the point till I have a pretty evil point, then hone the outside edge of the hook towards the point till it's lethal. Of the patterns which pass this test, I go for personal preferences. Hook batches can be very inconsistent so when

I've found a hook I like I buy a good supply. For lighter lines up to 10lb I use Drennan Super Specialists.

Rods

The rod I use takes me back to the California days. I bought a second-hand glass Tag Barnes rod for £15. Misfortune dogged it in its early days in my possession, in the guise of my wife who on three separate occasions broke the tip off in the car door. The more I fixed and rewhipped it the more I favoured it.

I also cut some off the butt so that it is now 1 foot long, and fitted the rod with silicon rings. During all these adventures I became interested in the explorer Shackleton and named the abused rod. 'The spirit of Shackleton', later shortened to just 'Shackleton'.

If I were designing a rod specifically for stalking I would have a bit more steel in the butt section because a stalking rod is as much a pushing tool (having to push fish away from bankside danger) as a pulling tool, like a general fishing rod. Some people favour carbon fibre and yet others split cane, but I find them altogether too precious. You really have to be able to hold the rod about a foot from the tip and be able to lift the rod with reel attached, because in very cramped situations you'll need to feed the rod back and forth without making any body movements. Those prized rods won't withstand that sort of abuse.

Reels

I couple my rod with a Mitchell 300 with a 410 bile arm because its still the best backwinding reel on the market. I can imagine a few furrowed brows at this remark, but I like to be in complete control of the situation and backwinding gives me that. I sometimes get bruised fingers but that is easily outweighed by the occasions when I manage to stop a fish from gaining distance by being firm and counteracting its various lunges and thereby stopping any momentum on the fish's part. This is particularly true when fishing shallow water – 4 feet and less – or surface fishing, where there is very little water above the fish's back and it cannot get any leverage. If you are firm it will break the surface and expend a great deal of energy for no reward.

I will not go through all the various bits and pieces of tackle – I'll mention them as and when they become relevant – but I do carry them all in a fly-fishing waistcoat, and I also have a small bag for carrying my bait.

CONCEALMENT

When fishing at very close range (within a few feet) concealment and stealth are obviously of paramount importance, but this be from the carp's point of view. A carp has an eye on either side of its head, which means basically that it has two completely separate monocular visions of its world, plus a prey mentality. The monocular vision means that perspective must be difficult and it seems to me that when they are viewing terrestrial objects they focus on the nearest object which may be sparse bankside vegetation or reeds. Therefore I like to keep something physically between me and the carp. Because of the prey mentality the carp is constantly on the look-out for danger signs so I try to avoid swift movements and breaking the profile of the bankside, remembering to try to gauge the profile from the fish's point of view.

Vibrations are another danger sign so I wear soft shoes. Voices seem to be a debatable point. I believe that they are detected by fish but are not necessarily associated with danger. Carp very often don't appear alarmed but they are aware, so I don't like voices above a whisper. Another important consideration is that because of the eye placement on a carp it has a blind spot above its head, so if possible I try to get above the fish. As regards clothing I just wear dull casual clothes. I feel easier in them though a case can be made for camouflage clothing.

Polaroids

Just as it is difficult for carp to view terrestrial objects, so it is also difficult for us to look into water. Polaroid glasses are a must. The pair I use

*Probably the most famous carp in this country – Basil – weighing in at 41 lbs 10oz.
And from where did Jan hook it? You've guessed it – up a tree!*

are Optic Cormorants. I know they are quite expensive, but because of the expense you are more likely to look after them. The curve on the lens is optically correct so there is less likelihood of getting headaches, and most important, the polarisation is very good. But really it all boils down to the technique of looking into water as opposed to looking at water, and making sense of the clues you find, because you are not always looking for carp. I use a string across the back of my polaroids so that I can take them off and put them on easily. For fogging on the inside on muggy days rather than wiping them I just take them off for a minute or two. In some lights I'm constantly taking them off and then replacing them, especially at sunrise and sunset, and very often I just like not wearing them when moving around not looking into the water.

SNAGGY SWIMS

You may be wondering what point there is baiting areas that you may or may not fish, but when fishing a lake I don't find any information irrelevant, so I'm perfectly happy to look at feeding fish to get information and possible clues to their downfall. Naturally a great many of the areas will be obstruction-free though because we are fishing margins, and very often overgrown margins, snags do come into the equation, as often the chosen ambush site is close to one of these snags. The first thing to observe is the speed at which the carp travel to and from the snags and, more important, once in them. This will give you a good idea of the obstacles the fish has to traverse. If they seem to be able to move at quite a speed in and through them then the chances are that though the snags may look horrendous from above there is probably be a clear channel below.

The dangers to look for are when the fish manoeuvre through the snags in stages, or they enter and exit from one direction only. This could indicate a labyrinth of tangles which could result in lost fish – and, ethics apart, hooking fish only to lose them is a complete waste of time. If the signs look promising, gardening may be required (assuming the fishery allows it). I don't cut anything above the water-line so to all intents and purposes it looks exactly the same, but below the water-line I cut out the twigs and small branches that risk fouling the line when a fish is hooked.

If you find that you need to remove more than a few then the chances are, first, that a you shouldn't be fishing there in the first place and, second, that by radically changing the swim you may drive the carp out of the area. Branches and debris in the bottom of the swim I leave alone. Others do like to clear the area in my view the

advantages outweigh the disadvantage. The disadvantage is that during the fight debris can get caught on the line. This is true and it has happened to me many times, but by keeping a clear head I simply remove the obstacle from the line and carry on playing the fish. As yet I haven't lost one. The advantages are that especially on the very difficult waters bait presentation has to be precise and even then you really want to see the fish take the bait. By making use of the branches and debris on the bottom, you can position your bait so that the fish can only take it in full view. This, of course, makes hooking so much easier.

SET-UPS

The two basic set-ups I use for bottom baits when stalking are float and leger. Both are simple.

The Float Set-Up

For the float I use a length of braided terylene just short of the depth I am fishing. If the depth is 4 feet I use about 3½ feet of terylene. This is tied to a swivel and the main line is tied to the other end of the swivel and with a running float, though a breakaway float can be used if necessary. I'll use any float that is substantial enough and if I haven't got a float I'll use a twig, but my preference is for bulbous floats with the long antennae. I put one or two shot about 6 inches away from the hook and one either side of the float to vary the depth, with the rest of the shot around the swivel on the terylene side.

The main function of the set-up is to keep the line where I want it to be. Second, when that monster comes into your swim and starts to wolf down the baits, though you might go into involuntary spasms and try unsuccessfully to hold the rod steady, your temporary St Vitus dance is not transferred to the bait to scare the fish. Of course the float can also be used as a bite indicator, probably one of the very best.

Not all waters are suitable for the float. The main stumbling block is the vertical line coming up through the swim. On some waters the fish don't mind and will often bump into the line, quite heedless of it; elsewhere they will scoot off at the first sight. To complicate things even more, on some waters certain swims will tolerate the vertical line while others won't. Just let the fish make the decision for you.

The Leger Set-Up
On the leger set-up I again use a braided terylene hook link, but about 1 foot long, then a swivel, a bead and a flattened Arlesey bomb of between ½ oz and 1 oz. The flattened bomb stops the rig rolling out of position on steep-sided lakes or when fishing gravel bars, and generally gives better control, letting you decide where to put the leger to your best advantage.

Depending on where I'm fishing, I'll either use terylene straight through or I'll use monofilament as the main line. Guiding factors are abrasion-resistance and visibility. Monofilament main line can be seen, and I don't know any lake that fish 15lb mono off the bottom won't scare.

I don't mind which method I use but the leger has the greater advantages, mainly the ability to effect a strike with the rod in the water (California style) and setting the hook by pulling the line with your hand without any disturbance to the swim.

Another variation to the leger style I use clouds over into ordinary fishing. I use it when I know there are fish present but I can't see them because of water clarity, depth or obstruction. The method is to use the same running lead but heavier (about 2oz), and a shorter link – about 8 inches unless silt is a factor, in which case it has to be varied accordingly. I then use a ½ oz back lead on the line. The rod is placed at rest, the line tightened up, and a bobbin is placed on the line with a 6-inch drop. The rest is just common sense. The important thing is to make sure that the main line comes away from the bottom at a point where it does not scare the fish.

I will only use this set-up as a last resort because of course it isn't selective and therefore undermines a major stalking advantage. The same is true when using the float purely as an indicator, but you can only fish the situations that

become available and I've certainly caught fish of over 30lb from very difficult waters using these blind stalking techniques.

PLAYING AND LANDING

Playing and landing fish hooked in the margins, very often in confined spaces, seems to present the greatest mystery to the average carp angler. I read and hear a great deal about various methods and theories and quite a lot of these folk tales are pure rubbish.

I dread bringing psychology into fishing, but really in playing large fish at close quarters it can't be dismissed.

Imagine yourself in an open field with a wood close by, then being scared for some reason and having to run to the wood for protection. No matter how frightened you may be upon reaching the wood you check yourself. Self-preservation dictates this, otherwise you would hurt yourself by crashing into a tree. The same is true of fish. How many times have you heard of cases where fish were charging towards some sort of sanctuary – lilies, reeds or snags – only to find them boil just before they reached it. The phrase often used is 'I stopped it just before it got to the snags' when what really happened is that on reaching the snags the fish, from a self-preservation point of view, has checked, the inertia has stopped, because of the pressure of the line pulling the fish boils and, having done so, cannot regenerate the power needed to make its way delicately through the various snags so then it shoots off again to find another sanctuary.

In principle the same is true in a stalking situation, only in microcosm. The thing is to keep unbalancing the fish by just veering it off line all the – time forcing it to find new sanctuaries expending energy until it eventually breaks surface, from which point is has to work twice as hard to gain momentum again.

In general fishing the rod is a pulling tool with absorption qualities, but in close-range playing of fish the rod is asked to perform other functions: apart from pulling it has to push fish away from danger, sometimes at your feet. Consequently, apart from playing fish in the normal way, the rod is pushed into the water – or, if you are using the California style, it is left in the water. In some cases I have only had the reel and butt above the water.

The essence is to gain line as soon as possible. Obviously the key word is playing, but in this context you will very often find that there comes a point where the fish seems to come straight in. Don't stop; keep winding. The only worry is if you have no barrier between the hook and the top ring, as in surface fishing or freelining. You don't want to bump the hook out of the fish's mouth by jarring the hook in the top ring. If you can get to a situation where the fish is on just a foot or two of line (set-up permitting) you are in such a commanding position that only bad luck or bad judgement will lose the fish. Obviously, line has to be given to land the fish, though I have on many occasions in tight swims landed the fish on a short line by passing the rod back behind and landing the fish on only a few feet of line. But you have to be very aware of your equipment and fish, and any sudden surge from the fish has to be countered by quickly bringing the rod back into play. Because the line is trapped between fingers and rod when playing fish this way (not as difficult as it sounds, fly fishers mastered it years ago), you have to be careful when using braided terylene straight through. I once had a fish I thought was beaten only for it to charge off on a long run, and by the time I managed to get back to the reel both my hands were cut to pieces trying to stop the run by trapping the line on the rod. Not to be recommended and something I won't do again!

I don't subscribe to the hit-and-hold philosophy – not that it doesn't work; it does, but only because of certain factors which stop momentum. These are that the fish isn't large up to 25lb or is larger than this but has been hooked in shallow water or on the surface. These last two have the same effect: leverage is non-existent.

The real problem with relying solely on this method is that should a fish gain momentum (and everyone has lapses of concentration or judgement) it could reach some sort of sanctuary, resulting in a loss. The contention then is that the line wasn't strong enough, so it is upped. I've seen people using in excess of 30lb line in the hope of stopping a fish. I can't tell you how stupid I think this is. Don't take my word for it, conduct a simple experiment. Tie some 30lb line to your scales, secure them some way and pull till you break the line. It should break at 30lb if your knots are sound. Remember just how hard you had to pull. The next dozen or so fish you land, look closely at the hookhold and ask yourself in all honesty what would happen if you were to bring 30lb of pressure to bear on it in a direct pull. You would tear the hook straight out of the fish's mouth. The euphemistic phrase is 'The hook pulled'; the reality is damaged fish, some of them irreparably so.

This would certainly happen in fish from 25 to 32lb. I hope I don't dent too many big-fish men's reputations when I say that this is the most difficult fish to land. The power generated by this class of fish under the rod tip, hooked on the bottom in 4 feet of water is frankly mind-blowing. Hook-and-hold is laughable in this situation, but such a fish can be stopped provided that we keep unbalancing it every time it tries to reach sanctuary.

The third class of fish, from 32lb up to veritable monsters, call for what I can only describe as psychological warfare. There isn't the sheer power of the second class but there is sheer bulk. The most difficult thing to control is yourself. You are generally talking of a personal best fish or one close to it.

You've done all the hard work. You usually know to within a couple of pounds how big it is. In your dreams you've gone through the capture a thousand times and there it is not four feet away from you well hooked. Believe me, there are a myriad ways to cock it up. The most common is freezing, but if you can land a 25–32 lb fish you can really land anything your mind will let you.

As regards the landing of fish, there are three windows of opportunity and I will list them in chronological order. The first window (mainly with very large fish) is almost immediately after

A mid-twenty from the notoriously difficult Wraysbury is gently slid back into the crystal-clear water. Stalking was the successful method.

it's been hooked. Sometimes the fish will just stop. It knows it's hooked, it has been there before and it knows running only aggravates the problem. So, provided that everything is prepared beforehand, it can be landed within a minute or two. I've read about myself that I have used my feet to land fish, which conjures up a picture of some ape-like creature using all its extremities in unison. Well, that is not quite true, but if possible I do arrange the landing net in such a way that by kicking the bottom of it I can move it to a position where I can land a fish, and I have indeed landed very large fish within minutes of hooking them.

The second window is roughly halfway through the normal fight, when the fish is still confused and can with positive pressure be lured into the net. The third window is the one everybody is familiar with, as its the same as landing fish in normal carp fishing: exhausting the fish till it rolls over the net.

For those who have not hooked a carp at close quarters before, what you have just read will be only of academic interest because there is no way of anticipating the baptism of fire you are about to experience. Hooking a carp of 20lb at your feet doesn't in any way compare with hooking the same creature at 80 yards. The sheer power – which might well result in a limp line will have you wondering how anyone can make any sense of anything that is over in such a flash. I know Einstein had a theory of expanded time. I'm not sure I understand it – in fact I'm not sure I understand anything he wrote – but if he means that we can get to a point where a second seems like a long time and a minute an age then that is exactly how it feels. A five-minute fight can seem like a lifetime; a surge from the carp one way can elicit a counter move on your part within a split second. Playing and landing a fish in close confines is just the same as in open water, but it is faster and instinct has a greater part to play.

I have perhaps dwelt long on playing fish at close quarters and close to snags because I feel it is the least understood. But of course on many occasions hooking a fish in the margins will result in fish running out into open water and a more

usual fight will ensue. The one thing to be careful of is friction as the line gets pulled at a ferocious speed across the roller in the bail arm and the line just seems to part. For this reason I still prefer to backwind. With the Mitchell all that is required is the forefinger pushed behind the spool housing acting as a brake. It might burn a bit but you will land the fish – and that is the object of the exercise.

RIGS

I have left rigs till last not because I think that they are least important because they are not, especially as our fish become more educated – not in the cognitive sense, but in the reflex sense as a result of frequent capture. Rigs are increasingly important in stalking such fish.

I will start by recounting some observations I have made at Longfield. I know it no longer exists, but, through constant pressure from some of the country's leading carp anglers and, more important, some of the country's leading thinking anglers, the fish there were the most problematic I ever came across. On finding a baited area the carp that were interested in feeding went through the same routine. First they cruised around the complete area checking for lines or anything they felt untoward. I know it can be dangerous to anthropomorphise fish behaviour but I am certain that that was what they were doing. If they felt anything amiss they left the area. Leads didn't bother them, mono lines did, rig tubing most certainly did, and in some areas a vertical braided terylene line did. The areas where they were tolerated were where physical objects (weed or fallen trees) traversed from the bottom to the top anyway. Once they assumed everything was fine they would proceed to feed. And once they started they would not leave the baited area but stayed constantly above it until they had finished or until something frightened them, in which case they would leave the area not to return.

Feeding was peculiar insofar as there were two distinctive types of feeding which were not interchangeable, in that particular fish fed either one way or the other. This was borne out in the catches made by the various groups and individuals who fished the lake. Very often the approach they employed caught either one group or the other. The first group sort of checked baits. They would suck a bait from about an inch away but before it entered their mouths they would partially close their mouths and check it with their lips.

I have seen a hookbait checked anything up to half a dozen times without it actually entering the mouth. The other group were clampers. These would open their mouths really wide and from directly above clamp down on the bait, trapping any line that came from a hookbait, and presumably they would suck. Of course all baits except tethered ones would get sucked up and eaten.

My first problem was one of approach. I like to walk a lake first and put bait in various places, then go on a circuit of these places until fish are found. But with the fish not moving once they started feeding this made putting a hookbait in place difficult. The alternative would be to set up in a chosen area and wait. The problem with this approach is that carp didn't visit all the areas all the time. So I chose to stick to my usual approach and rely on extra stealth to place hookbaits among feeding fish. This did not always work because even when the bait was placed unobserved they sometimes spooked on seeing a new bait in the swim. Whether I would have had more success with the other approach is debatable.

As to rigs to overcome the testers I used a simple pop-up rig 1 inch off the bottom, but it required nerves of steel. First the hookbait had to be placed in an advantageous way, along a sunken branch or right in close to a shelf or some other obstacle, which meant that when the bait was being tested it was in full view and then you had to wait while the carp went through its ritual of sucking and inspecting. Sometimes it would take a chance and take the bait into its mouth, but on feeling the line and hook it would of course spit it out. So there was that one split second when you had the chance of setting the hook – a very small window of opportunity. But,

provided that you knew what was required, it turned the situation from impossible to possible.

The clampers really did have me thinking hard. I went through a multitude of rigs and approaches to overcome the problem and originally my intention was to go through them to give you an insight to my thought process. But I have decided against it on the grounds that they were only partially successful and could in the end confuse. So I'll go straight to the one I ended up with, an adaptation of a simple stalking rig I had been using for a couple of years. It consisted of a bottom bait: a 1-inch hair tied to the eye and foam on the bend of the hook so that the hook was suspended above the bait. When the fish clamped down on the bait, the hook point was at least 1½ inches into the mouth and a pull on the line set the hook. I used both rigs in conjunction with float and leger.

When asked to simplify stalking I would always say place a bait as close to a fish as many times as possible, for as long as possible, and something will happen. But with the advent of the super-cautious carp it's not enough; something has to be manufactured. In the two half-seasons I fished Longfield not one carp made one mistake; every fish was earned. The float was never pulled completely under during a take. The only time the float went under was either when fish bumped into the line (as mentioned earlier, in some areas the line was tolerated completely) or when the bait was rejected, which was done with ferocity, the bait travelling anything up to 18 inches – which gave a lovely dip on the float, indicating only that the fish had gone. Of course, one never knew if a tester or clamper was going to enter your swim, which meant one couldn't rig up until you had observed what they were doing. This made for interesting fishing.

I believe that it is relevant to relate these Longfield experiences because one day many of our waters will be like this. The two rigs mentioned are the basis of my stalking rigs. The criterion I use is that I want to know where the hook is in relation to the bait, especially when in the fish's mouth. The rig also has to be efficient enough for the carp to pick it up unhindered but inefficient

The victor of another battle. This is 'Heart Tail' at 31lb plus from Longfield. Jan shows how devastating his specialist stalking can be.

enough so that should a carp you don't want to catch mouth the bait it can eject it without itself hooking.

The diametric opposite to Longfield was curiously just down the road at Wraysbury. As time goes by these large waters, which up to a few years ago were considered so impossible, will be the new targets for many a carper and on many of these stalking could be a practical approach. Obviously you are not going to get the ultra-cautious fish of Longfield in such places, in fact some of the carp will be quite naive, but the equation is simple: what you gain on relatively naive fish you lose on the location problem. Wraysbury holds about thirty carp. I have read various estimates on average so I won't confuse the issue any

further, but it takes one hour simply to walk round it.

So I hope I'm not overstating the obvious when I say that location can be a problem; indeed, you can lose the fish for anything up to a month. They could be around any of the numerous islands or just out in open water but still the same stalking procedure is relevant, but has to be adjusted. Every lake has a rhythm, but on the larger lakes the rhythms are more protracted. Nevertheless they are there and by working on them you can estimate to quite a high degree of accuracy where the fish are going to be. It wouldn't be appropriate to go into the various facets of fish finding, though obviously water craft plays a large part.

BAITING

On larger lakes baiting should be done only when fish have been located since baiting likely spots would be logistically impossible. Some bays of perhaps 15 acres or more might not be visited that year. But, once located, the fish are less suspicious of fishing hardware and time is on your side, as you are not likely to be disturbed by other anglers. But all this could lull you into a false sense of security. On the larger waters the fish are by nature nomadic, so, having found fish in say a particular bay, one is never sure whether they will be in residence for a day, a week, or a month, or whether they will visit each day for a period and then suddenly depart. Happily, they can be induced to extend their stay by baiting.

The tolerance of fishing hardware displaying by these carp could lull you into fishing clumsily. This could result in a spooked fish which might not stop for a quarter of a mile and your chances of putting a bait to that particular fish again might not arise for a few years. This is further compounded by the fact that carp are by nature gregarious, and by spooking one you spook the group. If the group consists of, say, six fish, that is twenty per cent of the Wraysbury carp population. Catching one fish can also spook the rest of the group, so it is imperative that you attempt to catch the right fish when the opportunity arises.

SURFACE FISHING

I have purposely left surface fishing to a minimum because I know that my old chum Chris Ball is doing a chapter on this topic (Chapter 8) and I don't want to go over the same ground. With a bit of thought, the methods he advocates can be adapted. There are just a couple of points to keep in mind.

First, because fish are almost stationary when taking marginal surface baits, the angle at which they take the bait is completely different from the situation in open water, in that it is almost perpendicular. This causes a problem: baits are easily inspected and rejected without the hook pricking. So manoeuvring the hook and striking to the side or over the carp's back is sometimes necessary, or, if this fails, a self-hooking set-up has to be employed – a bait on the surface and a short line direct to rod, which is either resting on something firm or held in the hand. But beware. Hook holds on marginal surface-stalked fish are notoriously bad, so fish losses are common and disheartening. The plus side is that fish are high in the water and without any traction can be landed quite quickly. Also, it is easy to be selective by simply lifting the bait from unwanted fish.

Finally, I'm sure there are many who having read this piece can see some of the logic, but are too self-conscious to fish known carp waters with the stalking approach. All I can say is that over the years more and more of the top carp anglers are adopting a stalking approach, at least in part. You wouldn't believe the ridicule I used to get wandering around with Shackleton, but in the end you don't get respect from the waters you fish, but from the fish you catch from the waters you fish. If you adopt a more intimate approach, chinks in the armour of the most difficult water will become apparent. More importantly, the problems that make waters problematical can be isolated and I suppose the greatest weakness I observe in carp anglers is that though they have at their disposal a multitude of solutions very often they are unaware of the problem.

7 SURFACE RIGS

I suppose surface fishing can almost be described as an attitude of mind, there are so many anglers who would not consider fishing on the top and in some respects class it almost as not serious carping. Boy, what a nonsense! Are they ever missing out on something! The problem, generally speaking, is that in surface fishing you have to use your eyes and be mobile, and many newcomers to the sport misguidedly think that carp fishing is only about hours of waiting, sitting behind multiple rods, incarcerated in their bivvy, perhaps entertaining themselves with the latest girlie magazine. I can tell that you this attitude will not only stop them enjoying so many other branches of carp fishing but will also guarantee that they catch fewer fish.

Carp are curious by nature and on most waters they will investigate just about any item floating on the surface above their heads. Another myth that should be dispelled here and now is that you can only catch carp on bright, hot, windless days. That statement is so far removed from reality that those of us who practise the art know better and consider it almost laughable. My good mate, Chris Ball, who has written the next chapter 'Floater Magic', has caught one of the largest, if not *the* largest winter surface carp at just over 30lb to endorse the fact that they can be caught on the top almost at any time of the year.

OBSERVATION

The whole crux of successful floater fishing is observation. Those of us who have eyes constantly searching the water will be looking out for tell-tale signs of carp moving on or near the surface. Never think that they will always be easily

seen, with inches of their backs protruding from the water. This does happen, but more often than not it will be just a flattening of the surface, a twitching of reed stems, a tiny movement beneath weedbeds or lily pads, or just a ghostly grey shadow patrolling almost out of sight.

Well, all that's okay by day, but what about location of carp at night? Any night-stalking angler worth his salt will sit quietly and watch out over and listen to likely areas of the lake, even on the darkest of nights. Carp feeding on the surface will make unmistakable slurping and clooping sounds as they sample floating items. Also, look out for oily ripples on calm nights and the slight flattening of surface ripples on breezy ones. Never ignore the margins, especially on quiet days when no one else is around or at night when the majority of anglers are tucked up in their bivvies. Go and investigate the windward side of the lake. Here there will be a vast accumulation of floating debris amongst which there are sure to be some tasty morsels which the carp will be rooting out.

Stealth is the name of the game – carp at close quarters do not suffer fools gladly. Dress in drab clothes, and move quietly, avoiding heavy footfalls and distinctive movements. Always keep low, even at night and try to avoid silhouetting yourself between the carp and the horizon.

Many anglers blow it the first time they get into this eyeball-to-eyeball situation with the carp, partly through wanting to get a bait to the carp as quickly as possible or to get a better look. It is far better once the carp has been discovered to sit and watch for a while. After all it is there of its own accord and will feel safe if left undisturbed. Sitting and watching and slowing the pace of the whole thing down will not only give you an opportunity of working out the best position to ambush the fish; it will also give you time to work out exactly where and how you are going to land it, assuming that you hook it successfully. As you sit there quietly observing the carp's movements a pattern will undoubtedly unfold. It may be a patrol route the fish is following, a particular piece of floating weed or something similar that the carp keeps investigating, or just the simple matter of selecting one of the fish which is larger than the rest milling about in the area.

FEEDING

When the time is right freebies can be introduced and the carp's response to them carefully analysed. It may need more to get them interested, however it is often the case that one or two are just enough. Never fire out free offerings over the carp's head; drift them down on the wind or wait till the fish are the farthest distance away on their routes.

Where carp can be seen at a distance the same will apply. The secret is never to hurry. Get the carp feeding and the rest will become a natural progression of selection.

Where many carp are in the swim a degree of preoccupation and competitive feeding is likely. This depends on free offerings being introduced at the correct rate. Only experience and continual observation will dictate just how much you need to introduce. You should see the difference once competitive feeding is achieved. A carp that started off looking very finicky and sampling free offerings with suspicion can in relatively little time be transformed into a ravenously feeding fish, racing its companions in eagerness to get the next free offering.

I will not dwell any further on the feeding methods, as I know that Chris has taken an in-depth look at this aspect of surface fishing. Instead I will look at some of the various rigs and set-ups that are currently being used with consistent success.

RIGS AND SET-UPS

Floating Breadcrust

Floating breadcrust is undoubtedly the most basic of all floating baits and it still accounts for hundreds of surface-caught fish every year. Pieces of crust are torn off from a loaf of bread and impaled on a hook of suitable size. The crust should always be mounted on the hook with the hard brown side up towards the eye, the white flaky side down on the bend. Pieces anything from ½ inch square to 4 inches square can be used.

The simplest method is to freeline the crust. Literally all that is needed is rod, reel, hook and line, no other casting weight is added. The crust is attached to the hook by the method described; it can then be momentarily dunked in the water to add some extra weight. It's surprising just how far you can cast freelined crust. When a carp comes along, predict its path and cast beyond and well in front. The crust can then be slowly edged back to intercept the carp *en route*.

Floating breadcrust. The most basic of all floating baits but one which has accounted for many thousands of carp.

The timing of the strike is critical. Some carp may well swirl several times at the crust before they finally take it. Make sure the bait is right in the mouth and the carp is moving away before you strike. It is imperative that the line is well greased so that it floats on the surface; if it sinks between the rod tip and the crust not only will it pull the bait out of position closer to the angler, it will also make bite detection and striking more difficult. The greased line adjacent to the crust can almost be used as the bite indicator. If you watch the taking fish carefully you will see the line start to disappear below the surface or snake across the top. A firm strike will usually be followed by an explosion on the surface as the carp dashes for freedom.

Margin Crust

The roaming freeline method is great for intercepting fish several yards out from the margins. Another exciting breadcrust method is to fish it static in the margins directly below the rod tip. This is a fabulous method to use for night fishing, even today, and one that is sadly overlooked.

This method involves setting the rod up on two rod rests, which should be positioned in such a way that the rod tip is directly above the area where the bait is to be presented. Obviously, the margins have to be reasonably deep and it's desirable to have good bankside cover.

The crust is attached to the hook in the normal way, the rod is then placed on the rod rest and the bait lowered onto the surface of the water so that it just sits there held in place with the line rising perpendicular to the rod tip, not touching the water at all. A little slack line is desirable but this should be kept to a minimum and it shouldn't touch the surface. At the reel end the bail arm should be left open and the line tucked in the line clip immediately above the spool or, with one of the modern reels, the free spool or baitrunner should be left in its slackest position. Naturally, a fish hooked at such close quarters is going to disappear out of the swim at an alarming rate of knots, so be prepared for this and have your clutch set quite loose so that line can be taken

fairly easily. To try to stop a fish at such close quarters could see the hook pulling out or, even worse, the line breaking.

This is a really fantastic method to use at night – it's real heart-stopping stuff. You will undoubtedly be aware of the carp's presence as it nears the bait then a slurp, a bit of a splash, the rod tip will kick over and the line will pull from the clip, peeling off at a hundred miles an hour. The other nice thing about this type of margin fishing is that, since there is no line touching the water, there is literally nothing for the carp to inspect that could possibly spook it. It is also guaranteed to anchor the bait in perfect position.

Naturally, the angler should not be seen and should ensure that he makes very little movement, if any at all. This sort of fishing is far better practised in solitude away from your mates – even a quiet conversation or a shuffling of bodies could be enough to deter the carp.

Specialist Floating Cake

On waters where there are many nuisance fish which would also like to feed on your floating breadcrust, a specialist floating cake could well be the answer. The cakes are made from one of the standard boilie mixes. I describe many of these in Chapter 11 but most of them can be adapted to make these special floaters. You will have to double up on the amount of eggs and add a level teaspoon of baking powder to about every 10oz of dry mix. Flavour and colour should be added at the same time, though in my view colour is only a confidence booster to the angler and a way of identifying different flavours if several types of cake are to be made up. The fact is that any floating item viewed from below against the sky is always in silhouette and appears black, so I personally pay very little attention to the colour of surface baits.

The eggs, flavour, colour and mix should be beaten up, ideally in a food processor. The secret is to introduce as much air into the mix as possible. I like to leave the mixer running for ten or fifteen minutes once all the ingredients have been folded in together. The mix, which should be now be of a soupy consistency is poured into a

Specialist floating cake made from powdered ingredients, bound together with eggs and baked in the oven.

The floating cake can be mounted onto the rig by just nicking the hook through the hard crusty skin.

greased square baking tin. Place it in the middle of a preheated oven and cooked slowly at about gas mark 7. This will probably taken at least two hours, sometimes quite a lot longer, depending on the type of mix. You will know when it is cooked as the mix should have risen and have a nice brown crust on the top. Once it has cooled down, turn out of the tin. You now have your own specialist floating cake which, although fairly dense in consistency, will be light enough to float since all the air introduced at the mixing stage will be trapped and make it buoyant.

The edges, the crusty bits, I use for hookbait. These will be very tough and give the abundant shoals of roach and rudd a hard time. Once the whole loaf has been cut into cubes and the edge bits put to one side for hookbaits, the middle non-crusty sections can be used as free offerings for baiting up. I personally like to see quite a lot of small fish worrying the baits as this attracts the attention of the carp. So these specialist floating cakes are very useful and can perform two roles.

The other advantage of adding flavour is that there is bound to be a nice leak-off in the water and the carp are very well equipped for picking up the scent, which all helps them to home in on the bait.

Rigs for Floating Cake
Cake can be used in much the same way as floating breadcrust, either freelined or margin-fished. In more open water or at long range the floating cake can be used in conjunction with a sliding leger rig. You will be using a bottom weight as an anchor as well as giving extra ounces to aid casting. The rig consists of a leger weight and a small length of line attached to an oval plastic curtain ring through which the main line runs. The floating cake is then attached to the hook and rests up against the curtain ring for casting. Once cast out the line is sunk between leger weight and rod tip in as straight a line as possible. Once this is done the bail arm is opened and line is payed out so that the buoyant bait starts to make its way to the

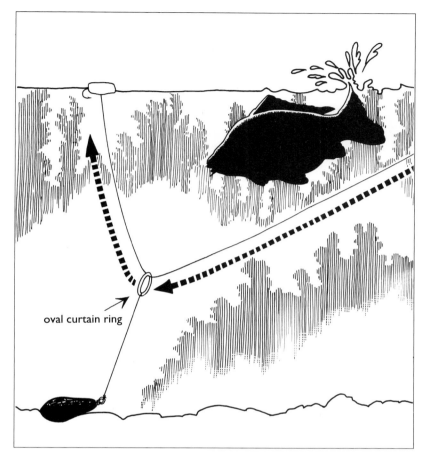

Floater rig for weedy waters.

surface. When it appears on the top the bail arm is closed and the rod is either hand-held or set up on rod rests. The length of line between the leger weight and the oval curtain ring depends very much on the type of water you are fishing. If there is a soft or silty bottom it may well need to be up to a foot in length. For hard-bottomed gravel pits it need only be a couple of inches. On very weedy waters this set up can really come into its own. The length between lead and curtain ring could well be extended up to about 6 feet to compensate for any weed growing up from the bottom. The line is kept well above the weed, allowing the angler to get the floater up to the surface with relative ease. I have fished this rig successfully on some big gravel pits up to above 80 yards.

If there is a drawback with this type of method it is that the bait is stationary so you are relying on the carp coming upon it *en route* or you must feed in free offerings adjacent to the hookbait to attract carp into the area. It's biggest advantage, however, is that it allows you to fish a floating bait at range in quite windy conditions when with most other set-ups the bait will be blown completely off course.

Alternative Floating Baits

As I mentioned earlier, carp will investigate just about any floating item, so there is a vast array of baits that can be used on the top. Just look at all the different floating breakfast cereals that are available in all manner of sizes, textures and flavours. Some of my favourites are Puffed Wheat, Rice Crispies or Coco Pops and Honey

Not the first floating bait that may enter your mind but Coco pops, like many breakfast cereals, make a good alternative to the more standard floating baits.

and Pedigree Chum, but how on earth do you fish such tiny baits? Well, I will tell you or perhaps first of all I will tell you how to get the free offerings out, for believe it or not this is probably more difficult than fishing these tiny little morsels on a hook. There is obviously little or no weight in any of these mini-floaters. This is no problem if we are fishing the margins or if a favourable wind blows them out into the lake.

Some of the cat and dog biscuits will take on water, adding extra weight and making them easier to catapult. But be careful when adding water not to add too much, or you will end up with just a soggy mess. It is far better to let them soak in only the minimum amount of water overnight. This has two advantages. First, it will add the extra desired weight to help in catapulting those extra few yards, and, second, it will soften up the bait to allow it to be easily mounted on a hook. I will come back to this in more detail later. To give you some idea just how much water you will need to put with the dry mix, as a rule of thumb I use approximately 100ml of water to every pound weight of dry mix. This has served me well now for many years. If you do a couple of test batches first then you can adjust the levels accordingly. This is also a good opportunity to add any flavour that you may fancy to enhance the bait.

The method of preparation is as follows. Put the dry baits into a large plastic bag; a heavy-duty freezer bag is about the best. Add flavour to the water and then add the flavoured water to the bag. Blow into the bag to fill it with air. Trap the air inside the bag and shake the contents until the liquid is evenly distributed amongst the floaters. I like to keep shaking them about for a good three or four minutes. Seal the bag so that no water evaporates and leave them overnight. Hey presto they are ready to use.

Now under favourable conditions you will be able to catapult small cat and dog biscuits 40 or 50 yards. To get them any farther I bind them together with Horlicks. As they are now already damp, the Horlicks will stick a dozen or fifteen of the individual biscuits together. Roll them in a ball to make them as aerodynamic as possible and

Nut Loops, but there are obviously loads more. Floating pet food biscuits are another favourite. Cat biscuits like Seanip and Meow Mix have accounted for many of my carp. Sadly, the best one of all of the cat biscuits, Felix Meaty Crunch, has now been discontinued, so if you ever see any of these about on the supermarket shelf take my advice and buy them up. Also, dog biscuits are taken avidly by carp. These again come in all different shapes, sizes and flavours and undoubtedly the most popular of all is Pedigree Chum Mixer, a firm favourite of Chris Ball as you will hear in Chapter 8.

I can hear you all now: It's all very well him saying he likes using Rice Crispies, Meow Mix

Just a small selection of floating cat biscuits in varying sizes and smells. I can assure you there are a whole load more for you to choose from.

Pedigree Chum Mixer, undoubtedly the most popular bait of our time.

The larger floating dog balls have a very high oil content, leaving a large slick on the surface, often flattening the ripples.

use a catapult with a large pouch to fire them out. You will now find that the distance has been increased up to about 80 yards.

Back to the breakfast cereals. Now these are obviously much lighter than the cat and dog biscuits and it's certainly no good soaking these in water as we all know what a yucky mess they turn into at the breakfast table. However you can still use the Horlicks powder for sticking them together but the method is completely different.

You will need some sort of mixing bowl or a large maggot box in which to apply the Horlicks powder. First wet the inside of the bowl or box. I like to use one of the atomising-type sprays to get an even distribution. Next sprinkle the Horlicks powder and then spray on a little more water. In goes the breakfast cereal and the mixture rolled

up into a stodgy ball and subsequently catapulted out into the swim.

There are a couple of things to remember when using this type of bait. First, make up as much of the Horlicks balls and breakfast cereal as you are going to catapult in immediately as you will find that the dry brekky biscuits will act like a sponge and soak up the water. This will make them soft and disintegrate too quickly. There is an added bonus when using Horlicks powder to bind the mini-floaters together to achieve extra distance. On impact with the water the balls break up but keep the baiting pattern tight, while at the same time the Horlicks powder clouds and flavours the water in close proximity to the free-bies. Carp definitely have a liking for Horlicks and they home in much more quickly.

Horlicks powder is an ideal medium for binding small lightweight baits together. They can be moulded into a larger ball and then catapulted a greater distance.

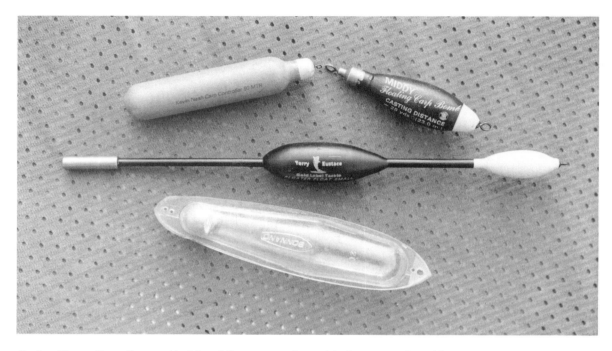

Surface Floater Controllers are ideal for adding extra casting weight for presentation with light floating baits. They also make a good visual indicator.

FLOATER CONTROLLERS

Floater controllers are used on the main line as a weighted aid for casting tiny floating hookbaits out to the same distance as the free offerings. There are several of them out on the market and they all have slightly different advantages, so I always carry a good selection with me. As well as adding extra casting weight, they also serve as a visual indicator. On some waters avidly feeding carp will tow them under or along the surface, giving excellent bite registration. On shy-feeding waters they will act as a marker so that we know the position of our hookbaits; inching the controller every now and again will make the hookbait move amongst the free offerings, allowing us to keep tabs all the time. On these harder waters we may well be striking at the moment the carp puts its lips round the bait or there is a swirl where the hookbait once was. The angler's experience must match the level of education of the carp if this limited opportunity is to be exploited. I'm glad to say that these waters are quite few and far between.

The controller is fitted to the main line and stopped in place with a swivel or something similar. To that is attached the hook link. The hook link should ideally be about 3 feet in length, and its material should be selected to be as unobtrusive as possible – what I said earlier about floating objects appearing as a black silhouette goes for line as well. The best line I have found for hook link material is Damyl Tectan. It has very little colour in it – in fact it is almost clear – and it does not show a stark outline. Alternatively, you can degrease the hook link so that it sinks just below the surface. If this is the chosen method the trick is not to degrease the whole of the hook link but only the third nearest the hook itself. The buoyancy of the bait and of the line closest to the controller will allow a small belly of line to sink a couple of inches below the surface. This is ideal.

rig tube
stop swivel

Drennan floater controller.

Here are few of my favourite controllers and how I set them up.

Drennan Clear Controller

These come in a couple of sizes, one for close to medium range and one for long range up to about 70 or 80 yards. They comprise a clear plastic body with an counterbalance weight encapsulated in the bottom. They are quite aerodynamic, giving a reasonably good splashdown as they enter the water. At the top end of the controller is a white sight blob fitted with a diamond-eyed swivel. I like to use these in a semi-fixed position. A short length of rig tubing is wedged through the eye of the controller so that it is a snug fit. This tubing needs to only be 2 inches in length. The main line is then passed through the centre of the tube and the stop swivel tied on. Hook, hook link and bait are then attached as normal.

Before casting, the stop swivel is wedged into the bore of the rig tubing. This is now in a semi-fixed position, which gives a much better and instant indication and also helps as an anti-tangle set-up when punching the rig out at distance. If the hooked fish should become tethered in a snag or weed the controller automatically jettisons itself so as not to leave it trailing in the unfortunate event of the line snagging.

Kevin Nash Controller

These are available in three sizes to give comprehensive cover up to 25 yards, 50 yards and 75 yards. They are made of buoyant balsa wood with an inserted brass counterweight in the bottom. The orange Day-Glo sight top is fitted with a very small diamond-eyed swivel. As illustrated, this is held in place by means of a stop swivel and a couple of float stops. The DAM float stops are slid onto the main line first. These float stops come complete with a wire loop for easy transfer onto the main line. I have always found that fishing with two gives less slip than using them

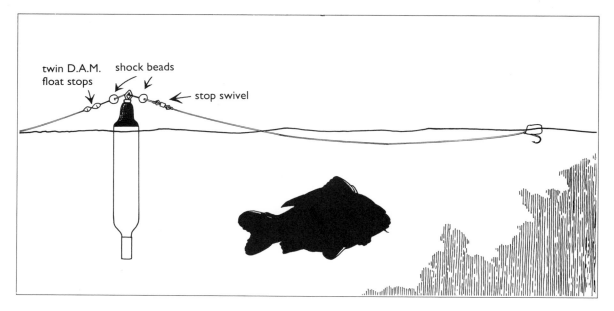

Nash floater controller.

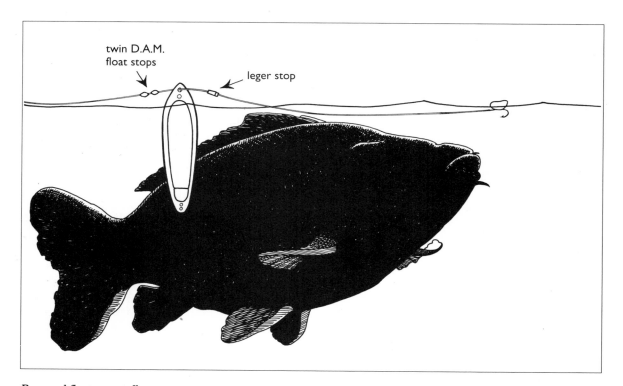

Bonnand floater controller.

singly. A small-bore shock lead goes onto the line next, followed by the controller, and then a larger-bored shock lead with a hole large enough to go over the stop-knot swivel, which is attached next. Finally it's a matter of attaching hook link, hook and bait.

For casting the float stops should be pushed up to within about ⅛ inch of the first shock lead in order to give a bit of free movement, but this free movement should not exceed about ½ inch. As before, this is a safe method; should the carp

become tethered, the controller automatically pulls free from the twin DAM float stops.

Bonnand Controller

These French-made controllers are injection-moulded from clear plastic, with a counterbalance weight encapsulated in the bottom. At the top there are two holes through which you can pass the main line. Some people like to attach a small link swivel through one of these holes. I am personally not bothered one way or the other as

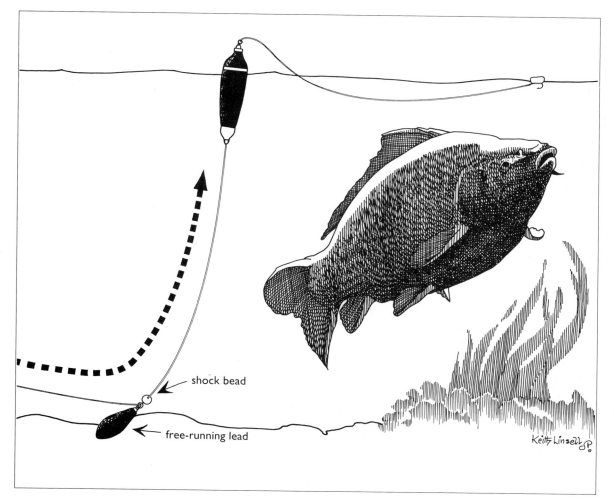

shock bead

free-running lead

Middy floater controller.

both methods work well. I use the Bonnand model mainly for close-range stalking, usually on quite heavy line, and I therefore find it almost unnecessary to use the kinder link swivel.

With this set-up I do not use a permanently fixed stop but an adjustable leger stop backed up with two DAM float stops. The reason for this is that while I am stalking I am always changing swims and I like to be able to decrease or lengthen the hook link at will rather than having to tie a new one on each time. This gives me a more flexible set-up and I now only use the smallest of these French controllers, which on heavy line enables me to fish up to 15 or 20 yards.

Middy Floater Controller

There will be times in adverse weather conditions where you want to anchor one of these small floating baits. It is in this situation that the Middy Doubled Eyed Controller comes into its own. As you can see from the drawing, the controller actually becomes an integral part of the main line, with a free-running leger weight and a shock bead passed on first. The top eye of the controller takes the hook link whilst the bottom counterbalanced end takes the main line. When cast out into the swim the line should be sunk as tight as possible between rig and rod tip. Then the line is

payed out until the controller emerges on the surface. The rod can then be hand-held or supported on a couple of rod rests. In this situation, rather than drawing the controller into the path of the fish we have to draw the fish to the controller. Careful baiting upwind of the controller should bring the carp within striking distance of the hookbait. Where drift, drag and undertow or a crosswind continually pull the normal controller off course, this set-up really works well.

MOUNTING HOOKBAITS

If you have used the method described earlier of softening up the baits you will be able to put two or three on a hook of suitable size so that the hookbait rides on the surface like the free offerings. When the carp start to wise up and get suspicious of free offerings as well as the hookbait, it is probably time to change the rig. This becomes apparent when the carp start bolting away as they suss that something isn't quite right with the hookbait. This is the time to consider hair rigs.

Mixer Rigs

Mixer rigs are equally suitable for most of the floating cereals and pet biscuits described above.

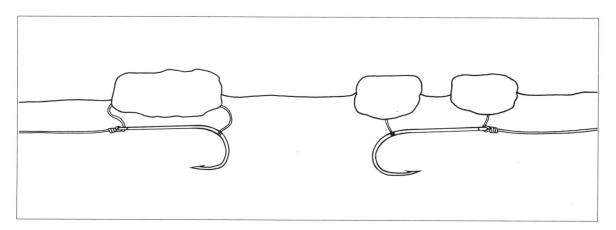

Chum Mixer rigs.

A Chum Mixer mounted on a 'D' hair rig. This ensures that the hook is presented directly beneath the bait.

Generally speaking, a single Chum Mixer is capable of supporting a heavy-gauge size 10 or a fine-wire size 8 hook. A fine monofilament hair of about 1lb BS is attached to the eye of the hook. It is then passed through the mixer at its widest point (a fine needle is by far the best way). The other end of the hair is attached at the top of the bend of the hook. The hair should be pulled up reasonably tight so that there is only about ⅛ inch play between the hook and the mixer.

In weedy or snaggy conditions a larger hook may be desirable, so extra buoyancy will be needed. Two Chum Mixers will support a heavy-gauge size 6 or a fine-wire size 4 hook and should be attached as shown, one to the eye of the hook and one to the back of the bend – again with only about 1/16 inch play. The hook will hang directly below the bait, ensuring that it always enters the carp's mouth first, which increases the chance of hooking finicky fish.

The next step in the battle against these spooky fish is to remove the hook link completely from the water. Remember the margin-fished crust. It is possible with the right set-up to achieve a similar presentation at distance with a single floating pet biscuit.

Gardener Suspender Rig

You can see from the drawing that this needs very little explanation. Basically it is another controller, one with a long extended arm that protrudes over the water at an angle. The protruding arm is made from hollow stiff plastic tubing inserted through a polystyrene ball. The underside of the controller has a brass counterbalance weight fitted so that it cocks the suspender at a slight angle. The suspender is threaded onto the main-line brass counterbalance weight end first. A stop swivel then holds it in place. At the end of the suspended tube is a silicone sleeve into which the stop swivel is pushed – this holds it in place. It is then a simple matter of attaching the hook link, which is around 6 inches in length. The hook link should be adjusted in such a way that the bait only just kisses the water.

The bait itself can be mounted just on the edge of the hook shank or on a short hair attached to the eye. Whichever method you use make sure that the whole of the bend and the point of the hook is exposed. As the carp comes up to inspect the bait, it will automatically prick itself and as the suspender slams down on the water the hook will be driven home even further.

Beachcaster Rig

This set-up first gained popularity at that famous Midlands carp water, Cuttle Mill. Constant pressure on the avidly surface-feeding fish began to take its toll and they started to become difficult to catch. Some innovative anglers began to adopt this method, which eventually became known as the beachcaster rig. The set-up is as follows. A larger leger weight 2oz or more, is tied on the end of the main line. A pike float or a buoyant-bodied controller is fixed slightly over depth. Into the main line above the pike float is inserted a three-way swivel or a Drennan ring. To this the hook link is attached and adjusted like the suspender rig, so that it only just kisses the water. The rod

stop swivel

silicone sleeve

Suspender rig.

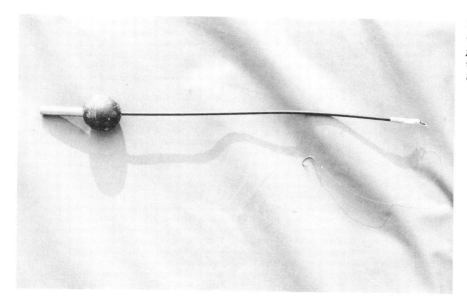

The Gardner Suspender Controller allows us to present a floating bait with none of the hooklink touching the surface at all.

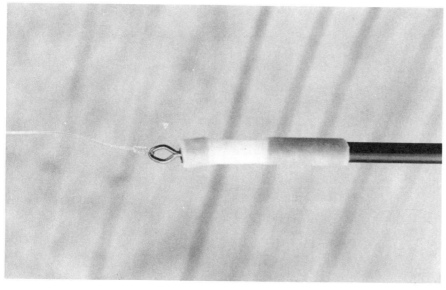

A close-up of the Suspender with the hooklink stop swivel wedged into the silicone sleeve.

is held in an almost vertical position, in a similar style to a beachcaster, whence the name. The line is then tightened up to the pike float.

Both of these methods allow the bait to be fished with no hook link lying on or just under the surface at all. With the suspender rig you are limited to cast of 60 yards or so but have the advantage of being able to draw the rig to any moving fish. With the beachcaster rig you can fish farther

and in more adverse conditions than with the suspender but you are relying on the fish coming to the bait rather than vice versa.

These are two extremely good methods. However, rather than going straight in and using the best that is available it is always far better to progress slowly and educate the fish at a sensible pace. We are already seeing far too many waters where the carp are wise beyond their years.

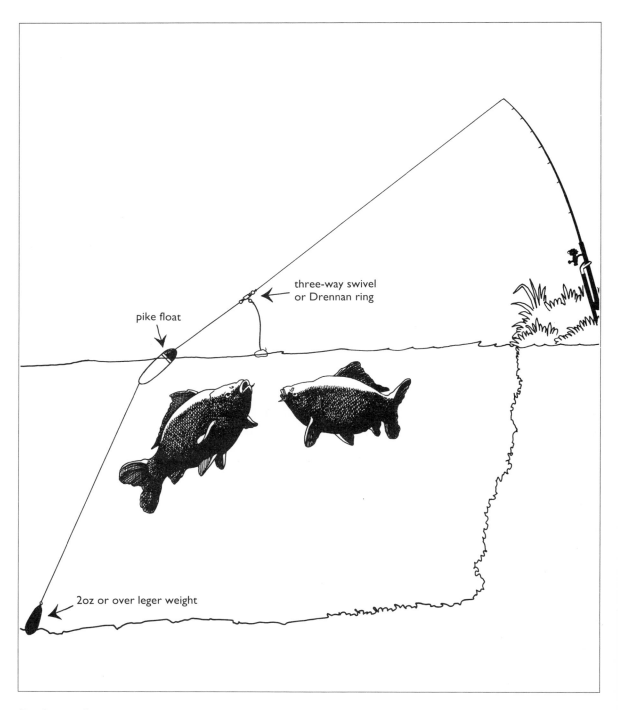

three-way swivel
or Drennan ring

pike float

2oz or over leger weight

Beachcaster rig

8 FLOATER MAGIC
Chris Ball

I guess the origins of fishing for carp on the surface go back much farther than you might at first think. You only have to thumb through the marvellous *Confessions of a Carp Fisher* by the noted carp angler 'B.B.' and you will find a whole chapter devoted to surface fishing. It was written by another carp angler, Flight Lieutenant Burton. This chapter by Burton, 'Floating Bait Method', gives all the basic methods that are still largely with us to this day. Naturally, there were other individuals who had experimented, but in fairness only a few had succeeded in mastering this specialised technique. Burton had studied carp and their behaviour with reference to the surface. This enabled him to make good catches, with some big fish amongst them, especially creditable when you take into account the time of his experiments with floating bread, in the 1930s.

As with many things associated with carp, the common denominator that turns up time and again is the name of Richard Walker. His emergence in the late 1940s gave hope to many. Dick was successful in pioneering a method that worked well at one of his local waters. It was what he called 'margin fishing' for carp. I believe it might have been Dick who first became aware

Any moment now! Another carp is just about to fall foul of Chris's fantastic floater method.

that carp would feed in this way – in the margins – and, once this technique had been mastered, he managed to catch them.

In the early 1930s Dick had regularly fished a pond which contained carp. The most effective method of catching them was floating crust, cast well out on a greased line. This method was also used by many other anglers, since an angling club had the fishing rights of the pond. The quantity of breadcrust cast upon its waters during the summer became considerable, and a great many carp were hooked, but few were landed. Some years later the fish had become very weary of floating bread. They would never touch the ordinary crust on a greased line; the nearest they came to doing this was to swirl violently close to it, repeating this until the sodden crust broke up and the hook sank. After a discreet interval they would return and devour the pieces.

During the summer Dick spent several nights carp fishing and soon could not fail to observe that as soon as dusk had come and other anglers had packed up the carp would come right in to the bank after crusts. Late that summer it dawned on him that to throw a crust 20 yards out into the pool was rather stupid, when he had seen numerous carp take crusts within a couple of yards of where he sat.

However, before that season had ended, he managed to land several by 'margin fishing', which encouraged him to persist. He learned that there was more in the method than just hanging a crust over the edge of the bank. Having the line taut would result in the carp sucking the crust clean off the hook, so Dick found it essential to have a foot or more of slack line between butt ring and reel.

The following year began with him feeling confident in the technique which had by then become so effective that he explained it to some friends. In the seasons that followed he caught some bigger fish in the 15–16lb range. Then came the war and with it little opportunity to fish, but when the war had finished he was back after carp once more and caught some big fish again. You might or might not know, but within a year of the war ending Dick was given a copy of *The*

Fisherman's Bedside Book by 'B.B.' and was so interested in what the author had to say about carp that he wrote to him. The letter appears in *Confessions of a Carp Fisher.* 'B.B.' went to stay with Dick Walker in 1947 and landed several specimen carp by margin fishing. Later Dick explained the idea to Bernard Venables, who featured it in his 'Mr Crabtree' fishing strip. The early 1950s saw the first twenty-pounder caught on such methods. In fact several such fish were caught and not only by margin fishing; with the greater acceptance of floating crust as a method to use, one or two big carp had been captured by people just slinging out a crust and finding that a large carp had snaffled it up

Dick Walker banged the drum as far as surface fishing for carp was concerned and the immediate effect he had on close friends was apparent. Maurice Ingham, that master carper from Lincolnshire and Carpcatchers' Club member, used this method when he first fished the Old Copper Mine, a water in Somerset. His catch on floating crust was important as it showed that the method worked on yet another water.

I think it was the first time that Maurice had used the method and he wrote to Dick Walker in an enthusiastically worded letter. Bernard Venables (Mr Crabtree) also used the method for the first time during this same period. His verdict: 'a creditable carp catching method'.

In the mid-1950s Dick Walker proved beyond doubt that carp could be caught by margin fishing by providing photographic evidence in one of his weekly *Angling Times* columns. Though catching carp by this method had been done before, it had never been photographed. So Pete Thomas, Pat Russell and Dick thought they would try and get some pictures for *Angling Times* readers. Pete did the fishing, Dick worked the camera and Pat stood by with a supply of flashbulbs and a powerful torch. It proved a difficult business, because an approaching fish was hard to see and it was exceedingly difficult to choose the right moment to shoot. After the flash had gone off, everyone was temporarily blinded, which did not make the proceedings either easy or safe, especially as Dick was perched on a small

Long hot summer days—just the job for catching carp on the top. They needn't all be huge to enjoy the sport. A single-figured fish comes to the net, one of a dozen taken during an afternoon's session.

36 lbs 10 oz Mirror from the notoriously difficult Oxfordshire water, taken in the early hours—a rod length out from the bank.

The first fish of the season are always special and this beautiful Leather was no exception. It was taken from a very small syndicate lake.

Towards the back-end of the season the weather started to cheer up, a new lease of life was injected into the lake and the fish responded accordingly. The result was a prime condition upper twenty pound Leather.

Left: *just what large, open gravel pits can offer the determined angler—the result of weeks of hard work. An upper thirty pound carp is gently slipped back.*

Below: *this is what winter carp fishing is all about. A 20 lb plus nearly fully-scaled Mirror. It just seems to glow in the weak winter sun.*

Opposite: *the smile that says it all—42 lbs of magnificent Bulgarian Mirror and no other angler for hundreds of miles. That's what carp fishing is all about.*

Left: *last day of the season and another old friend graces my net, although I did have to jump through a tree into the water to land it.*

Below: *a long, lean fighting machine contradicting all that I have said regarding the fight that carp give you in the winter. This one tore off with over a hundred yards of line on its first run.*

*On my travels again; a Brittany Mirror and a smile that shows my delight. This was the
first fish from a new water and the first of many upper twenties.*

A quiet period on a sunny afternoon, a good time to tie some more rigs up in readiness for the anticipated action yet to come as the temperature starts to fall.

Chris Ball with a 20 lb plus Mirror, naturally taken on the mixers, just beneath the bush behind him. 'That will do nicely' he said.

One of our rare, hot summers in England, the time to capitalize on surface-basking carp. This mid-twenty took mixers in the heat of the day.

Chris achieves some competition surface feeding—the bait, Chum Mixer again; now you can be selective!

Just to show that he can hold his own on any method, Jan with his personal best Common of 38½ lbs taken at long range on popped up Tiger Nuts from Salagou.

An ambition achieved—my first Redmire carp. This very famous Linear Mirror is even older than I am and that's saying something!

Winter Carping—it doesn't get a lot worse than this. A couple of hours before we were fishing but now the lake is completely iced over!

Junior Carp Society Fish In—a couple of future stars share a happy moment with me. Young John in the middle, who caught the 30-lbs fully-scaled fish that I am holding, was not strong enough to support it!

Yet another famous resident of Redmire—the Common with no pelvic fins. This fish has been handled by some of the most famous carp anglers in England, which somehow made it an even more special capture.

This could well be the offspring of a record carp; one of the Redmire youngsters looking fresh from the mould. Who knows, this fish may one day grow to even greater proportions than its parents.

First cast first carp from Salagou—a 42 lbs Mirror. Not a bad place, I thought to myself!

A couple of hours early morning feeding results in three 20 lb plus Commons, 29, 27 and 22. That's the way to do it.

It's the middle of March and the temperature is a stunning 27°C; time to relax after a hectic morning's sport at Lake Salagou in the south of France.

The south arm at the most famous carp water in France, St. Cassein. The French anglers opposite have just landed a big carp—the fish are obviously here. Will it be my turn next?

You can always get enjoyment both sides of the camera—it was my pleasure to photograph a cracking mid twenty Common for that very good angler Sean Harrison on a Midlands syndicate water.

Carp fishing is more than about just catching fish. My two angling companions, Jan and Chris—true friends who have shared the ups and downs of our never-ending search for carp. Cheers, guys!

This upper twenty was eventually fooled into taking the bait only 2 inches from the bank. A very cute fish that had alluded us all for most of the season, but persistence paid off. If I hadn't seen this carp take the bait I know that no bait registration would have been indicated.

Almost like fishing in a cloud, this is midday, not midnight. A 30 lb Common extracted from a huge French reservoir.

*It's autumn and the leaves may be falling, but Chris's surface action continues. A beautiful
20 pounder taken from a very tight swim in some dying lily pads.*

platform jutting out into the lake with 7 feet of
water only inches away. Margin fishing is an
exciting business for the angler but Dick concluded that it was even more exciting for a pho-
tographer.

Pete caught a 16lb carp for the camera and the
pictures proved it. Best of all, Dick managed to
photograph a carp that arrived unexpectedly. It
broke surface in a attempt to reach a crust that
was lifted several inches clear above the water,
because small rudd had been worrying it. This
picture alone gave evidence to the potential carp-
fishing public that carp were more than keen to
get their lips round a bait, even when it was not
in the water. It's from these humble beginnings
that the rise in popularity of surface angling for
carp started. Now we'll come forward forty years
in time and look at where we are today in the
world of floater fishing.

MODERN FLOATER FISHING

These days you would have to be a blind man *not
to notice* carp especially in the warmer months
when they frequent the warm upper layers of the
water and come across odd bits of food while
swimming around. If you introduce some food –
floating bait – you see something startling happen. They eat it! I know that sounds easy, and
perhaps I am stating the obvious, but in so many
people's eyes floater fishing is deemed largely a
waste of time. 'They don't take floaters here,
mate' is the battle-cry, but in my experience that
is rarely true. There can be times when carp are
more active on the surface and can be persuaded
to feed in such a fashion that you can catch them
in numbers and continue to reap the benefits year
after year. Sounds too good to be true? Read on...

A Mobile Approach

My main approach has always been centred on stalking tactics and this means that a mobile approach is vital to your fishing. You only need a minimum of tackle plus a small tackle bag containing a few items, so leave your bite alarms, bedchair and bivvy at home. I bet you feel better already!

Tackle

There are no hard and fast rules about what rod to use: your normal carp rod will do. If you become hooked on floater fishing – and that's not hard to do – you might invest in a specialist weapon later. You can also use whatever reel you use at the moment, but make sure you have plenty of spare spools. A guide would be 6lb, 8lb, 10lb, and 15lb. The line brand is a matter of personal preference, but I suggest you take a look at Maxima, Slycast, Berkley, DAM (various), and Brent. All are reliable and some have stood the test of time very well. The new Berkley Big Game line is going to be a winner for fishing near snags or heavy weed, so check this out as well.

Hooks, seen tremendous improvement these last ten years. I can recommend Drennan Super Specialist, Gamakatsu, and New Drennan Starpoint. Another hook which is strong yet lightweight and one I have used for years for open-water fishing, is the Drennan Specialist. It is a different pattern from the Drennan Starpoint. All these hooks are super-sharp (they have chemically etched points), which is of real benefit, for often our quarry are cagey and sometimes test the hookbait very carefully. These modern sharp hooks often prick the carp and make them bolt. They are a must.

In your tackle bag all you need is a small box with a selection of bits and pieces, spare hooks, swivels, and soon, a weigh-sling, scales and a keepsack. Other main items I recommend as essential are polaroids and a small pair of binoculars, plus a catapult. Naturally, a carp landing net is required. I have had one specially made. It has heavily bowed arms, which allow me to manoeuvre it into small, tight areas.

CONTROLLERS AND FLOATS

These days there is a good selection of controllers to choose from. Most of the major tackle firms now produce models. The most basic, the Bonnard, which is made in France, can be found in almost any tackle shop. I still use this type, for it casts well and is available in a wide variety of weights. Other manufacturers such as Gardener Tackle, Middy, Drennan, Terry Eustace and Kevin Nash produce a wide range as well. The idea of a controller is to add weight to your end rig, and they all sit up vertically in the water with a small amount visible, which is usually of a bright colour so they can be seen at range.

A great favourite of mine is the Gardener Suspender. This was conceived to overcome the problem of fish that were spooking away from the hookbait, frightened by the line lying on the surface. You will often encounter this when carp become wise to the dangers of surface baits. The idea behind the suspender was to keep the hook link off the surface in the immediate vicinity of the bait. How this is achieved is explained in Chapter 7.

I've seen a few hand-made floater floats of late. Some are good. Recently a friend furnished me with some excellent ones, made out of dowel with a biro tube through the centre. They lie flat on the surface, are painted a green camouflage colour and come in various sizes and weights.

With a normal controller set-up a general guide would be a hook link of about 4–6 feet; any longer and you might find it unmanageable to cast. Once cast out I don't like the bait too near to the controller at any time, so I try to keep it away if possible. Mending the line every now and then will do the trick, easy when the water is still but more difficult in a ripple. Another method that has received much publicity in recent years is the beachcaster rig, described in the previous chapter.

This will fool almost any carp, even where they have become most difficult to tempt. But, remember: familiarity breeds contempt. If everyone fishing your lake uses this method the effective life of the rig rapidly diminishes. One reason why this happens is simple. When there is a ripple on the water and you put out the beachcaster rig and some freebies, the freebies move with the ripple but the hookbait doesn't. Carp soon recognise this and avoid it like the plague.

PRESENTING THE SURFACE BAIT

There are many ways to present a surface bait. Each has certain advantages and disadvantages. The most straightforward way is freelining – just a hook attached. The bait, say breadcrust, can be attached easily: just pierce the crust with the hook point, then twist it round to bring it back so that the bend pulls down to sit on the crusty side of the bread. Try a piece about ¾ inch square with about ½ inch of flake showing. Don't worry if this looks big compared with a piece of Chum

Mixer. Look at the size of a carp's mouth! Even when dry, the bread will be heavy enough to flick out 5–10 yards, but you will find that a slight dunk in the water will help considerably. Be careful not to overdo this as the bread acts as a sponge and becomes flimsy, and you can easily cast it off. The line you cast out will float (or should) on the water surface.

This is floater fishing at its simplest and purest, and it does catch carp. For instance, you might find a carp swimming near some lily pads. Every now and then his mouth might investigate some item or other on the surface. If you don't frighten this fish, and cast ahead of it, there is every chance that he'll stop and investigate. If it does – and some won't – you stand a chance of hooking it. The first time this happens you will probably fluff it – either strike too early or hesitate too long as he investigates this unexpected goody.

Chris Ball showing that he is no slouch getting behind rods. Sharing a brace of twenties and a happy moment with the author. France's River Lot is the venue.

This is what I call 'sampling' by the carp. It happens so often that on some waters it represents a real problem when trying to hook fish. This is where rigs come into play.

For example, one or two soft-soaked mixers or floating boilies can be mounted directly on the hook (size 4–8). This rig will catch uneducated carp – no problem. But carp learn quickly on the surface, and soon they will mouth and reject this presentation time after time. By far the best method to use is a hair rig. There are many different arrangements, but start by tying the bait on to 2lb line. Just a slip knot round the bait will do but leave two long ends either side of it. Tie one end to the eye of the hook, the other to the bend. This makes the hook lie in the correct position for hooking. If you are quick, and able to watch the hookbait intently, fish can be hooked as they very carefully test to see if the food is attached to anything. If you watch even more carefully you might see our crafty carp check the bait by extending the top lip of its mouth over the bait. A quick strike and you are away – with luck!

Another variation is a mixer tied to the eye and another to the bend. This gives the same presentation as before but has the added advantage of being more visible in a bunch of free baits on the surface. Keeping your eyes on the hookbait at all times is something that I believe often makes the difference between success and failure. Remember this and I promise you'll catch more than your mates.

Don't forget margin fishing as well. Carp can be found close to the bank at all times of the day so keep your eyes about you and be *quiet*. There is considerable mileage in margin fishing straight under the rod top – when there is sufficient water, that is – at night. This method is rarely tried by carp anglers but you might be surprised at its success. Always pop a few baits along the margins where you are fishing at night and keep a careful eye on them. Make sure you have a rod set-up for this style of floater fishing so that you can react quickly when the opportunity arises. I have held the rod and just dapped the bait onto the surface next to where a carp has shown itself.

COMPETITIVE FEEDING

Most of the problems presented to the floater fisherman are to do with carp seeing or feeling the line. One way round this is to try and get the carp into a state of what I call 'competitive feeding'. By this I mean you get the fish into a frenzy, fighting over your surface food. This is something that is achievable with carp over a period of time. Sometimes it takes several hours, and it requires considerable patience on the angler's part. You must be observant and quiet and try not to give up. All right, I can hear what you are thinking: 'How can this happen on my water when I hardly ever see them take a floater anyway?' If I thought like that I would not have caught some of the very big carp I have. When building up the swim in this way you can catch carp on 20lb line, believe me! Cast only when the carp have been brought to this pitch of excitement and a mistake on the fish's part is highly likely.

This is what I am trying to achieve most of the time when I am out and about. If you can get your fish to this state you also stand a good chance of catching the largest fish that are present. This is because you can be selective. It works believe you me. However, the only way to see if this will work on your water is to stick at it. I've found this area of floater fishing something that's fascinating – it can teach you so much. First, because the fish show themselves quite readily and without caution, so you can often assess the size of what you are fishing for. Second, it's possible to find out which particular fish are more keen on surface food than others. This happens, and is especially noticeable when you are chasing a limited head of big carp – for instance at Wraysbury, the large gravel pit near Heathrow Airport.

Here my observations have revealed that the big common carp present are reluctant in the extreme to accept a surface bait. They rush around in the thick of the frenzy with the big old mirrors, but hardly ever have I seen a piece taken – this after years of looking at them. But once I did find a way to get them to take a floating bait – though by accident.

This happened when the carp were in and around some lily beds. These were in an area that was receiving a south-westerly wind and the dross, feather and scum was piling up around the pads. I found several good carp in this general area and after some time one or two of the big mirrors started to get interested. A further half an hour and they were really going for it. Then in came two common carp, well over 20lb in weight. They just wandered round the area watching the other carp having it! Some time later I noticed a pair of lips come up and engulf a piece of bait right in amongst the pads. I looked hard, and when he came up again for another piece I realised it was one of the commons. After this both these common carp had a field-day, but only taking bits that were deep in amongst the lily pads. I'd love to report that I managed to catch one. Alas I didn't.

CLOSE-SEASON RECONNAISSANCE

The close season is time to get yourself out and about and find what the carp are up to in your local lake. The close season offers a good time to investigate the habits of your particular carp. Really use your eyes. You might think the weather is too cold – early in the close season – but put free bait out anyway. However, if the weather is good the chances are that the carp will be somewhere near the surface.

What do you look for? To start with, any movement in the water. The all too obvious back breaking the surface as carp investigate or actually take some item off the surface is a great sight – though, inevitably, when you make your recce it might seem as though there's not a carp in the water. However, if you look more carefully you will notice much more subtle signs. For example, in a ripple a carp, even a stationary one, can show up as a different shade of colour, generally darker than the surrounding water. Polaroids and binoculars are so useful at this time of the year. Don't leave home without them!

Carp in your water might not be too keen on surface food to start with, but keep at it;

throwing out some cat biscuits and watching them drift out with nothing happening is only the start. Don't forget places like the margins, snags and lily pads. These are major areas to concentrate on. You might also find that the fish here react differently to the introduction of some floating food. They often do. In the season or close season, I find feeding the fish in this way as absorbing (almost!) as fishing for them.

PERSONALISED FLOATERS

Conditioning the carp to accept surface food in this way puts you in a good position once the season is under way. Try at this stage to make your floaters unique to you. By that I mean you should use some kind of flavour in them. Carp can respond better to a flavoured bait than to an untreated one. There is no point in baiting up for other people, although this is inevitable sometimes.

The reaction of carp to floaters can vary from the sublime to the ridiculous, with many variations in between. On some waters they can be almost suicidal in the close season especially. On others they show no interest at all in anything that floats, let alone food. However, I can tell you that there has not been a water where I've seriously fished for carp that has not responded to floaters. These cover many differing types of water, from gravel pits to old estate lakes, so it's not as hard as it might at first appear. Don't worry about stories concerning a particular lake, where people saying 'They don't take floaters.' In my experience they invariably do, or will! You have to work at it like any branch of carp fishing, so take heart in what I say: there's always a chance.

This conditioning of your mind is an important point. It is one reason why the successful anglers are successful. They think positively, and this shows in the way they assess any given situation. The fact that the carp in your water don't show any interest in floaters the first half-dozen times you try them, does not mean they do not take floaters.

BAITS

For years baits such as floating crust were the standard ones to use. I used to use the hard outside corner of a loaf; it lasted a lot longer on the hook. Also, you might be surprised to learn that carp anglers used to make their own bread loaves, which had a hard crust all the way round. The 'floater cake', made by baking in the oven a base mix for boilies but using double the amount of eggs, is another good bait. Here, as in boilie making, you can make the mix unique to you in smell and colour. Although not popular these days, it's a winner and an area I suggest you investigate. Good recipes are available in all the bait catalogues, so check them out.

Really you have no need to make any baits these days. The large range of preshaped pet foods and animal food pellets offer the floater angler a first-class bait. The sheer convenience that these packeted foods offer, with virtually no preparation, will appeal to nearly everybody. By far the most popular is Chum Mixers, which you can buy in different sizes of box or, as I do, in 10-kilogram bulk bags, which works out at 35p a pound. The cheapness of a bait such as Chum is bound to appeal to the younger angler. For those who like to play about with flavours, Chum will take a flavour and a colour as well. Munches are another good packeted bait, as are the multitude of cat-food biscuits. If you look carefully in some of the larger pet-food shops you'll find a bigger selection of potential baits, for there are all kinds of floating pellets you can try. One I've come across is Beta Puppy Food. It's dark in colour, high in oil content and has an unusual smell. It is also significantly different from other sorts of mixers in general use.

Preparing Mixers

Here are some ways to prepare Chum or any of the dog and cat food mixers:

1 Straight out of the packet. Carp love to crunch and grind the hard pieces of food. This makes them more addicted and can produce a feeding response that might frighten you.

2 Again straight out of the packet, but over-sprayed by an atomiser with your chosen flavour. I use ten quick sprays (10ml) out of the bottle into a bag containing 1lb dry weight of mixers. This gives the mixers the lightest of coatings, which in turn dissipates into the water immediately. Sometimes the overall effect can be devastating. Don't overdo this flavouring aspect and remember that all these kind of baits already have their own smell and attractor.

3 You can soak the mixers and introduce a flavour at the same time. Brian Skoyles's excellent method entails placing around 1½ lb of dry mixers in a clear airproof bag, then introducing 150ml of water plus a flavour and, if you like, a colour into the bag. Shake for 3–4 minutes so that every bait is covered. You'll notice that the inside of the bag will appear to go dry. Now leave for an hour and there you have your own unique mixer to use. This method produces a soft but durable bait, one you can impale directly onto the hook.

As you can see there is a vast choice open to you in the preparation of surface baits. These days as floater fishing becomes more popular, I suggest you start flavouring your baits. This can have a positive effect and make the all-important difference when you are out on the bank. Look at sweeteners as well; I believe they are an important additive (just as in bottom baits). So all those flavours you have in the cupboard and have never used can find their way into flavoured surface baits. The list is endless and should provide considerable scope in which to work – it's as much fun as making bottom baits. Good luck.

Well, there you have the theory of it all. In practice there is nothing quite like the excitement floater fishing can give. The sheer fact that you see the carp take your baited hook, often in a spectacular way, makes it heart-stopping and addictive. But beware. It might make you go prematurely grey on top and give you high blood pressure. What the heck! Without doubt it's *the way* to catch a carp. Go on, give it a try. You'll be far from disappointed.

9 WINTER FISHING

It really wasn't so many years ago that an angler who set his stall out for catching carp in winter was looked upon as some sort of loony. There used to be a myth that carp were virtually impossible to catch during the colder months, because they hibernated. The only exception to this rule, or so it was thought, were hot-water outlets like those of the power stations on the River Nene at Peterborough and the River Thames at Canbury Gardens. Fortunately, this old wives' tale has now been completely dispelled and, provided that the angler is sensible and goes about his winter campaign in an orderly fashion, there is no reason for him not to be successful.

Although the lake looks bleak and somehow inhospitable with a little thought the carp can still be regularly caught.

As the attitude towards carp fishing changed it was the easier, more heavily stocked waters that received most of the attention, but even that situation has almost vanished. Some of the hardest waters in the land are now intensively fished right through the winter and, to endorse the fact that the carp are catchable in such conditions, that very successful big-carp angler, Ritchie McDonald, landed a fabulous brace of winter forties from the ultra-hard Yateley complex.

These two fish were caught absolutely by design. The waters concerned are very lightly stocked and are extremely difficult, even during the summer. But Ritchie's determination and single-minded thinking targeted those two particular fish and when he had caught the first one – a mirror from the Lily Pad Lake – he immediately changed to fishing the adjacent Car Park Lake and banked the forty-pound leather. Quite a feat of angling!

WATER TEMPERATURE

It is generally recognised that winter carp fishing starts in earnest at the beginning of November and lasts right through to the end of the season.

Personally, however, I have always found temperatures during November very favourable and it is only at the start of December and in some cases during the run-up to Christmas that the temperatures really start to plummet. This is when I start to plan my winter campaign. It is during this noticeable drop in water temperature that the carp begin to show the first signs of a different feeding pattern. Although most years are different, so undependable is the English climate, there always seems to be a period, probably lasting about a week some time before Christmas, when the water temperature sees a drastic drop. This can be as much as 10°F (5°C) and normally puts the carp off of the feed altogether.

Fortunately, this is fairly short-lived and once the temperature begins to level out at the new, lower, level carp will resume some sort of regular feeding pattern. But it will be noticed that this pattern is completely different from any that they adopt during the warmer summer months. Their whole metabolism slows down, as does the pace of the whole lake's environment. It is rare to find the carp feeding more than once or twice in every twenty-four hours. The duration of these quite regular feeding periods is often less than an hour.

Naturally, much of this will depend on the stocking of the water. There are waters which can be classed as overstocked, where the carp's appetite never seems to be satisfied. On these venues winter feeding will be very similar to summer – perhaps more intense for an hour or two each day, while slighter slower in between times. On more balanced lakes where the stocking level is nicely married with the lake's environment these short feeding periods can become very predictable. On one or two waters of this kind that I fish it is almost possible to set your clock by these regular feeding periods. On rich, very lightly stocked venues feeding times are very spasmodic and extremely unpredictable, which makes this the most challenging winter fishing for the carp angler.

Having spent many winters painstakingly recording water and air temperatures and the like I have been unable to find what might possibly be classed as the ideal winter feeding temperature. For the greater part of the winter most of my local lakes will fluctuate between 40 and 50°F (4–10°C) and carp have been caught consistently all through this band. It is once it gets below 40° that fishing can get really difficult. Whether there is a temperature at which the carp will stop feeding altogether I really do not know. In the days when I was recording temperature and capture details the lowest reading that I caught carp at was 37°F (3°C).

I do wonder, however, if there are many lakes that drop below this anyway, as most waters will freeze over before the water temperature has had a chance to drop below this mark. It can only ever happen on large expanses of water in strong arctic windy conditions where the wind chill factor is subzero but at the same time the surface water movement stops the lake from icing over. That is a pretty alien environment and not one in which I am personally all that keen to sit out just for the sake of documenting the low-temperature feeding habits of my beloved carp. In fact, I have stopped taking water and air temperatures altogether these days. It's not that I didn't enjoy doing it or that I can no longer be bothered. The fact of the matter is that one day I sat down and coldly looked at exactly what I had learnt during all the years of scratching at my notebook. I actually think that I didn't learn anything at all. In fact it could have almost been detrimental to my fishing if I had slavishly followed catch rates in relation to temperature.

Let me describe a possible scenario. I have been merrily catching carp on a consistent basis while the water temperature registered 39°F (4°C) but when the temperature dropped to 37°F (3°C) I had no action. You can imagine how much confidence I would have if I arrived at the lake to find a water temperature of 37°F. Not a lot, but that would be quite crazy. Fish can undoubtedly be caught at 37°; in fact one or two of the largest fish in many of my winter carping campaigns have been taken at that temperature. I now find it far better not to know the temperature at all and just to go out full of confidence willing those indicators to move, even on the coldest of days. I certainly haven't been tempted to resurrect the thermometer from the bottom of the garden shed.

The most noticeable change between summer and winter carping is the environment itself. Gone are those long days of bright green foliage, the lake bursting with life and the sun streaming down on our backs. Most of the water plants have died back and hardly a leaf is left on the trees. The winter can transform a pleasant warm comfortable environment into something that seems bleak, intimidating and extremely inhospitable. But, as with most things in life, beauty is undoubtedly in the eye of the beholder. The winter holds its own attractions: frost-covered banks, cobwebs projected as fine white linen and icicles hanging daintily below old wooden fences have their own beauty. A carp landed against such a backdrop will always remain very special to me.

The carp's colours are almost enhanced by the bleak bankside. Chestnut- and orange-flanked

mirror carp seem almost to glow in the drab conditions. The countryside may not be at its best but carp undoubtedly are.

CREATURE COMFORTS

The well-being and comfort of the winter angler are just as important as his approach to the fishing. There is no excuse these days for being cold and uncomfortable on the bank. Purpose-made clothing is there to protect us from the elements. Rather than be cluttered up with multiple layers of shirts, jumpers and jeans, I prefer to wear a thermal undersuit in combination with a waterproof oversuit. These are very light and don't restrict movement. The best thermal undersuits I have come across are the Swiss-made Astro Thermo Wear, closely followed by Helly Hansen

Top-quality Astro Thermal Wear made in Switzerland ensures that you will be warm even on the coldest of days.

and Damart. Although these are rather expensive they are worth the investment and will keep any winter chill at bay. Waterproof oversuits will stop the icy winds from getting through and chilling the bones. There are several good makes around and you get what you pay for. The Kevin Nash and Mainstream one-piece models are brilliant. With these two garments you will need very little extra clothing – maybe just a jogging suit in between the two layers for looks rather than comfort.

Footwear has also come on in leaps and bounds and moon-type boots have now become the standard kit for winter carping. However, you should be aware that there are so many rather rubbishy models on the market trying to cash in on the backs of the one or two good designs. Head and shoulders above the rest are Skee-Tex and Boom 80s. These are of excellent design. I find that extra sets of liners are essential, as they do get damp through perspiration, especially if there is a lot of bank walking to do. The spare liners can be dried out in between sessions or taken with you if you are spending several days on the bank.

Do not suffer soggy woollen gloves; state-of-the-art Neoprene gloves are totally waterproof and many have thermal linings.

They are ideal for fishing on cold days. My own preference is for the Milo Match gloves, which have a fold-back forefinger and thumb so you can tie up rigs without taking the gloves off.

A good bobble hat, balaclava or cap will complete your winter clothing and allow you to get on with the task in hand without worrying about keeping warm.

On most waters there are bound to the fairly long periods of inactivity so it's always a good idea to have a brew-up on the bank to provide a bit of inner warmth and keep the enthusiasm going. Even for short periods it's worth taking a small cooking stove. Gas canister burners are of little use in cold conditions as the pressure drops to almost zero, leading to a weak flame which seems to take forever to boil just a kettle of water. I can really recommend the Colman Peak Multi-fuel Stoves. These will run on lead-free petrol

Moon boots are now standard footwear for the winter carp angler. The Skee-Tex make are amongst the best.

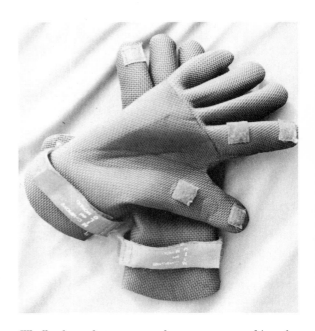

Woolly gloves that get wet and soggy are now a thing of the past. These Neoprene design are much more user friendly and even if they do get wet there will be no heat loss.

and are totally unaffected by freezing conditions. They have an amazingly high output of heat (about 8,500 BThU), which will have your kettle of water boiling in minutes. One word of warning, though. Please don't cook inside the bivvy with the door closed. Toxic fumes given off are extremely dangerous and can be fatal. Either cook outside or, at worst, at the entrance of the bivvy with the door open, and never ever run the stove with the door down just to warm up the inside of the bivvy.

Another item of equipment that you may well need in extreme conditions during winter sessions is a small tube or bottle of glycerine. A small smear of this applied round the rod rings, bail-arm roller and monkey-climb or swinger indicators will stop them freezing together as the air temperature drops below zero.

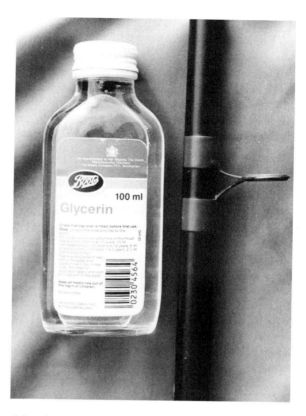

Often the air temperature will be sub-zero and ice can form in the rod rings, but a small smear of glycerine around each one will ensure the line is kept free running.

With low temperatures in the winter, standard camping gas loses most of its pressure, this is when the Coleman Peak Multifuel Stoves come into their own.

The rest of the tackle will remain much the same as you use for the summer. On normally weedy summer waters line strength and hook size may well be reduced as the weed dies back. Your bite indication systems should be set up so as to register the tiniest line movement, for, although the carp will feed quite confidently in winter, their movements slow down dramatically. They become very lethargic, and spend more time inspecting the bait, so on many waters bite indication is more slighter than during the summer. Often just a tiny nod of the rod tip will produce a well-hooked carp, if struck at the correct time. Of course, there are occasions when the fish scream off as they do in the summer, but this is an exception rather than the rule so your rod-end set-up should be adapted accordingly.

THE MENTAL BRIDGE

Having equipped yourself with good clothing and adequate food and drink and sorted out your bivvy to combat the environment, you now have only to cross that mental bridge in order to start putting a few carp on the bank. If you start to get despondent and the task begins to look impossible, pack up and go home; don't just sit it out regardless. Back in the warmth of your living room you can reassess the situation, charge up your batteries and go for it again with new vigour. I have seen so many anglers fall at the first hurdle just because their confidence has been broken during the first couple of fishless sessions. Believe in what you are doing. I can assure you that carp *can* be caught even during arctic conditions.

LOCATION

The first challenge is location. Because the carp's metabolism slows down they show very little in comparison with the summer months. That's why I always find it a good idea during the winter months to fish waters that you know intimately. It is not really the time of year to start tackling a new water unless you are part of the 'in' carp grapevine. It has often been said that once winter sets in the carp move to the deepest part of the lake and stay put. My own experience shows that this is often far from the truth. On most of the lakes I fish summer hot spots are also normally winter hot spots and it's only in very shallow water on extremely cold days that I would not expect to find the fish.

Unless I am fishing the margins I favour areas where the swim changes considerably in depth over a relatively small distance. On gravel pits this is usually a steep drop-off over the edge of a bar or a large plateau rising towards the surface from a deeper surrounding area. In this sort of place the carp have to move only a short distance to find the most comfortable water temperature. I believe that the carp rise and fall within the layers as the temperature changes, even by as little as half a degree or so. Studying carp in gin-clear water throughout the winter months has convinced me of this.

By far the most productive areas throughout the winter are under fallen trees and overhanging bushes. Carp at any time of the year love a canopy over their heads and have a great fondness for any woodwork protruding into the water. Once they are in such an area and their movements have slowed down it is often possible to observe the fish at close quarters for many weeks at a time.

During this period it is unusual to see the carp move more than a few yards out of position every day. They will forage round for a few hours, seemingly just topping up their food supplies, before adopting an almost motionless state once more. The one thing that has been very evident throughout my winter carping observations is that they do not move with wind conditions as they would during the summer months. A southerly wind pounding into the northern end of the lake for several days does not mean that the carp will be found frequenting that area, as they probably would during the summer months.

Other areas where carp can be found in winter are dying lily pad beds as well as reeds. The water here need not be that deep, in fact, one venue springs to mind where reeds spread out into the water some thirty or forty yards from the bank and for most of the winter the carp can be found foraging around in them in only 4 feet of water Twenty-five yards away there is 12 feet of water, so this certainly dispels the deep-water myth.

If we are lucky enough to get two or three days of consistent sunshine with no frosts at night, shallow water may well warm up enough for the carp to venture into it and it's even possible to catch them on the surface during this period. In fact on some lakes where the carp can be easily observed it seems that the best chance of catching them *is* on the surface. Where they are holed up under bushes and trees a floater offered on the surface a few feet above their heads will often rouse the carp's interest. There are waters where they have even been caught in holes on iced-up lakes. I remember my mate, Chris Ball, a few years ago wandering round one of our local lakes trying to stalk carp from some semi-frozen swims. He happened on a carp lying in midwater close to the bank and, although it refused a bottom bait, he eventually tempted it with a floater, saving a blank day.

Once my winter campaign starts I like to choose two or three waters that are close to home and if at all possible ones that are clear enough to observe the fish. Fortunately, as all the inhabitants of the lake have slowed down, less feeding takes place and the water tends to get clearer. This is not possible for every angler and sometimes compromises have to be made but it is certainly worth putting yourself out to try to select waters accordingly. This alone will help you be far more successful during the winter rather than jumping willy-nilly from one water to another as you hear of a good carp capture.

Three such waters are ideal to my way of thinking, and if they can all be visited within the same day so much the better. The mood of the fish will be constantly changing and rather than sitting on just one water throughout the winter I like the opportunity of ringing the changes. As one lake fades another will often come to life.

I like to bait up as regularly as my job allows even if it means two or three trips out after dark in the evenings each week to drop a few baits in. I am of the firm belief that consistent baiting throughout the winter is the greatest key to success. The baiting will be completely different from that of the summer: the little-and-often rule is paramount at this time of the year. If you put too many baits in at one time there is a good chance that most of them will be eaten and satisfy the carp's hunger for many days, so it is far better to feed just enough for their daily requirements. This not only keeps up their interest up but also sustains a consistent feeding pattern. Baits for winter can be as varied as in the summer. Boilies are the most consistent of all, if only because they are the most used.

The constant question is just how many boilies to introduce. There is no easy answer to this. All I can say is that if you can't see the fish feeding you will get a feeling when it is right. But as a helpful guideline – though a flexible one – I like

to work on the formula of about ten boilies per carp per day. Naturally, in clear waters where you can see the fish this can be finely adjusted to suit just how many carp there are in the swim and the length of time they are feeding. But out of the angler's eye a fair bit of guesstimate will come into play. Assessing how many carp are in a given area at a given time is always a nightmare, and some assumptions have to be made. Realistically speaking we have to assume, depending on the stocking of the water, that there are, say, between five and ten fish in your swim at a time so therefore you should be introducing between fifty and a hundred baits per day. Baiting up daily is obviously the ideal but it rarely can be achieved in reality. I am happy if I can visit the water every other day, but that would almost be the minimum requirement.

CONFOUNDING THE WILDFOWL

Winter fishing brings other problems – wildfowl for one. Winter-visiting tufted ducks and resident coot can be a nightmare as they easily capitalise on your regular baiting and they just love boilies! Don't think you are safe when you are baiting up in fourteen feet of water. This presents no problem at all for a tufted duck, and I am always amazed at their ability to home in on a baited area. This can be very frustrating and where the problem is exasperating night baiting is often the only answer.

If that isn't bad enough flocks of seagulls move in during the winter months for easy pickings around carp lakes.

At times it seems just about impossible to get a free offering into the water at any sort of range. Their aerobatics are quite remarkable; a boilie is rarely missed. When you encounter this situation it is far better to bait up with the aid of a rod and reel.

Winter Baiting Rig
This is my winter baiting rig. It is nicknamed by my mate, Pete Springate, the 'headache rig'. It is set up on your spare rod with a lead of suitable

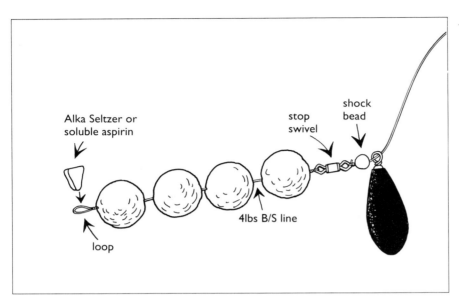

My winter baiting rig, the 'headache' rig.

Alka Seltzer or soluble aspirin

stop swivel

shock bead

loop

4lbs B/S line

size to achieve the given distance. This is stopped by a swivel with a shock bead in between. To the free eye of the swivel attach about a 4- or 5-inch length of 3 or 4lb BS line. At the end of that line tie in a loop with about a ½-inch diameter hole. Thread on four or five boilies using a large-diameter baiting needle (the baits must slide easily over the end loop and the larger the hole through the boilies the better. Into the loop push a broken piece of Alka Seltzer or soluble aspirin tablet. The boilies are then pushed down against the tablet to hold them in place. The rig is cast out into the swim and left for between 45 and 60 seconds for the small pieces of tablet to dissolve. Then a light strike will deposit the free offerings accurately in the swim and out of the way of the ever-hungry seagulls.

On the days when I actually fish I cut baiting back to the bare minimum, swinging any opportunity of the carp picking up my bait firmly in my favour. On some waters I will fish hookbait only, whilst on others I will use a stringer set-up.

Stringer Set-Up
This is my stringer set-up. It consists of a long loop of PVA (polyvinyl acetate). This is a water-soluble material and is available in many different forms. My own preference is for the finely braided variety, which dissolves in about three minutes or so even in very cold water. The end of the loop is closed off with a double overhand knot, leaving the tails about ½-inch long to act as a backstop for the boilies to rest against. With a long stringer needle slide the desired amount of boilies down onto the loop as shown. It is then a simple matter of passing the open end of the loop onto the bend of the hook. For security the freebie boilie nearest the hook can be pushed up tight to close the loop off, minimising any chance of the free offerings flying off the rig during casting.

On wet and rainy days you have to act quite quickly with this method because the PVA dissolves as soon as it gets damp. I like to tie up several loops of PVA in the comfort of my own home, and store them in sealed polythene bags ready to use. The boilies are put on the stringer needle before I even take any of the PVA loops out of the bag. Likewise the rig is at the ready, with the hook and bait dry.

If you gear yourself up in this way the whole procedure will take a matter of seconds. Once

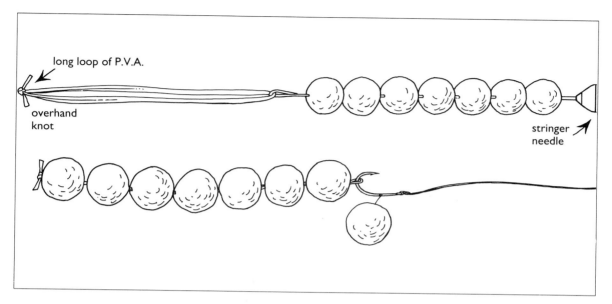

Stringer set-up.

you have cast out you will have 30 seconds or so to draw your bait into position. This usually applies only to gravel pits, where you are fishing over bars, plateaux, and the like, and 'feeling' for a feature. Once the PVA has dissolved you can be assured that you have a small group of free offerings lying in close proximity to your hook-bait. My own preference is to use boilies coloured to blend in with the bottom during the winter. This has absolutely nothing to do with the carp. It's an attempt to hide the boilies from the ever-preying coots and tufted ducks. It's bad

This Stringer has been made up on one of the new braided PVA materials, ensuring that even in low water temperatures it melts quickly.

enough that they home in on the baits anyway. Why make their job any easier by using brightly coloured baits that they seem to be able to see from a mile away?

Bait Flavours

Over the years I have changed my mind several times about the best flavours to use during the winter. I used to think that natural flavours were by far the best but in recent seasons I have had great success with ethyl alcohol flavours, my favourites being strawberry jam, Caribbean fruit and plum. I use these in combination with a clear sweetener and a sweet enhancer. Another change of mind: I always used to increase the flavour level during the winter but now throughout the year I stick to exactly the same level as recommended for summer. This also goes for dipping the bait in flavour soaks. I still think this is a good idea but now I greatly reduce the concentration level instead of using it neat as I used to. You have to have flexibility of mind; this is not an exact science and there are very few hard and fast rules.

If you are tempted to use oil-based baits during the winter make sure that they have an inbuilt emulsifier, or if they haven't, add one in order break down the oils in the cold water. A lot of anglers are very successful with this type of bait in the colder months but until I experience otherwise I will carry on using the ethyl alcohols for the time being.

Particles in Winter

It has always been said that particle baits are only of any use during the summer and autumn and it is certainly a fact that their power to attract does wane as the temperature drops. But there are a couple of exceptions to this rule.

Sweetcorn and Tiger Nuts

Sweetcorn is an amazing bait and even on waters where it has been used for many years it still produces the goods. On waters that have been boilie bashed all summer, sweetcorn will often outfish boilies during the winter. The same minimum-amount rule applies: no more than about 4oz per

fish per day as an inducer when not fishing and when you are fishing, two or three grains on a short hair backed up with about another dozen or so grains on a PVA stringer. You will need to dry the corn out to use it with the stringer rig because straight from the tin it will dissolve the PVA before you have a chance to cast out. It is a simple matter of straining off the water with a fine sieve and then laying out the grains of corn on absorbent kitchen paper overnight.

Tiger nuts go on and on – another magic bait and just as effective in winter as in summer on many waters. Use similar amounts to the sweetcorn and again dry out the freebie nuts for stringer use. So it's well worth bearing in mind that there are a couple of successful particles that can be used during the winter.

Baits for Winter Stalking

For stalking any of the aforementioned baits will work but a couple that are often overlooked and are very successful as well as being flexible in their use are luncheon meat and bread. Luncheon meat can be cut into all manner of shapes and sizes: square cubes can be fished on a bottom set-up in place of your boilies; thin strips can be cut so that they flutter down provocatively through the water in front of the carp's nose on a freeline set-up; smaller oblong shapes can be fished under the float and be presented to margin feeders. Even in the high-tech days of the super-boilie there is still a place for luncheon meat.

Bread is another bait that seems to be all but forgotten these days. In fact I doubt if a lot of the modern carpers have come into the sport in recent seasons have ever used this fantastic bait. For stalking during the winter months I would not be without a loaf of good old Mother's Pride. Pieces of flake can be pinched off from the centre and allowed to fall through the water at a rate and in a manner that any carp find hard to resist. If the flake is just pinched on very lightly with all the fluffy bits left hanging, tiny particles will break off and drift down at different rates, which all enhances the bait's powers of attraction. Pieces of crust torn off the corners can be

I have usually got a couple of tins of luncheon meat tucked away in the bottom of my bag – always an instant carp bait.

One of the most under-rated baits around, the breadflake can be adapted to so many situations. This is an ideal stalking bait, especially where the fish can be seen.

suspended like a pop-up boilie. So whether you are freelining, float fishing or bottom fishing on the lead, it's worth remembering to give a good old loaf of bread a try.

Maggots

Now to my favourite bait for winter and one that is going to surprise a lot of people – maggots. I can almost hear the grunts of disbelief since it's true to say that on most waters during the summer it is almost impossible to be selective when fishing with maggots. The swim will normally be full of hordes of greedy roach, rudd and perch devouring every maggot before it hits the bottom. In cold-water conditions it is a different ball game altogether. The smaller inhabitants of the lake have also slowed down, apparently to a greater degree than the carp. Of course you are still going to catch the odd smaller nuisance fish but where carp can be seen and fished for individually the humble maggot will almost certainly outfish any other bait.

How on earth do you fish a maggot on a size 4 hook? The truth of the matter is that you don't fish one at all; you fish multiples, and they can easily be mounted on the hook itself or a couple of other special set-ups described below.

Maggot Rigs

This is my free-swimming maggot rig, and it is about the most basic of all. It is important to use a light fine-wire hook with this set-up and my favourite is a Gamakatsu 6318 in size 10, 8 or 6. This is for relatively open swims where heavy pressure to extract the carp should not be necessary. The hook is tied to a soft multiflex-type hook link of about 7lb. This will give the rig a high degree of movability. Depending on the size from half a dozen to ten maggots are lightly nicked through the skin and pushed round to cover the bend and shank of the hook. Just on the back of the bend I insert a piece of white buoyant foam. This is cut into a rough maggot shape so as not to be too conspicuous. The best foam I have found for this is the type they sell for lining fly boxes. It is quite dense and has a waxy, water-repellent finish. The rig is balanced out so that the hook only just sinks. This is done by adding or subtracting maggots to give more or less weight to the set-up. Larger hooks may well require two white foam maggots to get the correct balance.

Once you have achieved almost a neutral density the hook will literally be free-swimming, neither resting on the bottom nor suspended perpendicular off of the lead. The light, semi-buoyant multiflex hook links are a great aid with this type of set-up. I like to have a hook link of at least 9 inches to give the bait plenty of opportunity to move around. When fishing on the lead this is simple enough: the hook link can be attached to the main line via a swivel at the desired distance. A float-fishing set-up should be arranged similarly, with tungsten putty moulded around the swivel to give the float the right cocking weight.

It is quite amazing how carp respond to a live moving bait, even when they seem to be in a semi-dormant state. If you come across a group of carp lying close to the bank, approach very quietly and gently catapult out small pouchloads of maggots. Try and let the maggots sink about a foot or eighteen inches in front of the carp's nose. Keep a steady stream going into the swim but make sure each pouchload contains only from six to ten maggots. With any luck the action of the maggots falling through the water will stir the carp into action and they will usually investigate immediately. Keep introducing the maggots until the carp start to root out every freebie, then gently drop your free-swimming maggot rig in place.

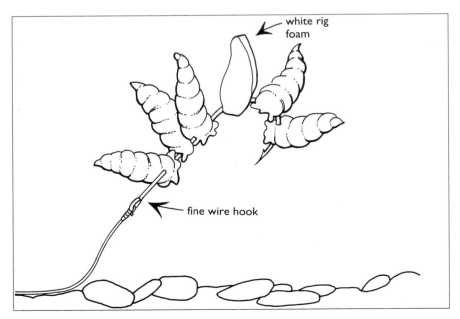

Free-swimming maggot rig.

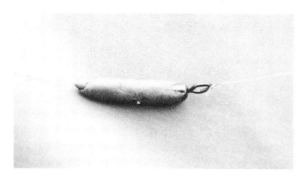

Rather than use splitshots I much prefer Tungsten Putty moulded around the swivel.

Not on top of the carp, obviously, but a few feet away. Keep the steady stream of maggots going in, concentrating them round your hookbait, and with any luck it shouldn't be too long before the carp fall foul of this almost irresistible rig.

I have found that it is very important when maggot fishing not to introduce so many that they start lying around on the bottom. Maggots are less active in cold water and just lying there as they often do they seem to be of very little attraction at all to the carp. It's the free-falling ones that seem to get them going.

Unfortunately, the more heavily snagged swims offer the best opportunity for fishing with maggots and therefore you will need to use larger and heavier-gauged hooks. Heavy-wire hooks will just burst the maggots open as you try to push them over the thick wire, making them almost useless with regard to presentation. There are a couple of rigs that fish well with a heavy hook set-up.

Quick Maggot Rig

The illustration shows my quick maggot rig. I use about a size 18 or 20 hook to nylon for this set-up. This is whipped to the shank of a size 6 or 4 heavy-gauged hook. A tail with the hook on of about 1–1½ inches length is left hanging loose. This forms a hair on which to mount the maggots. The strength of the hook to nylon length is usually between 1 and 2lb BS, which is ideal for this set-up. I bend the point of the hook in towards the spade end, which stops it pricking in the carp's mouth when the bait is sucked in. The maggots are easily put on the hook and passed round onto the hair as shown. Again, one or two pieces of white foam can be added to get a free-swimming rig. The nice thing about this set-up is

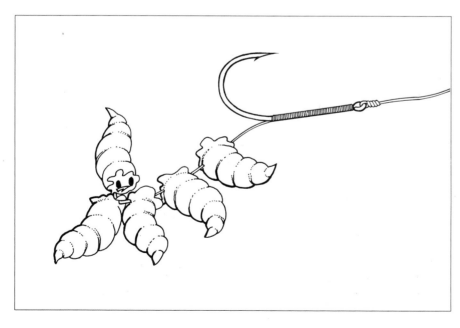

Quick maggot rig.

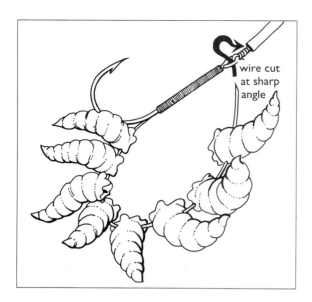

Maggots mounted on fuse wire.

the speed with which the maggots can be put. This is obviously useful when the odd small nuisance fish in the swim keep crushing the maggots.

Fuse-Wire Rig

This is the other rig that I use with heavy-gauged hooks, especially in real hit-and-hold situations where a heavy-gauged size 4 is usually called for. A length of 5-amp fuse wire is whipped onto the back of the shank of the hook. The free end should be cut off so that it is about 2 inches long. When it is cut it should be cut at an acute angle so as to give a pointed end. The maggots can now be mounted on the fuse wire as illustrated. On the hook link just above the eye is a small piece of 1 mm rig tube. This need only be about ¼ inch long and acts as a retainer into which the end of the fuse wire is pushed. You should now have formed a loop of maggots that stands off the back of the hook. You will probably find that it takes at least three foam maggots to give you a free-swimming rig, which always seems to outfish maggots lying on the bottom.

What normally happens is that when the carp enters the immediate area of the bait the vortexes caused by its pectoral fins which it uses for

manoeuvring itself around, cause the maggots to waft up off of the bottom. If your hookbait is set up in free-swimming mode it will do exactly the same. The carp do not seem to be bothered by the almost natural-looking large bunches fished in this method. In fact they almost seem to take them in preference to the single freebies floating around in the swim.

Good as maggots are, and they are certainly a firm favourite of mine, they can really only be used practically in margin swims where the carp can be seen. But for me that's what winter carping is all about, and it makes the whole thing so much more interesting in a very bleak environment.

THE FIGHT OF WINTER CARP

It has often been said that carp don't fight as well during the winter. Strange that I haven't noticed it myself! I believe they fight just as hard. The only difference, if any, is that they don't seem to take off on such long runs, but plough around under the rod tip for an incredible amount of time. You often wonder if they will ever give up. When you have landed your winter carp I am sure you will be quite amazed at their truly enhanced winter colours. They are magnificent beasts out of their watery environment.

Please be careful when handling them. I know this should go without saying and I will be covering the subject further in the next chapter, but I can't leave winter carp fishing without stressing that cold carp should only ever be handled with equally cold hands. I know it will be unpleasant but it is fairly short-lived. Damp your hands with cold water and touch the fish only for the minimum amount of time. Never ever lay a carp down on frozen grass – the frost will quickly be transferred to it. Having spent so much effort in capturing your valuable winter prize, please take care of it.

I am sure you will find – as many already have done – that the time spent on the bank in wintry conditions is well worth the effort and that a carp landed in such circumstances is a very special fish indeed.

10 PLAYING, HANDLING AND CONSERVATION

Most of this book deals with the catching of the fish, successful rigs, baits and the latest tackle. Unfortunately the well-being of the carp is often overlooked, when in reality it should actually be top of our list of priorities. I know it's a boring subject and not very exciting, and possibly in real terms it doesn't put any more fish on the bank. But next time you are thumbing through your gallery of trophy shots and remembering the fight that wonderful looking carp gave you, spare a thought for the next angler who may well catch the same fish. We are now so successful and there are now so many of us at the sport that multiple catches of individual fish are the norm and not just an odd occurrence. Each time the carp is hooked, landed and returned it is in a vulnerable position. Its well-being is completely in the hands of the capturer and those around him. We are very fortunate in that we now have some good items of carp-care kit, which, to my mind every angler should carry. So let's have a look at what happens once a fish picks up your bait and you hook it successfully.

PLAYING

I guess that seventy-five per cent of fish hooked will suffer very little in the way of damage on the way to the landing net, but even this isn't good enough. How can damage occur while we are actually playing fish? The mouth area is the prime area for damage. An angler with over-heavy tackle dragging a poor helpless carp back to the net in double-quick time can inflict unnecessary damage to the carp's mouth. Immense pressure can be exerted on the hookhold and a small carp beaten too quickly into submission on over-heavy heave-and-hold tactics will undoubtedly suffer some sort of damage. This is why even when stalking I will not use lines any heavier than 15lb BS. If I consider that the swim calls for heavier gear I really should not be fishing it. With balanced tackle even a hard-fighting carp – assuming it is properly hooked – can be landed with no damage.

We all talk about hit-and-hold when it comes to stalking. In realistic terms that is fine with fish up to about 20lb or in some cases possibly even 30lb, but a powerful fish over that size that has just been hooked under the rod tip is virtually impossible to stop in its tracks. It has to be played out and the swim should be such that this is possible. So if the swim calls for anything heavier than 15lb BS I just don't fish it.

Hooks

The hook itself – depending on the pattern, size and where it has entered the fish's mouth – can inflict some damage even without excessive pressure on the part of the angler. Hook patterns are a controversial subject as I am sure you are all aware, and like most such subjects it is often skirted around. But I'm sure we are all caring anglers deep down and must look at things in realistic terms and not skate over them with sweeping statements.

It well known that one or two patterns of hooks definitely inflict unnecessary damage in the carp's mouth. These are the long-shanked streamer or lure-type hooks that have been bent at an angle halfway along the shank so that the point of the hook faces the eye directly. Here terminology comes into play. These patterns have been called bent hooks, when clearly all hooks are bent. Personally I am totally against bans, hoping that the anglers' own sensibilities will tell them what is right and what is wrong. I would hate the term 'bent hook' to be used in any ban, since it is wide open to misinterpretation. There are very successful and caring anglers who modify all sorts of patterns of hooks. Many of these are short-shanked and even when they are tweaked and the shape slightly altered they are not detrimental to the carp.

It is basically the long-shanked models that, when bent, have the ability to keep winding themselves in under pressure, causing double and treble hooking. In fact I have witnessed the sorry sight of about a size 4 lure hook bent in the way described deeply embedded in a carp's mouth so that only the eye and a tiny piece of the shank were visible. Please think about the carp's welfare. This sort of pattern must be avoided at all costs. With luck there will then be no need for bans.

Large barbs on hooks can also tear the mouth more than is necessary under heavy playing pressure. Thankfully micro and whisper barbs are in vogue at the moment – long may it last!

Tail and Fins

There are other ways of inflicting damage during the fight. The tail and fins of the carp often come into contact with the main line as the carp twists and rolls on the line during the course of the fight. The spiny dorsal fin is undoubtedly the most susceptible. On many gravel pits we have to use shock leaders to combat sharp bars, snails and mussels when fishing over a very uneven bottom. Some of the new ultra-thin high-abrasion-resistant shock leaders seem to account for more split fins than standard monofilaments. I wonder if it would not be better to cover at least the first three feet or so of the shock leader with some sort of protective tubing. This would increase its diameter and avoid the effect a cheese wire cutting through the vulnerable skin between the rays of the dorsal fin.

Fail-Safe Rigs

The only other aspect of playing the fish that I suppose we should concern ourselves with is the question of what happens if the carp wins. If the hook pulls as a result of straightening or breaking or simply because of a poor hookhold, then we need not worry, I am sure. There will be no twinge of anxiety, though there will be disappointment for sure. Losing a fish is hard, no matter how experienced the angler may be. But if the line actually breaks that is another matter.

All the rigs described in this book I consider to be safe rigs. In the case of a break all of them will automatically jettison most of the terminal tackle that could get caught up in snags, thus tethering a fish and leading to even more damage. Permanently fixed leads, controllers and the like are bound to get caught up in some underwater snags. It's bad enough that the carp has broken the line and is now roaming around with a hook still in its mouth, but if the end tackle subsequently becomes tethered the carp has less chance of getting rid of the hook.

Methods of Playing

When fishing the margins behind static rods, in other words in any situation other than stalking, I always set the clutch reasonably loose. The reason for this is twofold: the speed at which a hooked carp can depart from beneath your rod tip is at times quite unbelievable; it is virtually impossible to keep up with by backwinding. Once the carp is under way at speed I start to tighten down the clutch gradually, at the same laying the rod over at the appropriate angle to keep the fish clear of danger zones.

Once I start to get the fish under control I screw the clutch down until it only can just take line and switch over to playing the fish by backwinding. Line is gained by pumping the fish gently back towards the bank. Not screwing the clutch down completely tight gives me a safety margin if the carp bolts unexpectedly at the last minute.

The second reason for initially playing the fish on quite a loose clutch is that I am of the firm belief that a good deep hookhold comes only after a period of constant pressure. The only exception to this is when you are stalking and the power of the strike drives the hook fifty per cent of the way home. But when a screaming take occurs I am positive the carp is only lightly pricked. If you try to clamp down and really hang on tight there is a good chance of the hook 'gaping' – the hook springs open momentarily losing the valuable initial hookhold. If you let the carp have its head, as it were, and then gradually tighten down, I believe the hook will be pulled progressively deeper and deeper into the skin. This obviously means there is less chance of the hook pulling.

At medium range I will wind down to a fast take and sweep the rod steadily over my shoulder. I always try to think of this as pulling the hook in about as far as the barb. This ensures that it will not immediately fall out if the carp runs towards me or starts kiting left or right. Again the clutch is set so that line can only just be taken, so that should I get it wrong catastrophe is avoided. For the rest of the fight the carp is played by the backwinding method. Only after the fight has been under way for a couple of minutes am I convinced that the hook has well and truly gone home.

At long range – over 100 yards – a strike is almost superfluous. I have conducted quite a few tests and, even on dry land with a mate hanging on to the hook at a hundred yards and me striking for all I'm worth at the other, it is very difficult to pull the tackle out of his hand, let alone drive the hook home. I imagine that in water this problem can only be magnified, so I often smile quietly to myself when I see anglers giving it the real big strike at about 120 yards.

My set-up is as follows: the clutch is all but screwed down and once the take starts I re-engage the free spool and keep winding until I feel the fish. I then steadily pull the rod back as far as I can. Sometimes this process is repeated two or three times before I really feel that I am in direct contact with the fish.

It is very rare for a carp at long range immediately to pull line off the angler's spool. The distance is so great and there is so much stretch in the line that the carp can probably go a good fifteen yards away from the angler before you are in full contact.

One of the big problems of playing a carp at long range is the distance the fish can travel to either side of you by kiting. This is when the carp comes into the bank on a tight line. You can imagine the problems that can be encountered when, for instance, you are fishing a 100 yards out in the lake and 50 yards to your left you have a snaggy island and 50 yards down to your right a big bed of dense lily pads. I'm sure that if you were a carp there is no way you would obligingly swim straight back to the angler, is there? Laying the rod over to one side and lowering it as close to the water as possible increases the angle between you and the hooked fish. This has the effect of bringing the carp round in a large arc, inching it back towards the angler. Once you feel you have its nose pointing in the right direction back towards you, you can return the rod to the normal position, gaining line fast and, with luck, averting danger.

NETTING AND LANDING

Once the carp is under the rod tip, especially in deep margins, there is always a danger in trying to bundle the fish into the net too soon. This will probably be the most intense part of the fight, with the carp making its last few desperate bids for freedom, and this is invariably where the inexperienced angler will make his mistake. Always try to coax the fish gently to the net, never chase it around and always practise netting the fish yourself. Then if you are unfortunate enough to lose it you only have yourself to blame. I can tell you there are very few people that I would trust to net my fish for me!

Keep the net still and draw the fish completely over it before attempting to lift it. It can be very nerve-racking and seemingly go on for ever as the carp continues to boil away from the net at each attempt to get it in. Don't lose your cool, your patience will be rewarded. If the fight has been prolonged then the hookhold may by now be getting loose. Any extra uncalled-for pressure might just pop it out at the eleventh hour which would be disastrous!

Landing Nets

Most carping in the United Kingdom is for doubles, twenties and thirties. A large net, triangular in shape with 36-inch arms is more than capable of landing any of these fish. There is a trend to go for the larger size of triangular net with 42-inch arms, and if you are fishing for thirties and forties this obviously has a positive advantage. But where you know the upper limit on your lake is going to be a big twenty always bear in mind that the smaller 36-inch model will be much easier to manoeuvre through the water.

I'm glad to say that it's almost impossible to buy a bad landing net. There are some ultra-light

A good quality landing net is essential. This is the standard 42 inch bowframe variety with a reverse tapered handle.

models around which must be treated with the utmost care since they have very thin-walled arms, but standard models from companies such as Gardener Tackle and Keenets cause few problems.

Some thought should be paid to the size of the landing net mesh. Thankfully, gone are the days of knotted nets. They are now all knotless and very kind to the fish. Generally speaking, the finer the mesh the kinder it's going to be to the fish – but we are talking about carp so not as small as micro or minnow mesh. There is a trend towards dual-mesh nets and I personally think that this is a marvellous development. The top two-thirds of the net is equipped with a large open mesh some ¾ inch or so in diameter while the bottom third of the net is made from heximesh or, in some cases, fine woven nylon sacking. The idea is that the large holes in the top allow for easy movement through the water while the fine netting in the bottom helps protect the fish once it's lifted from the water.

The depth of the net, though very much a personal preference, really should be a minimum of 30 inches on the 36-inch model and 36 inches on the 42-inch model. I have seen some ridiculously deep nets – up to about 6 feet on 42-inch arms. These can only be unmanageable and a distinct disadvantage, since I'm sure they will be forever getting caught up in bankside snags and underwater debris, as a great deal of the net will be lying on the bottom.

Most modern nets consist of two tapered arms with a cord drawstring along the front making up the third side of the triangle. The two arms are slotted into some sort of spreader block under tension. The spreader block is usually screwed into or is a permanent fixture on the landing net pole. The pole itself is some 5 or 6 feet in length. My own preference is for the Ultracult Carp-Mix Specimen Landing Net. I have both the 36- and 42-inch models, which cover all of my carping requirements. The heavy-duty carbon arms are spigoted into a solid alloy spreader block. In the spreader block is a countersunk slot which can house a large black isotope – very useful for night fishing. It illuminates the spreader block itself,

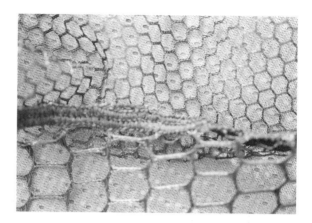

You can see here that two different meshes have been used. The larger carp mesh around the top section allows for easy movement through the water. The finer free-flow mesh on the bottom is kind to the fish and ensures that the terminal tackle will not fall through.

This is the Spreader Block off the Ultracult Carp Landing Net. The milled slot will accommodate either an Isotope or Starlite to give direction when netting fish at night.

This tapered aluminium spike is fitted to the end of the Ultracult Landing Net Pole. This is useful when pushing the net handle into the ground to keep it vertical, especially when fishing in reeds.

which allows you to judge far more easily when the carp is over the net. The 6-foot handle, which is permanently fixed into the spreader block, has a reverse taper and is finished with an aluminium spike, which allows it to be pushed into the lake bed when I am wading out to net fish in shallow water. Alternatively it can be pre-positioned out on the edge of vast reedbeds whilst I am fishing shallow mere-type waters. Both nets are of the combination of heximesh at the bottom and carp mesh at the top.

Landing Carp

Once you have successfully netted the fish it is always better to hold it still in the water for a couple of minutes rather than dragging it out immediately. This gives the carp a bit of a breather. It

has already done battle out in the lake and it is now going to spend several minutes out of the water while being unhooked, so a couple of minutes recovery time is quite vital. I will assume that your unhooking mat his already in position, so you are now ready to transfer the carp from the water onto the mat. Never try to lift the carp out by just hanging on to the landing-net pole – no matter what the quality of the landing net you are in great danger of snapping the arms clean off if you trying to lift the fish out in this way. One of two methods should be used. Either grab an arm of the net with each hand and lift it straight out and onto the mat or gather the net beneath the arms and take the weight of the fish solely in the net. Now is the time when the carp is most vulnerable damage. Panic will already have set in in the mind of a novice angler if he has suddenly been thrust into the whole new world of landing a very big and lively carp. There is a code of conduct that should always be practised and the fish should at all times be protected adequately. Where possible, transfer the carp from the landing net to the unhooking mat before you attempt to remove the hook. Single handed this is not always possible, I realise, but there is always a danger that part of the rig could become snagged in the net and if the carp starts to thrash around the hook could be torn from the mouth so please be as careful as possible.

Unhooking

As well as all my carp-care equipment I always carry two pairs of forceps, one straight and one curved. Both are 9-inch models. I also carry a good set of quality side cutters. These are always close to hand when unhooking. The method is as follows. Support the carp under the cheek that is lying closest to the ground, lifting it slightly upwards. If you can, straddle the carp with your body at the same time in case it starts to flap. If the hook cannot be teased out – and I do emphasise teased out – by gripping it with thumb and forefinger, then use the forceps to help get a more positive purchase. But remember that a lot of pressure can be applied through a set of 9-inch forceps. If the hook is difficult to dislodge cut the

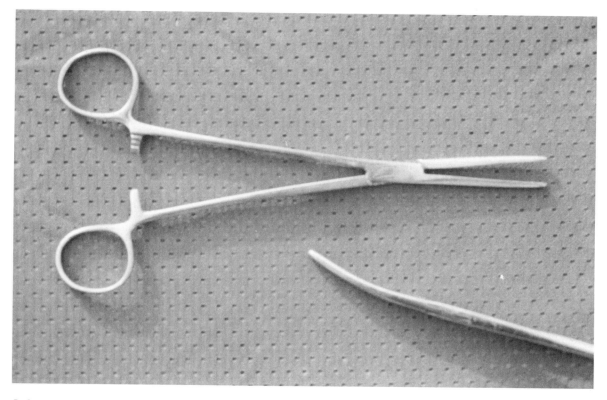

I always carry two sets of forceps to help unhook the carp – one straight and one curved.

hook link and gently work the hook back out through the skin, point first.

Be very careful not to tear the flesh. If things are looking difficult, do not hesitate to use the side cutters to snip pieces off of the hook, which will make it easy to extract. When trying to get the hook out eye first, if you cut the point and barb off – if they can be seen – you will be amazed at the difference it makes; and if you are trying to extract the hook point first, it will slide out easily once the eye has been removed. I would far rather cut up a hook, even if it has taken me ages to set it up on the rig, than risk damaging the carp in any way.

Unhooking Mats

An unhooking mat is absolutely essential and I will now take a look at some of the better models available. I suppose it should be said that any unhooking mat is better than none at all, but there are a few things to watch out for. Every item of carp-care equipment that is going to come into contact with the fish should be well and truly wet. Imagine the situation on a very tight swim with steeply inclined banks. You have a basic unhooking mat which consists of a flat piece of protective of material. On a flat surface this would be fine; but put it on some sort of slope and do you think the carp is going to stay put? Not on your life! The wet mat will simply act as a slide, possibly causing more problems than it solves.

There are designs available which have overflaps to secure the fish in place or have peripheral walls in which to contain the fish. The two best models I have come across are the Romart and the Ultracult unhooking mats. The Romart has

Carp care has come a long way. This fish will remain unharmed in the confines of the Ultracult Unhooking Mat.

an inflatable base, which gives positive protection between the fish and the ground. All sharp stones and rocks will be ironed out. There is an overflap that can be Velcroed in place holding the fish firmly between two layers of nylon. The Ultracult model has a thick protective base with inflatable walls, ensuring that the carp will not slide out.

Inevitably you will be confronted with the carp crashing around on the unhooking mat – it happens to us all. The instant reaction is to try to pin the carp down by pressing both hands firmly on its body. This can in fact do more damage than it does good. They are very strong animals. You won't stop them flapping, just concentrate their movements into a tighter area, which is usually when damage to pectoral fins occurs. It is far better to get your hands underneath the fish while kneeling over the unhooking mat and

drawing the carp lightly to your chest whilst at the same time keeping the carp low over the unhooking mat. Supported in this manner, there is nothing for the fish to thrash against and do damage. Always remove any items of jewellery or badges and the like which could get caught on scales and possibly remove them, and be especially wary of heavy-duty zips on Barbour-type coats. T-shirts, sweatshirts and soft jumpers are far kinder to the carp.

Weigh-Bags

Like unhooking mats there are a lot of good-quality weigh-bags about. Companies such as Kevin Nash, ET and Ultracult all offer good models. Always wet slings and weigh-bags before putting carp anywhere near them. Check that the fins have not been caught up or bent back against the body. The scales should be zeroed before

Another variety of inflatable mat; this is the Romart.

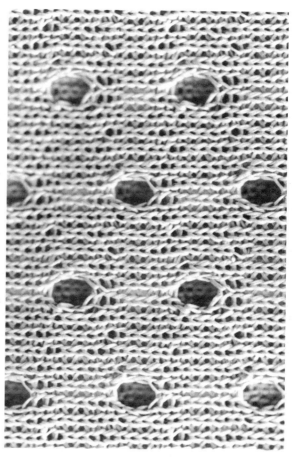

This is the material from a good-quality sack – the holes are actually knitted in and not punched, giving the ultimate in water exchange.

weighing commences. You will then have an accurate reading with no weights to deduct. There are some good multipurpose weigh-bags-cum-sacks which you may consider if you are going to retain the carp for photographing. All the aforementioned companies make one of these models.

Sack and Sacklings

We have been brought really up to date with modern sacks. They are so far removed from the old hessian models of yesteryear. Water exchange is the key to a good-quality sack. Thousands of tiny holes which are either punched or knitted into the material allow water to pass through the sack. A good sack once immersed in the water and lifted clear will immediately drain while a bad sack will balloon out taking some time for the water to drain away. The latter should be avoided at all costs. A dark environment will also be beneficial to the carp's quick recovery as it will feel safe when it cannot see out. Dark-green, brown or black are the preferred colours.

There are basically two types of sacks available: long triangular models with the drawstring at the neck and squarer designs with a full-length

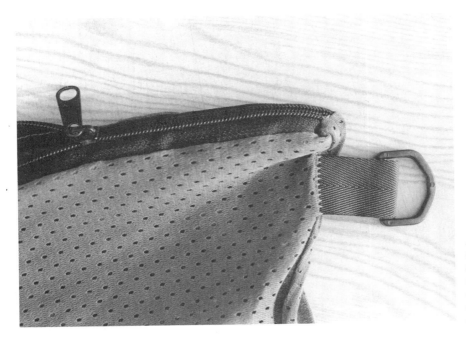

Full-length zips are far easier to cope with when transferring fish in and out of a sack. Also make sure that there is a good securing ring for staking the sack out.

The Ultracult Sackling is a combination of sacking and weighbag. This is very useful as the carp only have to be handled once.

zip along the top edge. The latter are my own preference. They are much easier to get the carp in and out of as the full-length zip exposes a larger open area of the sack. The carp can be easily placed right in the bottom of the sack. With the drawstring type they more or less have to be slid down to the bottom. All the good models of zip sack are equipped with D-rings at each top-edge corner, which means that they can be staked out in exactly the correct position. These zip sacks can also be equipped with weighing handles so that there is no need to transfer the carp from a weigh bag or sling into a separate sack. I have the greatest faith in this type of model and my own choice is the Ultracult Sackling. It is made of woven supersoft nylon with literally thousands of holes knitted in. The corners are nicely radiused so that the carp cannot suck the corner into its mouth. Unfortunately this has been known to happen with some square-cornered sacks.

Positioning of the Sack

If you are going to sack the fish up ensure that it is only for the minimum time, never in shallow water and never in hot, low-oxygen conditions. Try and find a shady quiet spot in which to position the sack. Make sure that there is a good depth of water and that the wind won't batter the sack against the bank or sunken trees. Only ever put one fish in a sack at a time – even if you have had a fantastic catch never be tempted to double fish up in the sack.

Always ensure that the sack is adequately staked out between two good bank sticks, and it's not a bad idea to attach a secondary lanyard tethered securely back to the bank. If the carp is suddenly disturbed for whatever reason, particularly after it has recovered, it could well bolt for freedom, pulling out insecure bank sticks – which would condemn it to certain death. The chances of recovering a fish once it has swum off in the sack are very minute.

Weighing

Weights are obviously a personal thing but I'm sure you will all try to get as accurate a reading as possible. There are many good sets of scales

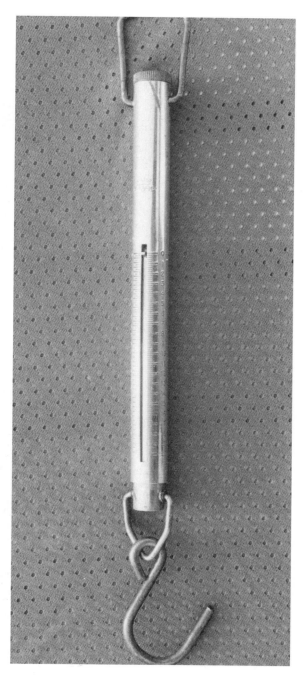

Although weights of the fish are very much a personal thing I always like to get as accurate a reading as possible. These brass Salters are the model I choose for stalking. Although they are quite small and lightweight they are very accurate.

Undoubtedly the most popular dial scales around. The Kevin Nash system offers a selection of two weight variants.

available. For my wandering, stalking fishing I use a set of good-quality brass Salters. These weigh up to 44lb in 4oz divisions. In the car as well as my main fishing bag I carry a set of dial scales. There are three good makes on the market: Avons, Kevin Nash and Reuben Heaton.

Basically you get what you pay for. Avons go up to 40lb with 1oz divisions and are the cheapest. Kevin Nash have 56 and 120lb models with 4oz divisions in middle price range. The most expensive are the Reuben Heaton which weigh up to 60lb in 1oz divisions.

The Fox International Weigh Bar – this is always better to use than trying to support dial scales on the top hanging ring.

When weighing with dial scales there is always a tendency to support them on the bottom half of the body – naturally enough, as this is the easiest way of picking them up. However, carp weighed with scales supported in this manner will be registered inaccurately. For some reason – and I confess I don't understand the mechanics – supporting the scales on the underside always gives a higher reading. The correct way of weighing is to hold the scales in an absolutely vertical position by the weighing eye on the top. On the Nash and the Reuben Heaton scales the weighing eye is quite small and you can only get a few fingers through, which is next to useless with a big fish.

By far the best method is to use a Fox weighbar. This is a purpose-made little tool with a central large dogclip which hooks in the weighing eye. A plastic-covered aluminium bar which extends either side of the dogclip allows a good positive double-handed grip. Always weigh the carp over the unhooking mat and only just lift the weigh bag or sling clear of the ground.

PHOTOGRAPHY

Of course we all want a good permanent record of our capture, and why not? But when the fish has just been landed and is lying unattended in the unhooking mat is not the time to go rummaging through your tackle bag for your cameras. Always have everything set up at the ready. The couple of minutes recovery time the carp spends in the landing net while still in the water can be utilised by your companion to set out unhooking mat, forceps and side cutters, scales, weigh-bags and sacks – and, of course, cameras. It should be then a matter of just a couple of minutes before the whole unhooking, weighing and photographing operation is proficiently executed.

Imprint this safety code firmly in your mind. If necessary, do a practice run. So next time you put the net under another beautiful carp you have everything at the ready and then you can watch as it swims majestically off into the lake no worse for its brief encounter outside of its watery world.

We spend a lot of time, money and thought in our quest for catching carp and all enjoy that magic moment as another whacker slides over the rim of the net. From then on in the carps wellbeing is firmly in your hands. Please look after them so that others who follow after may enjoy the same experience. And just a thought – this doesn't apply just to big carp it applies to all carp. The five-pounder of today could well be the fifty-pounder of your tomorrow's dreams!

11 SPECIAL BAITS

PASTE BAITS

Sadly, paste baits appear to be going out of favour these days in preference to boilies, but on some waters where nuisance fish aren't a problem or where you can stalk, the paste baits are still worth considering. After all, in pre-boilie days that is all we had to use. Paste baits are quite simple to make. It is just a matter of mixing powdered-type bulk ingredients together with a binder and liquid. The consistency of the paste should be such that it moulds easily and does not crack open. Something like Plasticine would be about right. The storage of paste baits is probably the key to consistency as much as the bait itself. Once the paste has been made up I store it in polythene bags inside a sandwich-type plastic box so that the sun and air cannot get to it, and dry it out. Some of the best paste baits I have used are based on recipes on the good old trout pellet. The trout pellets themselves are ground up to a fine powder in a coffee mill. Fortunately they have a lot of binding qualities themselves so it's only a matter of adding some more bulking ingredients and a little sodium caseinate, which helps to make a smooth paste.

A typical recipe will be something like: 6oz ground trout pellets, 2oz biscuit meal or layers' meal and 2oz sodium caseinate. All the dry ingredients are mixed together in a polythene bag by blowing air in and giving the mixture a good shake-up. Water is then added to the mix until the correct consistency is achieved. There will naturally be some drying out as the absorbent ingredients take up the water. This will give you a really nice smelly paste that has accounted for many hundreds of carp in years gone by – and I'm sure on certain waters will be as good today.

To ring the changes, as it were, the trout pellets can be replaced with one of the dried cat biscuits, which all have their own individual smell and taste. These are ground down in the same way and can be mixed up as before. There are now so many of these cat biscuits about that the choice is almost endless.

I also like tinned-fish pastes. Tinned sardines and pilchards are ideal. These are dropped in the liquidiser and then bound together. They have such a strong smell that no extra attractants need be added. Rice powder or fine semolina together with a little wheat gluten added to the liquidised fish will make a good paste. Sardines and pilchards are available in their own natural oil as well as in tomato sauce, which gives additional options.

Soft meat pâtés and liver sausage make yet another substitute. Add 2oz breadcrumbs, 4oz biscuit meal, 2oz wheat gluten and 2oz sodium caseinate. Pâtés and soft meat are quite hard to blend in with the dry ingredients so a little warm water to soften them up will help fold the dry ingredients into the paste.

Probably one of the oldest of all the pastes is sausage meat mixed up with groundbait or breadcrumbs. This was certainly the first special that I remember using. This was closely followed by Kitekat and groundbait or breadcrumbs. The state we used to get into mixing that lot together – let alone the smell! It's a good idea to make your paste baits in bulk. This gets it over and done with in one go and helps achieve a good consistency. Several 10oz or 1lb batches can be made up at a time. Leave them a little on the sticky side, put them in polythene bags and drop them into the freezer. This gives you instant access to bait without having to worry about making it up before you go out fishing. Leaving the paste a little on the sticky side ensures the right consistency when you come to use it, as the freezing and thawing out removes moisture and dries the bait out a little.

BOILED SPECIALS

As these specialist carp baits were developed we soon found that they attracted not only carp but lots of other unwanted species as well. I'm not sure who was responsible for the original idea of boiling up the paste but whoever it was laid the foundation of a whole new industry. The paste baits were rolled into balls of anything between 1 and 2 inches in diameter which were then dropped into boiling water for between 30 seconds and a minute, resulting in a cooked skin on the outside. The skin made the baits much more resistant to the attacks from some of the smaller, unwanted species. Thus we had a more selective bait and so the boilie was born.

Those original lightly boiled baits look enormous by today's standards. We used to think that heavy leads on the line deterred the carp from taking our baits so freelining was the method of the day, and the bait itself had to carry enough weight to allow us to cast – hence their size.

BOILIES

Today's boilies range from about 10mm up to about 24mm in diameter. These are the most convenient to use with modern set-ups, such as the hair rig. As time has gone on boilies seem to have got harder and harder in an attempt to counter the attentions of nuisance fish. The water that was originally used as the medium for mixing various components of the bait together has now been replaced with eggs, which when boiled give a much harder finished product. On some waters where large tench and bream are problematical, baits that have been boiled for up to 5 minutes are not unusual. This has the effect of making them rock hard.

I am much happier using baits of between 10 and 18mm diameter. I am sure the carp find these much easier to take. They are thrown back to the pharyngeal teeth and crushed far more easily than a bait of, say, 24mm diameter. The other advantage is that generally speaking you will be able to introduce more free offerings of a smaller size into the swim. This builds up confidence as the carp takes more and more bait before eventually taking the hookbait. It also looks better. With lots of small free offerings scattered around, the area can be more comprehensively covered, drawing carp into the baited zone. The odd one or two large baits scattered haphazardly around might easily be missed as carp pass through the swim.

The other nice thing about boilies is the length of time that they can be fished in the swim. Paste baits, which have no cooked outer skin, soon begin to disintegrate. As the paste becomes softer even the tiniest of fish will start pecking pieces off. But a boilie may well take several days before it starts breaking down, increasing the chances of a carp finding it before it is either whittled away by a small fish or dissolves. It's lovely to think that baits cast out in the evening will still be there in the morning if they are not taken by carp during the night. Before the days of the boilie we must have wasted hundreds of hours of fishing time with no bait on our hooks. Large chunks of paste cast into the swims at nightfall might easily have disappeared by midnight, and by then you might have been well into the land of Nod. Of course you can always make yourself get up in the middle of the night to recast but that in itself can be problematic if you are trying to fish holes in weedbeds or tight against the far bank with overhanging trees. I think we all fish with a lot more confidence knowing that our bait will stand up to the attacks from smaller nuisance fish.

Bought Boilies
Such is the popularity of boilies as a bait that many companies are now offering a comprehensive range of packeted boilies. These either come in frozen form or have a limited shelf life. When

A bag of ready made boilies – these off-the-shelf boilies give the angler the opportunity of fishing at any time without having to worry about making bait first.

The range of commercial boilies now available to the angler is quite enormous. As well as the standard fifty-fifty mixes, which come in all manner of flavours, there are now bird-food-blend type, fishmeal mixes, bird-food mixes and white-seed mixes. It just goes on and on and as far as I am concerned long may it continue. I am glad to be able to use them. I never ever liked making up boilies; it was a chore. All those hours of mixing and rolling in the kitchen are now spent in pursuit of carp instead.

HIGH-PROTEIN BAITS

As carp fishing has become more popular, so our thoughts on boilies have changed. I used to have a lot of faith in my own mixes and ingredients outfishing anyone else's, and I was very much a fan of Fred Wilton's high-protein theory.

The idea was to give the carp what were conceived to be the perfect pellets. Within that little round bait all the ingredients were chosen to give the carp the best nutritional value that was thought possible. Just about all of these early high-protein baits were based on milk protein, and I am sure carp still like the taste of milk protein powders. The theory was that this perfect pellet should be introduced regularly into the lake. A flavour was added to the baits to make them identifiable to the carp and it was thought that over a period of time the carp would become accustomed to picking up these baits, which would fulfil their daily dietary needs. The idea was that once a certain level of feed had been introduced the carp would pick up these baits in preference to anything else.

I am convinced that in the early days of protein baits this was very much the case. But things have changed so much today that I very much doubt whether the carp ever get the opportunity or indeed are capable of detecting the best bait that is introduced to any lake. There are far too many permutations these days and the chances of finding a unique flavour which would label one bait different from the rest are long indeed. Imagine spending hundreds of hours mixing, rolling and

they first hit the market in the early eighties I don't think many people thought they were actually going to take off since at the time there was much secrecy surrounding boilie recipes, with everyone looking for the ultimate mix, and if you were successful on a particular bait you were as sure as heck not going to tell anyone else. To use a bait that someone else has made, without really knowing what the ingredients were, or what level of flavour and indeed in some cases what flavour, was at first treated with great scepticism. But a decade of factory-made boilies on and even some of the top carpers in the country are using them. Anglers such as Peter Springate, Albert Romp, Ritchie McDonald and Rod Hutchinson all use production boilies – what more convincing argument do you need?

cooking a top-class protein bait, then spending many more hours baiting up and assuming that you had then got everything right and the carp had latched on to your bait, when Joe Soap wanders along the bank with his shelf-life boilie of very similar flavour to those you have been introducing. Do you really think the carp could tell the difference? I am not so sure.

I certainly wouldn't condemn making your own baits out of hand. There are many people who actually like making bait, (I always knew there was something strange about carp anglers). Whether it's a question of confidence or whether some anglers get a bigger kick out of catching carp on a bait they made themselves I do not know, but I am certainly not going to knock it. If that is what it takes, then so be it – this game is all about getting the maximum pleasure. If making up your own bait is what it's all about and gives the angler more confidence, this alone will lead to more fish on the bank.

Bait Ingredients

Boilies are made up from multiple ingredients – generally fine powders – bound together with eggs, colours, flavours and enhancers added before they are eventually rolled and cooked. I suppose that really you could include in your boilie any food item that could be made into a powder, but the more standard ingredients are milk powders, wheat gluten, soya flour, nut meal (hazelnuts, peanuts, etc.), special cage-bird feeds (such as PTX, Nectar Blend and Robin Red), and the endless amount of fishmeals (mackerel, shrimp, whitefish, razorfish, etc.). Most of these ingredients are familiar enough but some of the milk proteins may seem a little alien to the beginner. So let's have a quick look at a few that are commonly used.

Casein

This is the main protein extracted from raw milk and usually has a protein content of about ninety-five per cent. It is available in varying consistencies and a mesh size is normally stated. The higher the mesh number, the finer and more flour-like the casein will be. For angling purposes a mesh of between 60 and 90 is ideal. Buy only food-quality casein; there are industrial caseins about, which should be avoided.

The bait connoisseur has never had it so good. There are hundreds of different ingredients to choose from to make his own recipes. But always make sure that they are of the best quality. For the ultimate in freshness I prefer to buy the powders in small sealed bags.

Lactalbumin

This is an eighty-six per cent protein powder which is derived from the whey of cow's milk. It is usually used in conjunction with casein but with a much lower amount to achieve a well-balanced, high-nutritional-value bait.

Sodium Caseinate

This is a ninety-five per cent protein powder which is a soluble form of casein. It is very light and fine and tends to be quite sticky because of its soluble form. It certainly helps to smooth out paste baits and give them a nice texture and it will go some way to help create a buoyant boilie or neutralise some of the heavier ingredients in the mix when we are looking for a bait that will only just rest on soft silty bottoms.

Calcium Caseinate

Another soluble form of casein, this too is a ninety-five per cent protein powder but it is treated in a slightly different way so that it is not quite so sticky as the sodium variety. Calcium caseinate was one of the earliest and most freely available milk proteins that the angler could use. It was sold in a lot of chemists' shops under the name of Casilan.

As well as the milk proteins here are some more commonly used ingredients in a boilie mix. I often think descriptions actually give you a better understanding of the bait.

Wheat Gluten

This is a protein that is extracted from wheat flour at an eighty per cent protein level. It is ideal to use in combination with milk powders and is also one of the best binding agents used in the bait-making industry. Whenever you are having trouble getting one of your mixes to hold together, a couple of ounces of wheat gluten might well be the answer.

Soya Isolate

This is a ninety per cent powdered protein extracted from soya beans. It is rarely used at a greater rate than 1 or 2oz in a 10oz mix. It makes the baits go out of shape and flat when they are boiled and you can end up with a gungy mess if it is used at any higher level. But because of its high protein content it does help balance out any HNV bait.

Soya Flour

This is a fairly low-protein powder at about forty per cent. It is made from ground soya beans and quite a high percentage of the natural oil content is retained. Adding one or two ounces of soya flour to your mix certainly aids with the rolling and it also makes quite a good binder to use with any paste baits.

Wheatgerm

Though of low protein content at thirty-five per cent, wheatgerm contains a lot of fibre and vitamins. It is particularly high in vitamin B. It is made from the leftover flour millings and will provide good roughage in any bait.

Egg Albumen

An eighty-five per cent protein, egg albumen acts as a good supplement egg replacer or at least goes part way to reducing the amount of eggs used in the boilie mix. It has excellent binding qualities and when used in low amounts (between ½ and 1oz in a 10oz mix) it often helps bind difficult ingredients together.

Colours

Most people like to colour their boilies and safe food dyes should not be detrimental to any bait. Colours are a personal preference and unless I am trying to disguise the bait for one reason or another I am really not too worried what the colour is. I do sometimes wonder if anglers pay too much attention to colours. I don't believe the carp are good sight feeders; they rely much more on other sensitive organs to detect water-soluble attractors.

Flavours

There are now so many flavours available that you could just about fill a book with them. A solvent medium is used to carry the flavour. On sweetie-type flavours which are nice to taste

Flavours are often based on personal preference as there are so many successful ones available. The tackle shop shelves are full of them.

glycerol is usually used as the base. These are fast-dissolving and are used at quite a high dosage. Ethyl alcohol flavours are the vogue at the moment. They are very strong so · the dosage is quite small. They are extremely long-lasting and even baits that have been out in the water for two or three days will still retain a lot of that attractive smell. Natural oils are also used as an attractor, with mackerel, herring, sardine and pilchards at the top of the list. Essential oils have been used for many years and appear to be making a bit of a comeback at the moment. Some of the best are black pepper, lemon grass, geranium, bergamot, ylang-ylang, eucalyptus and garlic oil. Other useful additives are enhancers and sweeteners.

RECIPES

As you can see, there is a whole industry around those little round things that we chuck in for bait. Here are a few recipes that you may consider using, or you can at least use them as a guideline when creating your own bait.

A good high-nutritional-value bait may well consist of the following: 4oz casein, 3oz lactalbumin,1½ oz calcium caseinate, 1oz gluten, ½oz vitamin and mineral supplement.

Along similar lines: 5oz casein, 2oz lactalbumin,1½ oz calcium caseinate,1oz gluten, ½oz Equivite (vitamin and mineral replacer).

A good animal protein based on fishmeal is as follows: 3oz white fishmeal, 2oz shrimp meal,

3½oz casein, 1oz gluten, ½oz Equivite.

Another of my favourites, consisting almost entirely of fishmeals, is as follows: 3oz white fishmeal, 2oz shrimp meal, 2oz anchovy meal, 2oz gluten, 1oz Codlevine.

Bird-food type mixes have again made a bit of a comeback in recent years. Here is one of my tried and tested recipes: 5oz Nectar Blend 2oz PTX, 1½oz Robin Red, 1oz gluten, ½oz wheatgerm.

You will see that all of these have been made up into 10oz mixes. The reason is that it is far easier to calculate the protein level by doing this. Here is an example to help you understand what I mean.

5oz casein	5 x 95	=	4 7 5
1oz lactalbumin	1 x 86	=	8 6
2oz soya flour	2 x 40	=	8 0
2oz wheat gluten	2 x 80	=	1 6 0
Total ingredients	10oz		8 0 1

By dividing the total protein content by 10 you will get an approximate protein level: 801 divided by 10 = 80.1, giving a protein content of about eighty per cent before any liquids or flavours are added.

All the ingredients should be placed in a large plastic bag and given a really good shake to ensure that they are well mixed together.

Pre-Mixed Ingredients

As well as making up your own recipes you can go halfway by buying pre-mixed dry ingredients. It is then a matter of adding your own flavour and colour. Commonly available ready-made mixes are well put together on tried and tested recipes, so at least you can be assured of using something that you know works. Five of the most popular are: 50/50 mix, protein mix, nutmeal mix, fishmeal mix, and bird-food mix. Always use the flavours, sweeteners and enhancers at the recommended dosages, which should be displayed on the labels. Most flavours are in liquid form and good colours normally come as powder, so add the powdered colour to the dry mix and the liquid flavour to the eggs.

The halfway house. Add your flavour to a ready-mixed bag of bait – just add egg and then roll.

You will need the following kitchen utensils: a set of good-quality kitchen scales for weighing out the ingredients; a large mixing bowl with wooden mixing spoon; an egg whisk; a large saucepan for boiling and a flour sieve. A large cutting board is ideal for rolling out your baits. The colours will stain, so use your wife's best board at your peril!

Method

The operation is as follows. To make a 10oz mix weigh out all the ingredients, put them in a poly bag with the colour, and mix them well together. Six large eggs together with the correct dosage of liquid flavour, sweetener and enhancer are beaten up in the mixing bowl. Make sure that the eggs and flavours are really well mixed together.

The kitchen utensils you will need for making boilies.

Knead the paste into a smooth consistency similar to Plasticine.

I always find it best to add the dry mix by hand to the beaten eggs. Do this slowly, stirring all the time until you have a really thick soup consistency. This should then be allowed to stand for about five minutes so that all of the liquid is completely absorbed by the dry ingredients. Next, knead the mix, possibly adding a little more of the dry ingredients until you have achieved an even Plasticine-like consistency.

If you are not going to roll the bait out straight away the lumps of kneaded dough should be put into a plastic bag and sealed. This stops them drying out and making hard work of rolling. When ready to start rolling, break off several lumps and roll them into long, thin sausages slightly larger in diameter than the finished boilie. Then take two or three lumps at a time and roll them into balls in the palm of your hand. If you are new to the game, start by rolling one

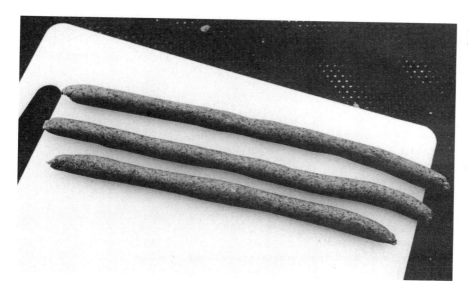

Roll the paste out into long thin sausages.

bait at a time, progressing to three or even four if you have got big hands. Rolling is made easier if your hands and the board are lightly greased with margarine. This may not be necessary if there are a lot of natural oils in the bait itself.

Once you have rolled the whole mix you can now put the saucepan of water on to boil. By the time it comes to the boil the last boilies rolled should already have formed a slight skin on their outside. If they haven't, wait for another five minutes for them to do so. This will stop them sticking together when boiling. If it is the sort of mix that won't form a skin in the air, sprinkle a little of your dried mix over them as if you are dusting them. This will have the same effect of preventing them sticking together.

Slugs of bait are taken from the sausages and rolled between the palms of your hand into neat balls.

The boilies should then be put into the fine flour sieve ready for boiling. Do not try to do too many at once; between twenty-five and fifty is plenty, depending on the size of saucepan. Immerse the sieve in the boiling water and time the cooking. It will usually take 1–4 minutes, depending on the sort of mix and how hard you want the baits to be. It is essential that the water does not go off the boil. If it does the baits will become waterlogged and soggy. As soon as the time is up, shake off excess water and turn the baits out onto an absorbent towel to dry. The longer they are left the harder they will become. Sometimes I leave them out overnight if I want a good hard bait to withstand long-range catapulting. If you are going to freeze them in batches don't let them dry out too much. Put them straight in a heavy-duty freezer bag while steam is still coming out of them. This will trap moisture inside the bag and stop them drying out and cracking once they have been thawed.

Only boil a few baits at a time – ensure the water is kept from going off the boil.

It's always a good idea to label up the bag with the date, flavour and mix and then you can use them in date order. I know some anglers who still spend the whole of the close season making

Lay the baits out on an absorbent surface to soak up any excess water.

up boilies. It's always worth keeping back a few unboiled baits for making into pop-ups. They can either be slowly baked in the oven or put in the microwave to make them buoyant and float.

If you intend making up lots of boilies it may well be worth investing in one of the labour-saving devices. Gardener Tackle seems to have cornered this market and offers a great array of implements to speed up home production of baits. Rolling tables will make sausages of precisely the right diameter every time; likewise their powerful bait guns, which turn out an endless rope of boilie mix. The sausages are then transferred onto a rolling table or side-winder machine. A couple of backward and forward movements of the table or a few turns of the handle on the side-winder and round boilies will be dispensed automatically. Sticky mixes can bind up the works of these labour-saving devices but if you smear all contact surfaces with oil or margarine smooth running should be achieved.

BOILIE PARTICLES

As well as the perfectly rounded boilies which are ideal for accurate distant catapulting, specialist boilie mixes can be turned into particle-sized baits for fishing the margins or fishing at close range. These are much quicker to produce than the boilies themselves and there are two methods of manufacture that are easy to learn and execute. First, long thin ropes of paste can be rolled out to roughly the diameter of the finished bait. These can be as small as ³⁄₁₆ inch in diameter. The long ropes should then be placed on a foil tray and placed in the freezer overnight. When they are solid they are easily cut up into short cylinders with a good-quality kitchen knife.

Before they thaw out they should be placed in boiling water in a sieve as before. Literally thousands of particle-size boilies can be produced quickly in this manner.

The Gardener Tackle Rolling Table will give you consistently sized sausages every time.

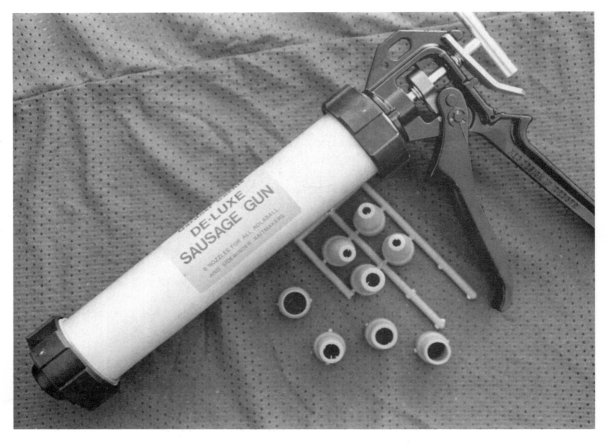

*The Bait Gun. A whole mix can be put inside and extruded as a long thin rope.
Note the various sizes of nozzels.*

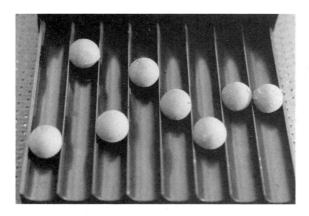

*The Gardener Rollaball will undoubtedly speed up
production of boilies.*

Alternatively, the whole boilie mix can be cooked first. Once kneaded into a Plasticine consistency, the mix can be formed into a brick shape. This can then be wrapped in greaseproof paper with two or three polythene bags Sellotaped tightly around the outside to stop any air from getting in. The whole sealed brick can then be cooked for about half an hour. It is then taken out and left to cool. The brick of bait should now be cooked right through. This can finally be cut up into particle-size shapes of your own design.

Both these methods give you a chance to ring the changes and get away from the more standard spherical boilies.

The Side Winder. We are really getting down to high speed bait making now.

A brick of paste bait that is boiled can be cut into all manner of various shapes to ring the changes.

SPECIAL BAITS

SPECIALIST FLOATING CAKE

You can turn most of the aforementioned boilie recipes into a floating cake by simply adding twice as many eggs and some baking powder and cooking them slowly in the oven. The method is as follows.

For a 10oz mix break twelve large eggs into a mixing bowl. Add flavour, sweeteners and enhancers as normal. Beat the eggs together, trying to force in as much air as possible. A good food processor is normally far better for this than an ordinary egg whisk. I like to leave the mixer running for a good five minutes or so – you should get a good froth on the surface ensuring that you have got plenty of air in. Add about a level teaspoon of baking powder to your 10oz dry mix and shake it in well. While the food processor is running on low speed slowly add the dry mix. You should now end up with a thick soup-like consistency. A further 5-minute run at medium to high speed will push a lot more air into the mix.

The mix should then be turned out into a greased baking tin. One of the high-sided square jobs is ideal. This should then be put into a pre-heated oven at about gas mark 7. Cook slowly on the middle shelf for a couple of hours. The cooking time may need to be adjusted depending on the type of mix, but you will know when it is done when it has risen and a nice light-brown crust has formed. Take it out of the oven, allow it to cool and cut it into cubes. The outer crusty edges are used for bait while the softer centre cubes are used for freebies.

So much myth and misconception is talked about special baits that a whole book could be devoted to the subject. So, rather than writing reams and reams about theoretical mixes, attractors and the like, I have addressed myself only to what I know is fact. I make no apologies for this as there are far too many bait barons trying to capitalise on vulnerable carp anglers.

Take my advice and stick to honest-to-goodness mixes or even pre-made boilies. At least then when your bait is sitting out there and you are not getting takes you are pretty well assured that it's not the bait to blame. Maybe the carp just aren't feeding. Baits and rigs are the two easiest things for the angler to blame for a blank, but they are rarely at fault. Just use a good bait and a good rig and concentrate on the more important things – like finding the fish!

12 PARTICLE BAITS

Before I get down to the nitty-gritty on these very interesting and extremely successful baits I would first like to thank a couple of people for their involvement in the art of particle fishing. First, to the old master himself (sorry, Rod, none of us is getting any younger), Rod Hutchinson. He was undoubtedly the first angler to inspire many of us to try our hand at particle fishing and I believe that his forward thinking on the subject laid the foundations of all that followed. It was in the late 1960s and early 1970s that I first became heavily involved with particle fishing, and the following story about Rod, which will always remain firmly fixed in my mind, dates from that time.

Like all success stories – of which this is certainly one – it resulted in a good catch of carp, but for the life of me I cannot remember just how big those carp were or indeed how many he caught. Suffice it to say that it was an extraordinary capture for that particular water. The water concerned was the then ultra-hard Johnson's Lake in Kent. At that time it was a clear, fairly young gravel pit with a relatively light stocking of good-sized carp. The season was well under way and I was quite smitten with myself, having already caught three carp, when Rod turned up on the water.

There are a couple of things I should tell you that make what was to follow even more special. I was a fairly local angler, visiting the water most weekends and for the odd session in the evening, so I thought I knew it rather well. Certainly the hours of observation had led me to think that. Now Rod could by no means be called a local angler, making only the odd trek down from the Humberside area, so it was very much on instinct that he approached the water.

The sequence of events that followed was to change my thoughts on particles and baiting for ever, and I am not sure even today whether Rod realises what an impact that session had on me. At the time I was using sweetcorn, the revolutionary wonder bait of that era. Most of the fishing was conducted in the margins and I would normally spread out three rods in an area and put about the contents of one large tin of Jolly Green Giant around the hookbaits. The water that year

Sweetcorn – the current British record carp caught by Chris Yates was taken on these golden grains.

was very weedy and Rod set himself up in the car park corner and actually had to clear a spot before he could begin fishing. It was what happened next that left me gobsmacked: he emptied the contents of a huge bucket of particles into one very tight area, and when I say huge it was like more than all the bait I had used so far that season.

As I lay there that night on my bedchair, dozing in the dreamland of big carp, I thought: that guy is crazy; with all that bait there, he will have to wait three months to get a take! For me the night passed peacefully and uneventfully and it was some time after first light that I dragged myself from the comfort of the bivvy. I peered across to Rod's swim and it was like the wreck of the *Hesperus*! Anyone who knows Rod will know exactly what I mean – rods all over the place, bivvy on the point of collapse, buckets and bits strewn everywhere. But there must have been an aura of success beaming out of the swim and, although I couldn't actually see Rod, I just knew that he had caught and of course he had – and what a caning he had given them!

As I say, I can't remember exactly what he caught. It was probably three or four twenties in that very short night. What amazed me was the vast amount of bait he had put into the swim. It was at that moment that the penny dropped with the loudest of clangs and a whole new world opened up to me. I had previously had no conception of just how much bait carp are capable of eating.

The other person I would like to mention is Paul Gummer – in fact not just Paul but Dickie Caldwell and the rest of the Chad Valley Gang. I first came across this bunch of guys at Brooklands Lake, Dartford, Kent, and they looked more like a group of long-haired, pot-smoking, beer-swilling hippies rather than carp anglers. As always, appearances were deceptive and in the next decade or so this small group of friends took the Darenth valley apart using particles. If Rod's exploits were not enough, if you get half a dozen guys fishing together as a group on the same bait and on the same water they are surely a force to be reckoned with. I was very fortunate to be let in on the periphery of their circle and a new friendship was struck up and many carp shared, along with several buckets of maples and many gallons of tea.

Being taken into the confidence of a group like that was very refreshing since about that time there was so much mystery, rumour, speculation and secretiveness that there were times when the lone angler could feel totally out of touch with what was going on. This did have its advantages, however, as most of the carp that were caught came as a result of creating the chances oneself. So it was nice to have met guys like Rod and the Chad Valleyers who spoke openly to me about what they were doing, and particularly about our shared love for particle fishing. I pay tribute to their kindness.

PRINCIPLES

The whole idea behind particle fishing is to try to simulate in some way the abundance of natural food that is freely available in most of our rich waters. As logic should dictate, the richer and harder the water, the more successful particle fishing becomes.

It is one of the few methods by which a high degree of preoccupation can be achieved. Particle baits – which include nuts, beans and pulses and anything from Hemp to brazil nuts – are of all the same size, colour, texture and flavour. When carpets of these are introduced into the swim (rather than being treated as individuals, as with other baits) they are often grazed upon and treated almost like a field of grass rather than a manger of hay. This is the key to success. Suspicion is thrown out of the window as literally hundreds if not thousands upon thousands of baits are consumed by the carp before they come across a hookbait, whereas in most branches of angling the hookbait may well be the tenth or the twentieth to be sampled.

Life Expectancy
Particle baits continue to be effective for an amazing length of time. Because of the great

numbers of baits involved the chances of the carp sussing out that something is wrong are greatly reduced. In fact on some waters where the carp are individually recognised multiple captures of the same fish on the same bait are by no means unusual. However, it's not just a matter of bunging out as many particles as you can; it's knowing when and how much to introduce to guarantee success. Some perspective must be put on baiting. A lot of bait will attract the carp into the swim but the right amount must be judged accurately so that it will be consumed in a given period, giving the angler the chance of a take or two. A newcomer to particle fishing is often frightened by the amount of bait that successful anglers use and will not have the same sort of confidence.

To get an idea of how much bait can be eaten, weigh out a pound of boilies. Depending on size, you may have about 250 individual baits. Over a weekend's fishing on many waters this would be considered an insignificant amount. Now weigh out a pound of, say, tares. There will be literally thousands and thousands of individual baits, and it's fair to assume that the multitude of tares will be consumed just as easily as a couple of hundred boilies and will give the angler the same chance

of a take. The difference is that the carp will have to work a lot harder in searching out each individual particle than it would with the boilies. So, as a starting point, the beginner to particle fishing might well relate the amount of bait introduced to the weight of boilies that he would be happy fishing with. As I say, this is just a starting point. I firmly believe that carp will consume as much as six times the weight of particles as boilies in the same period, and this brings about a degree of preoccupation which often results in better catches.

CATEGORIES OF PARTICLES

Mass Baits

The smallest of particles I usually term as 'mass baits'. They range in size from a minute pinhead to about $3/16$ inch in diameter. Moving up in size from the smallest first, here is a list of the mass baits that I use: salmon fry crumb; pinhead oatmeal; red, white, Japanese and panicum millet; red and black rape seed; linseed; red and white dari seed; moth beans; hemp and buckwheat.

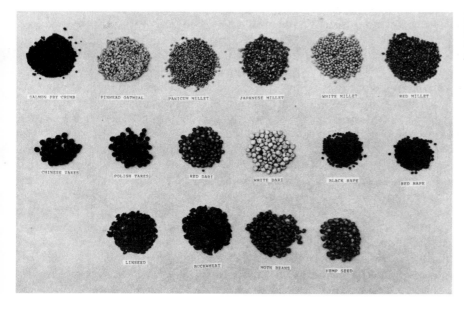

This selection of particle baits can loosely be grouped together as the smallest and so called mass variety.

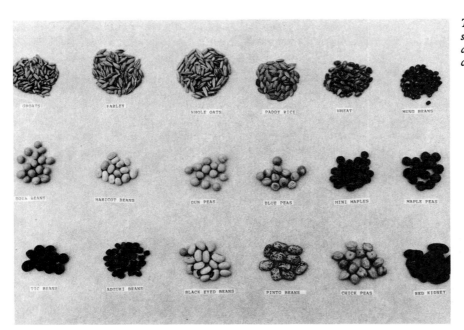

These are bracketed as standard-sized particles and are among the most commonly used today.

Standard Size Particles

These are probably the most commonly used. Again starting from the smallest, here are some of the successful ones that I have used: groats; paddy rice; oats; barley; wheat; mung beans; Chinese and Polish tares; adzuki beans; mini-maples; soya beans; dun peas; maple peas; black-eyed beans; haricot beans; blue peas; chick peas; tic beans; maize and sweetcorn.

Large Particles

Again here are some of my favourite beans: pinto beans; red kidney beans; sweet lupins; tiger nuts; pistachios; large, small red and medium peanuts; cashew nuts; lima beans; hazelnuts; almonds and brazils.

That little lot should give any would-be particle fanatic a very comprehensive choice.

Best Quality

Always insist that you are only ever supplied with the best-quality and latest batches of particles. Although all the ones listed are dehydrated, storage is of paramount importance as they will absorb moisture easily and become mildewed if not stored correctly. So it's always the fresher the better. Look for clean particles free from dust, stones and part seeds. When buying in bulk (which usually means 25- or 50-kilo sacks) ask for the bags to be opened up before you part with your money. Believe you me, I have seen some real old rough stuff about! If you have any trouble in finding a good-quality supply at a reasonable price I can strongly recommend that you get in touch with Hinders of Swindon. Bryan Jarrett, the proprietor, is a good carp fisherman in his own right and knows exactly the requirements of his clientele. He offers a fantastic helpline service also, so if you have any problems get in touch with him.

Like good wines, particles also have good years and batches will undoubtedly vary from time to time. It's amazing what things contribute to a short supply or poor-quality particles. The weather obviously plays the most important role and we seem to be in an era of hurricanes, floods and droughts. Wars also take their toll, not only in human terms, but in their effect on the distant carp angler. Currency fluctuation doesn't help either.

TIGER NUTS   FRENCH MAIZE   SWEET LUPINS   BRAZIL NUTS

PEANUTS   ALMONDS   HAZEL NUTS   LIMA BEANS

These are the largest of all particles that are commonly used in carp fishing.

PREPARATION

Once you have found a good supply of good-quality particles preparation is of equal importance. Most of these nuts, seeds and pulses are dehydrated. If they are thrown into the water unprepared and the carp eat them straight away this could have a devastating effect on the fish. Dry particles in the gut of the carp take in water and swell up, sometimes expanding to twice or three times their dehydrated size. You can imagine the effect this has on the carp's digestive system: fatalities are inevitable, so please take care.

Another problem with unprepared particles is that if they are not denatured they will start to grow and, whereas rice fields in the margins may look very pretty, I don't think the landowners would be any too pleased. Even if there is no chance of the carp ever eating the unprepared particles, still don't chuck them in the margins of the lake because you will give them the optimum conditions for growth.

There are several ways of preparing particles, most of which involve soaking them overnight –

ideally for a minimum of ten hours; far better twelve or fourteen – and then cooking them. Some of the mass baits (millet, rape, linseed and dari and moth beans) are exceptional in that they only need scalding with boiling water to denature them before being left to soak overnight. For virtually all of the rest boiling or pressure-cooking after the soaking process is required. When boiling in a large, open-topped saucepan always make sure the water does not go off the boil. Cook them for between quarter and half an hour, depending on how soft you want the bait.

The only trouble with boiling in an open pan is that a great percentage of the natural flavour in the particles is boiled out and just evaporates into the atmosphere. For this reason I am a great fan of pressure-cooking. As well as keeping in the flavour it also takes less time. Again depending on just how soft you want the bait, 10–20 minutes once you have got steam up is plenty of time. A further advantage of the pressure-cooking method is that baits are much more easily prepared on the bankside provided that you have got a decent stove.

Pressure-cooking particles ensure not only are they cooked well but all of the flavour is not boiled away – definitely my favourite method of preparation.

DANGEROUS PARTICLES

One or two particles must be looked at individually as they have been labelled killers of carp. I do not altogether agree with this, provided that a code of conduct is followed.

Red Kidney Beans

These have been banned on a lot of waters because the governing bodies have had evidence that they are detrimental to the well-being of the carp. This is very true if they are only partially cooked. They need to be soaked for an absolute minimum of ten hours – longer if you have the opportunity – then boiled for a minimum of 25 minutes, better 30 or 35 minutes, or pressure-cooked for a 15–25 minutes. If this is adhered to there should be no danger to the carp.

Peanuts

The problem with the peanuts is not so much with the preparation (though of course that has got to be right) as with the quality. We experienced a period not so many years ago when some bad-quality peanuts were being brought into the country. These had been lying on the ground for quite some time and a dangerous mould started to grow, which was not easily visible to the human eye. This was called aflatoxin. Fortunately this problem seems to all but have disappeared but to make sure always ask to see the anti-aflatoxin certificate that is supplied to the sea merchant with good batches of peanuts.

Almonds

The problem with almonds is quite simply that they do go off very quickly. Particles that are rank are very often quite attractive to the carp, but not so almonds. Where overbaiting has taken place and the almonds have lain around for several weeks they really are quite horrible. I must say that I am of the strong belief that when they are like this the carp don't pick them up anyway and eventually they will decompose and become part of the lake's natural food chain for other organisms. However, it should be said that this is not a desirable situation and should be avoided at all costs. I can't believe anyone wants to see beds of rotting particles lying around in the margins.

FLAVOURING

Although most particles will have their own individual flavours, which contribute to their success, there are one or two that benefit from a boost of extra flavouring and below are some examples. Dun peas for example, certainly take on savoury flavours very well. Whether you use a concentrated flavour – such as blue cheese, walnut and nutmeg – or add a packeted soup mix, you will find that their attractiveness level is increased. Soya beans can be treated in the same way, and black-eyed beans and haricot beans benefit from being boiled up in tomato soup. Blue peas and chick peas seem to take sweet flavours more readily. Butterscotch, tutti frutti and strawberry jam are my favourites for these two peas. Some liquid sweetener will also give an extra little boost. Most flavour companies give recommended dosage on the label, say 10ml to every pound of dry mix. Though primarily intended for powdered boilie mixes, the same rate is suitable for dehydrated particle seeds. With soups, the packeted powdered varieties can be used at one sachet for every 2lb dry weight of particles, and tins at a rate of one medium tin again to 2lb of dry weight.

COLOURS

It is only on the hardest of waters that colour seems to make much difference. Light-coloured particles fished over a dark bottom could well, spook wary carp, but in the main I am sure that carp are drawn to the particles by smell rather than by sight. If you do come across such wary fish, light-coloured particles such as lima beans, sweet lupins, chick peas, soya beans, dun peas and haricot beans can all be coloured to make them less obtrusive. Use good-quality salt-based dyes when colouring the particles, and only at the minimum recommended dose.

FERMENTATION

Many particles gain extra appeal once they start to ferment. Maples, lupins, maize and tick beans are prime examples (but don't forget what I said about rank almonds). Once they have been correctly prepared I like to leave them in sealed buckets, ensuring that there is at least a couple of inches of water covering them. Depending on weather conditions, these can be left for two or three days until a chemical reaction starts to take place. When the water starts to go milky and the particles give off a distinct aroma they are just right for use. If they are left too long a mould will start to develop on the surface. The baits are now past their best and should not be used.

Tiger nuts start to ferment in a slightly different way. Sugars within are converted and the water in which they are soaking is converted into a sweet, sticky liquid. Again depending on weather conditions, this will take a couple of days after the initial cooking. Carp respond in a very different way to fermented tigers from freshly cooked ones, homing in on the baited area at a great rate of knots.

PREBAITING

I have seen some absolutely extraordinary prebaiting campaigns carried out where particles are concerned. In deed, I have to admit that I too have fallen foul of this temptation. Because we are introducing a slightly alien food into the carp's environment it might be thought that a period of introduction would be necessary for the carp to get used to the new bait. In recent years I have completely changed my ideas about this and these days I never bother about prebaiting with particles at all. What I do occasionally do is bait up an area consistently if I want the carp to keep visiting it once they have found this new food larder. To prebait with a new particle for the sake of recognition is just not necessary, and in fact it could do more harm than good. This is because whilst the life expectancy of most particles is extremely long the initial reaction is often phenomenal and is not repeated. Carp continue to accept them with gay abandon but they almost seem to get used to them and they get rather less excited as time goes by.

With prebaiting the initial impact might well be lost. To give an example of this, a couple of years ago I fished a French water that I know had never ever seen tiger nuts and I caught fish within two hours of introducing them. That week was one of those weeks to remember: I caught many fish with apparent ease. This information was passed on to two or three of my close friends, who repeated the performance in much the same way. But after about four months of fishing with the tigers the catches started to slow down to what was considered a normal level. The introduction of a new particle, sweet lupins, increased the catch rate once more. With so many particles available, it is certainly possible to keep ringing the changes to achieve good catches, especially on these naive waters where the carp have not been exposed to the extraordinary angling pressure they undergo on some of the circuit waters at home.

PREOCCUPATION

A degree of semi-preoccupation always seems to be easier to achieve when there are numbers of carp in the swim. If you have the baiting level right and have attracted a nice group of fish into the area, competition as well as preoccupation seems to occur and the carp seem to feed more eagerly in large numbers than they do singly or with only two or three fish in the swim at the same time.

The only problem with preoccupation is that it can lead to overconfident feeding, with the carp mopping up everything in sight. Baits are drawn into the mouth and thrown past the pharyngeal teeth almost as if they are on a fast conveyor belt. This often includes the hookbait as well. This situation should be avoided at all costs. Deep

hooking for the sake of catching a carp should never ever be practised. Not only can it cause unnecessary damage to the carp's internal organs, with the pressure of the hook being pulled from below the pharyngeal teeth, but in extreme cases it can lead to a bite-off.

PREVENTING DEEP HOOKING

If you do experience a bite-off (when the hook link is severed by the carp's pharyngeal teeth) or if you are getting hookholds deeper than usual (anything farther back than a couple of inches) the rig should be adjusted to alleviate such hooking. There are several ways of achieving this.

Simply increasing the thickness of the hook link and at the same time shortening it will cause the carp to feel the extra resistance before the bait is thrown right back. A 6-inch hook link of 15lb BS wiry monofilament should do the job. If the problem persists then I will introduce a frightener into the rig. This consists of a 1½–2-inch length of biro or rig tubing pushed onto the hook link as shown and fixed about 2–3 inches from the hook itself. As the carp takes, the frightener will come

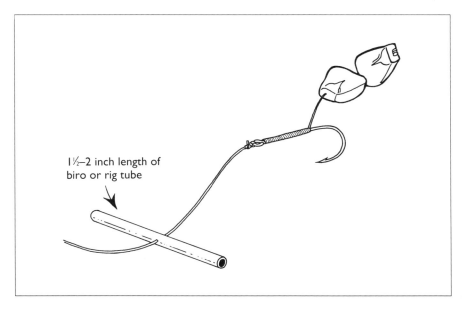

1½–2 inch length of biro or rig tube

Frightening rig.

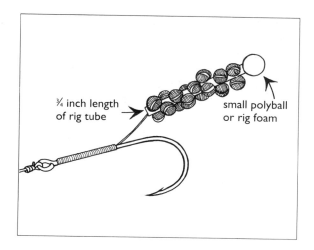

Mini seeds set-up.

up against its mouth, causing the fish to bolt and usually at the same time hooking it squarely in the corner of the lip.

SET-UPS FOR MASS BAITS

I am sure that by now many of you must be wondering how on earth to mount some of these tiny seeds on a hook or hair rig. In fact it is quite easy.

My favourite way is to superglue the mini-seeds on a short length of rig tubing about ¾ inch long. The hair is attached in the mid-shank position with about ¼ inch play between the hook and the end of the rig tube. The seeds are stuck all round the outside of the tube. If you wish you can actually stick seeds to seeds to get more on the tube. A small piece of rig foam or a polyball, which can be coloured to match the seeds, is attached to the other end of the rig tube. This has the effect of making the tube with the mounted seeds sit up perpendicular in the water, which adds to its attractiveness. On waters where the hair rig is banned the mini-seeds can be stuck to the shank of the hook itself. Do not worry if so many seeds clustered together look slightly artificial. It is virtually impossible for carp to pick up a single individual mini-particle on its own; many will be sucked into the mouth at once.

PARTICLE POP-UPS

I like virtually all of my particles to be fished in this manner. On all but the hardest of waters I am strongly of the opinion that a couple of particles suspended above the rest will often be sampled before the others that are lying around.

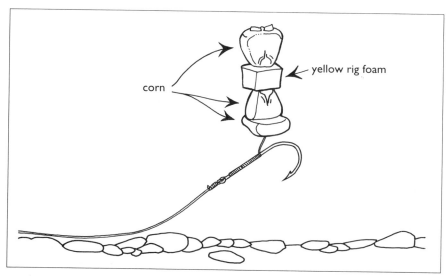

Pop-up corn rig.

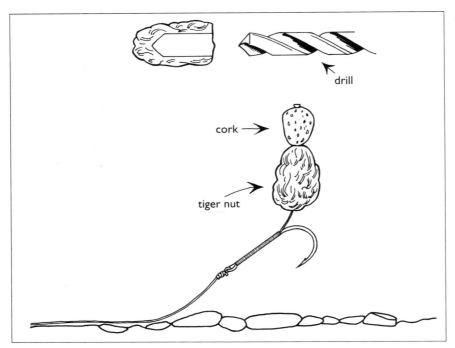

Pop-up tiger nuts rig.

Naturally, sticking up and standing out as they do they are more accessible. Here are a couple of examples of other particle pop-up rigs.

Sweetcorn or maize can be suspended as shown with the help of a small piece of yellow rig foam. This can be cut down until the rig is literally free-swimming – in other words, until it only just sinks under the weight of the hook. Alternatively, it can be given positive buoyancy by means of a larger piece of foam counterbalanced by some tungsten putty attached to the hook link so that it sits up a couple of inches off the bottom.

Tiger nuts can be made into pop-ups by drilling out the centre as shown and replacing the void that you have made with some rig foam. Another way is to cut a piece of cork to resemble a tiger nut. As cork is of similar colour and texture, it makes a natural partnership with the tiger nut. Again, buoyancy can be adjusted so that the rig only just sinks or pops up proud, counterbalanced with tungsten putty.

It's worth remembering when you are hair-mounting any flat-sided particles that they do spin like a propeller in the water. This is more evident if you mount them across the middle or

the shortest side; if you mount them longways on the hair they will spin a lot less. It can be really aggravating when you have taken some time tying up and critically balancing a rig only to find that the first time it is retrieved it ends up like a cat's cradle, so it is obviously worth paying it little thought to the matter.

WHICH PARTICLE?

Important factors in making the right choice may well be the make-up of the lake bed and the distance at which you are fishing. If you are fishing over a soft, silty bottom, flat-sided beans such as lima, pinto, red kidney beans and sweet lupins will land softly and their relatively large area in relation to their weight gives them a good chance of lying exposed just on top of the silt. The very high oil content of nuts such as brazils, almonds, cashews, pistachios, hazelnuts and peanuts is a buoyancy aid which helps touchdown softly on silty bottoms.

Hard-bottomed gravel pits are ideal for maples, tick beans, dun peas, soya beans, chick

The ultimate mass particle mix. This Heinz 57 mixture of mini seeds has often proved to be more attractive than just offering one variety on its own.

It's really the massed baits that are problematical. Something like linseed has very little weight and unless you are fishing literally under the rod tip they are a real bind to get any distance. It is here that the bait dropper comes well and truly into its own. My favourite is the Gardener Bait Rocket, described in Chapter 4. The other baiting implement which is ideal for baits any size but obviously of greater benefit with these tiny particles is the radio-controlled boat. But please refer to my comments in Chapter 4 about this slightly controversial piece of kit.

MIXED PARTICLES

All the particles described will stand up in their own right when used on their own but you can add another dimension to these fascinating baits by mixing several together. Although I occasionally mix middle-sized baits such as soya beans, dun peas and tick beans, the small mini-particles are where you can really score. One mixture I have had a great deal of success with is equal amounts of red and white millet, black and red rape seed, red and white dari seed, moth beans and hempseed – a real Heinz 57! Carp love them.

CANNED PARTICLES

So far I have considered only dehydrated particles, but there is an alternative. Some varieties can be bought ready-cooked in the can, and these are particularly suitable for anyone tempted to try this type of bait for the first time, since they at least do away with the worry of preparation. Another advantage of the canned jobs is that having a supply ready in the larder means you can be off a moment's notice without the hassle of the planning that the dried ones involve.

There is a drawback, price and availability. A lot of the bigger supermarkets carry sweetcorn, red kidney beans, black-eyed beans, pinto beans, haricot beans and a few others. They are all prepared in a nice attractive sauce, which can only enhance their effect.

peas, black-eyed beans and the like. These are all fairly dense so they will sink quite quickly and find their way between small stones and rocks where the carp love to root them out.

On very weedy waters I love to use mass particles. Any of these tiny seeds will sit in and amongst the weed and the carp will naturally forage on these areas. For areas where silty pockets lie between harder gravelly areas, mungs, tares, adzuki beans, wheat, barley, oats and groats are all useful. Distance is the second important factor in choice of particle bait. Obviously, somehow or other the particles must be delivered into the swim. The larger varieties should pose few problems since most will catapult out with relative ease, though one or two of the flat-sided beans can be a bit of a problem – not so much in distance as in accuracy. One tip when using sticky fermented particles, especially tiger nuts, is always to wet the catapult pouch between loads. This will prevent the particles from sticking to the pouch and so keep a tighter bunch and give a little more distance.

Middle-sized particles such as maples, chicks and soya beans, also catapult out very well and because they are quite dense can almost give you the same distance as larger particles.

STRIPED SUNFLOWER SEEDS   SAFFLOWER SEEDS   PINE NUTS

There are some floating particles too. Here you can see sunflower seeds, safflower seeds and pine nuts. These will not disintegrate floating on the surface for a considerable amount of time, maybe giving the carp extra time to get used to them.

FLOATING PARTICLES

A few seeds actually float on the surface because they have an air pocket trapped within the kernel. The main ones are sunflower seeds, safflower seeds and pine nuts. These have all caught carp with great success. There is one major difference between floating particles and the standard floaters that we are used to: they do not break down in the water, but just float backwards and forwards until they are eventually eaten either by the carp or by any wildfowl on the lookout for an easy meal. I cannot decide whether this is a good or a bad thing.

The best way of mounting these three floating particles is simply to superglue the seed to the back of the shank of the hook. This way they stay more buoyant than they would if they had to be

Presentation is easy – simply glue the floating seed to the back of the hook.

drilled out for hair mounting. They can be used on the controller set-ups described in Chapter 7.

I hope that this chapter will have whetted your appetite and that you will now give particle fishing a go. It is, as they say, another string to your bow.

13 CARPING ABROAD

For someone who said five years ago that I had no urge to go carping outside the United Kingdom I seem to be spending an awful lot of time behind my carp rods in foreign lands. This is a sign of the times. The fact of the matter is that there are just so many carp anglers at home with relatively few waters to service them that anglers are now looking abroad to fulfil some of their carping needs. It is said that we have more than fifty thousand regular carp anglers in the United Kingdom. That is a large number fishing for a single species. Although a large percentage of that number will be more than content to sit round busy lakes and there will be others who have the advantage of fishing small clubs or closed, private syndicates, there are many among the ranks who are always on the lookout for new ventures.

When I originally started carp fishing it was indeed rare to see another carp angler on the bank so I have been fortunate in having had three decades of progressive fishing on many different waters up and down the country, moving on from one to another as the pressure from the ever-growing band of carp anglers increased. Some five years ago I suddenly found that I was beginning to run out of waters. That's not to say that there are not any waters in here that I consider worthy of fishing; it's just that the challenge of fishing new venues overseas began to have a greater attraction.

My first encounter with carping abroad was in France and it suddenly dawned on me that here was a whole new world for the pioneering carp angler. This situation suited me completely as I always enjoy a new challenge and a chance of catching a fish that has seen neither hookbait nor angler before, let alone been given a name.

Of course I had already heard stories of the fantastic captures that had been made in France by some of my colleagues. Some of these were huge fish, almost doubling the size of anything that I had ever caught at home. I was a little worried that going to France and catching some of these monster carp would take the edge off of fishing here in England. In fact I am glad to say that I need not have worried as I still get great enjoyment out of my English carping. It's almost like fishing for two different species in two different countries and I draw very few comparisons between the two situations as they are in reality completely different.

Here we know virtually all of the waters that contain carp, and on most of them we know just how big those carp grow, how many there are and how to catch them. At the moment, with very few exceptions, carping abroad is a complete mystery and there are thousands upon thousands of venues around the world that have never ever seriously been fished for carp. It is that fact that for me offers the greatest attraction. So a forty-pound carp from England offers no more and no less enjoyment or sense of achievement than one caught anywhere else in the world.

Here we at least know, generally speaking, where to fish but abroad it's a matter of starting from scratch, for I can assure you that not every foreign carp water holds forty-pounders. So it's back to basics: find your waters, find the fish and hope to reap the rewards of positive groundwork. One thing is clear: once carp are found in an accessible fishing spot where they are happy to feed they are definitely easier to tempt than their British counterparts, simply because they have been subjected to little or no angling pressure.

FRENCH STILLWATERS

France was one of the first natural choices simply because it is so easy to get to. Car ferries across the English channel are relatively inexpensive and the journey is quick. France is a huge country compared with England and there are so many waters to choose from. Regarding the size of fish, other than a few known waters you will have to rely on local hearsay and your own feelings.

I always used to think that the farther south you went the larger the carp were, just because the temperatures are so much higher in the south of France than in the north, which means more feeding time, more food available, and, generally speaking, larger carp or so I thought. In fact, this doesn't appear to be the case at all. As more venues are discovered every year, it has now become apparent that there are huge fish in waters all over France. And the fishing isn't restricted to lakes; many of the rivers also contain a vast head of carp and there are huge sheets of water that have been artificially created by the construction of dams. These concrete walls are built across river valleys to form huge reservoirs, some of them several thousand acres in area. One or two cover more than 10,000 acres, which can be mind-blowing for an English angler on his first visit who has never before faced anything much above 100 acres.

Rules and Licences

Except on privately owned waters night fishing is prohibited throughout the whole of France. Be warned: it is not just a telling-off if you are caught – tackle can be and generally is confiscated by local police. You will also need to buy a French national licence from a local tackle shop, or from some restaurants which are often found adjacent to the water.

This licence allows you to fish with up to four rods unless otherwise stated. The licences are valid for different areas rather than the whole country, which you should definitely be aware of if you are thinking of travelling from one region to another.

Cassien

Probably the most famous venue in France is Lac de St Cassien. This has been regularly fished by English anglers since the early 1980s and has produced some truly outstanding captures. It is strongly believed by many in the know that Cassien offers the best chance of a carp breaking the mythical hundred-pound barrier. Several over seventy pounds in weight have already been caught.

This venue is also very popular with the German, Dutch and Belgian carp anglers. It has now become quite a difficult water and offers a real challenge to anyone in pursuit of megacarp. But it does get very busy for most of the summer. The night-fishing rule is now strongly enforced at St Cassien and in fact there is a band of ranger patrols to enforce it.

Salagou

Lac de Salagou is probably the next in the popularity stakes and is certainly much more heavily stocked than Cassien. I am sure that the full

Before you start fishing ensure that you are adequately equipped with appropriate licences. This will make certain that you don't have a run in with the local law which could ruin an otherwise successful holiday.

potential of this water has not yet been realised. There are so many twenties and thirties it is impossible to be selective. Undoubtedly, massive commons of more than fifty pounds do exist.

The problem with a lot of these French dammed rivers is the huge amount of snags that the angler has to encounter. When these reservoirs are created no land is cleared and the water floods trees, fences, roads and in some cases massive vineyards. Trying to extract hard-fighting fish can often be a nightmare.

Both Salagou and Cassien are in the south of France, some 700 miles or more from Calais. Whilst these two popular venues certainly have great appeal, I have no doubt that many carp of forty, fifty, sixty and who knows how many pounds are passed on the way.

FRENCH RIVERS

Many of the large rivers that run throughout France are certainly worth a look and have a sneaky feeling that this is where some of the largest carp in France are to be found. The Loire, the Seine, the Lot, the Saône, the Seille and the Tarn run for hundreds of miles and in places are wide and deep. Sixties and seventies have already been caught from some of these rivers.

TACKLE AND BAIT

The nice thing about travelling by car in France is that you can take with you all the gear needed for a week's fishing. Generally speaking, because the waters are larger and more snaggy the fish fight harder but at the same time are more naive, so much heavier tackle is required than is used at home. Rods of from 2½ to 3lb test curve matched with 15lb line and size 2 hooks are the order of the day.

Other than on waters that have already seen a fair bit of carping pressure, heavy baiting should be carried out to ensure success. Boilies are rarely successful at first. I have always found it far better to introduce particles while at the same time

baiting up with boilies so that the carp can be weaned onto them. Maize is available throughout France and costs very little. A 50-kilo bag, depending on the time of year, will only set you back about 100 francs (about £10). It should be cooked up on the bank for 15–20 minutes after being soaked in the water overnight in carp sacks. Sweet lupins are also easily obtainable and act as a good back-up to the maize.

It can be quite astonishing just how much bait you can get through during a week's intensive fishing on these waters. A recent seven-day trip to Salagou saw me using a 100 kilos of maize and about 25 kilos of boilies. While this amount is not always required, it is not at all unusual.

Generally speaking in France there is no close season, which gives English anglers visiting the country during our own close season the chance to fish all the year round. However, at certain times of the year there are areas of the water that are cordoned off for spawning. These are usually well signposted and should under no circumstances be fished. Wherever you are tempted to fish abroad please remember that you are ambassadors for your own country. Act accordingly. Don't break the laws, don't leave litter everywhere and please, please respect the countryside and the country people. Let us not queer our pitch.

HOLLAND

Holland is the next most popular country with the English angler. Again it is convenient to visit from the point of view of travel. Before you start fishing you must obtain a Dutch national licence (sportvisakte), which enables you to fish with two rods for the whole of the year. The licence is obtainable from most tackle shops or from post offices at the relatively cheap cost of about £4 at the present exchange rate.

Many waters throughout Holland can be fished on this licence alone. The vast network of canals interlinked with large lakes offers enormous variety. There are some private waters where an extra charge may be made but this is usually quite small. As in France, there is no close season in Holland, night fishing is allowed only in June, July and August. The only exceptions to this are a few private and club waters, where they seem to waive the ban outside the permitted months.

Many foreign countries will have unusual by-laws, and it always pays to find out as much as you can beforehand so as not to upset local authorities. One such law in Holland is that catapults are banned. This rule is not enforced strictly on all waters but it is on the more public ones, especially near towns.

Although there are a lot of carp anglers in Holland there are still many untapped waters. It is in many of the huge canals and vast rivers that some of the best pioneering carping can be sampled. There seems to be a profusion of 20lb-plus commons scattered throughout most Dutch waters and these are undoubtedly the biggest attraction to visiting English anglers.

Many of the canals and rivers are strewn with large mussel beds so quite heavy tackle is called for. The canals especially should be tackled with a good snag leader, as the mussels are usually to be found in abundance just on the drop-off and lines can be severed quite easily. The most frustrating thing that I have encountered on the canals and rivers are the massive ocean-going barges which at times can come through in a seemingly constant stream. The wash is such that free offerings can be moved quite some distance, leaving the angler never really knowing exactly where his freebies are. I have spoken about this problem to a few of my Dutch carp-fishing friends and the only way they can overcome it is by using quite heavy and dense boilies some 30mm in diameter which have been slightly flattened to help hold the bottom, so this is a tip worth remembering.

Quite a lot of secrecy surrounds the very large fish that have been caught from rivers such as the Meuse and Ijssel and the Rhine Canal. Certainly fifty-pounders exist in all of these waters and rumours of sixties are definitely bubbling under. As far as I know the largest that has been authenticated is 54lb.

BELGIUM

Belgium, although a very small country, has loads of very good carp waters. However, carp fishing has really taken off in the last decade and many waters now see a fair amount of pressure. A government licence must be obtained before fishing and will cost round about £6 at the current exchange rate. As in Holland, night fishing is generally allowed only during the months of June, July and August, the odd exception being private and club waters. It is essential that you find out the rules beforehand.

Boilies have been extensively used in Belgium for some time and in fact there appears to be a trend back towards particle fishing on a few of the harder waters. There are a lot of lakes in the Ghent and Brussels area and many large carp have been caught in this region. One of the largest I can find which has been fully authenticated is a big mirror of 51lb taken from a sandpit on the outskirts of Ghent.

GERMANY

We are actually quite lucky to be able to fish Germany at all for the German anglers themselves have to take an examination which includes a long written paper before a fishing licence is granted. Fortunately, foreign visitors have been excluded from this examination but they must still obtain a government licence before fishing. These are available at post offices at a cost of around £6 per year at the current rate.

Night fishing is banned by law throughout Germany. There are, however, a few private landowners who do allow it. The Green Party is very strong in Germany and they have managed to get laws passed that all fish captured should be killed, since returning them afterwards is deemed to be cruel. Now there's a contradiction in terms! Fortunately, I know a lot of German anglers and they definitely do not agree with this law. All the fish that they catch are returned without any harm caused to them whatsoever. Most German waters can be fished on a day-ticket basis, allowing two or three rods to be used at a time.

Carp seem to be plentiful throughout the whole of the country with a lot of good waters between Cologne and Frankfurt. Between Nuremberg and Regensburg is another good area. There are a few large canals containing carp as well as some very big lakes and reservoirs.

Just what is the top weight for carp in Germany is hard to ascertain but twenties and thirties seem to be fairly commonplace and many fish of 40lb-plus are caught every year. I have not been able to fully authenticate a fish of over fifty pounds but a fish in excess of that size is reputed to have been taken from the River Rhine.

FARTHER AFIELD

Spain, Portugal, Italy and Austria have all been fished by exploring British carp anglers. Just how far are people prepared to travel for their carp fishing? I believe just about anywhere.

I have reports of carp catches from all round the globe – the farthest away in Australia. A good friend of mine, Paul Gummer, lived there for a few years and in certain parts the carp are extremely well established. The problem is that locally they are treated rather as vermin, though there is a group of specialist carp anglers who are starting to change that. In fact in the last couple of years they have started to organise regular carp fish-ins.

On the other side of the Atlantic Ocean, South America, the United States and Canada all have good heads of carp. As lure fishing is the most popular style in all those countries the carp again has taken a bit of a back seat. But the spear-fishing record in America is over eighty pounds. What a way to find out that you have got a big carp!

Several anglers have already ventured out to South America in pursuit of their beloved carp. So who knows which will be the next country to figure on the carp angler's map. I have been looking at new waters around the Black Sea – in southern Russia, Romania, Bulgaria and part of Turkey. All have carp. For the last year I have been making regular trips to Bulgaria and I am confident massive carp will be taken here in the not too distant future.

PROBLEMS OF THE LONG-DISTANCE CARP FISHER

All this is a bit different from just jumping in a car with all your gear. The pioneering carp angler who has to rely on air transport to get him to his destination has to think seriously about the sort of gear he is going to take with him. I can tell you from bitter experience that the stringent baggage allowance allocated to you on most airlines can be a real nightmare. At best 20 kilos of hold luggage and 10 kilos of hand luggage is about the limit. A lot of the smaller planes allow considerably less, so you have no chance of taking thousands of boilies with you on these trips.

The best that you can do is hope that you can pick up some sort of seed particle when you get to your destination. Corn, barley and maize are grown fairly extensively around the world and all make attractive baits for the carp. With a bit of homework a few sacks can usually be purchased at a very reasonable price. These can be soaked in the margins in carp sacks and then for a few extra pennies I am confident you will be able to find someone who will boil them up for you.

I always like to take at least a couple of bags of shelf-life boilies with me and these are fished on at least one rod over the top of the bed of particles. It's strange how on some waters boilies are accepted instantly whilst on others the carp have to be weaned on to them. On one of my recent trips to Bulgaria I caught carp on boilies fifteen minutes after casting out, and that was on a water that had never been fished with rod and line, let alone with boilies.

Boats are a great asset and can often be hired locally. With very few exceptions the travelling angler is received enthusiastically by the locals, although they cannot really understand the logic behind anyone travelling so far to catch a few carp only to photograph them, give them a kiss and return them. But who ever said that carp fishing is logical?

Tackle is also a problem when flying. Until recently my normal 12- or 13- foot two-piece rods were protected by a heavy-duty drainpipe tube. That was until disaster struck when the tube had a fight with a baggage-handling conveyor, so I'm now the proud owner of three 26-piece carp rods. This completely converted me and I now use telescopic carp rods. At long last they have got these right. For so long telescopic rods were treated as a bit of a joke but I can tell you from first-hand experience that the new 12-foot Tele Specialist Carp Rod from DAM is brilliant. Three of these, a landing net, a rod pod and a specially designed two-piece landing-net pole fit into one small bag and go on board with me as hand baggage. A second piece of hand luggage contains breakables such as cameras, reels and Optonics.

I'm afraid the comforts of a good-quality bedchair have to be forgone because of the weight, and likewise the normal umbrella and bivvy setup. These are replaced with a very light weight ET bivvy dome and a pump-up lilo. These together with a light weight sleeping bag, a few items of clothing and as many boilies as I can get in to make up the rest of the baggage allowance go in a Ruck-A-Bag as hold luggage.

As airport baggage examination is tightened up, my few leger weights I put through the X-ray machine in a small pouch since they seem to send the monitoring machines into overdrive, with the assistant foraging in the bottom of your bag trying to discover what these bomb-shaped items are. So it's best to show them first and explain what they are and put them through the X- ray machine as a separate item.

THE ECHO-SOUNDER

The other thing that really gets the baggage handlers going is an echo-sounder, or fish-finder, as they are fondly known. I personally wouldn't be without one of these on my pioneering foreign trips. Although they seem to be very controversial, they are my eyes on the lake bed. Having spent a lot of money and many valuable hours travelling you really need to put a few things on your side. Imagine being confronted with a lake of say 5,000 acres. You have done your homework; you know carp exist; there are numbers of them, and of size that is going to make them interesting to catch. But where do you fish on such a huge inland sea? All the basic watercraft learned at home goes right out of the window. Some of these lakes, as well as being of an enormous acreage, are also very deep. It is not unusual to find depths of up to 150 feet. Carp just do not act in the same way on these waters as they do in our much shallower, smaller venues.

I have converted my landing net pole by spiggoting the two pieces together so that it is now short enough to take on board the aircraft as hand luggage.

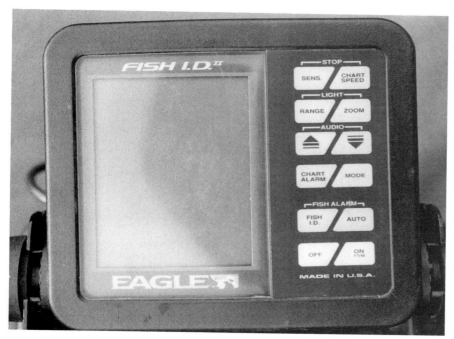

A controversial piece of equipment on my trips abroad, this Echo-Sounder is my eyes on the lake bed. Although it will locate fish I am far more concerned about the topography of the water. Some of these foreign lakes are huge by our standards. The Sounder lets me get to know them far more quickly.

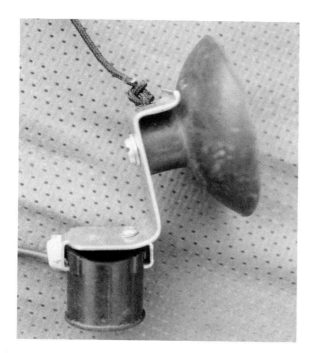

The Echo-Sounder's Transjuicer. This has a rubber sucker that can be attached to the bottom of the boat. This sends down the solar beam to the lake's bed.

At one time I was convinced that the carp rarely fed at depths of more than about 30 feet and with very few exceptions that is probably true of British waters. But foreign carp are different animals altogether. My first encounter with deep-feeding carp was in the south of France, when I was fishing Lac de St Cassien.

I had seen fish crashing around in the north arm. This had been happening on a regular basis over a couple of days and it was obviously too much for me not to investigate. This I did and I was staggered to find out that the area where the fish were heaving themselves from the water was 150 feet deep. Although the carp were not going right down to the bottom I was able to plot some of their movements on the echo-sounder and without exception they were all swimming in a band of water some 45–55 feet from the surface. I just couldn't imagine what sort of food life could be living at that depth, or indeed whether the fish were really feeding at all. But a few days later I was rewarded with a take from a bait that had been presented in 52 feet of water and the result was a 40lb-plus carp. That was a real eye-opener. If I hadn't seen it with my own eyes I would have been slightly sceptical if that story had been related to me.

In further overseas experiences on similar waters I have found the same situation has been repeated. In fact, even in the height of summer when the shallower water warms up considerably, there are certain lakes where the carp prefer to frequent a band 40–60 feet deep. The greatest depth I have caught a carp at is 57 feet; the deepest I have seen them show up on the echosounder is 65 feet, though I can't be absolutely certain that they were carp. They were certainly big fish, but they might have been catfish.

The portable echo-sounder that I use is an Eagle which is lightweight and runs either on two 6-volt bell-type batteries or on a larger 12-volt car battery. This is ideal as dry-cell batteries are often

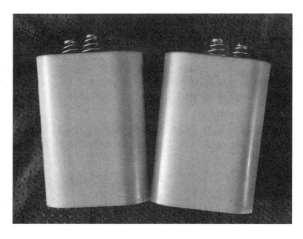

The power supply for running the Echo-Sounder – two dry-cell 6-volt batteries. Alternatively, it could be wired up directly to a 12-volt electric outboard motor battery but I personally prefer to keep them separate.

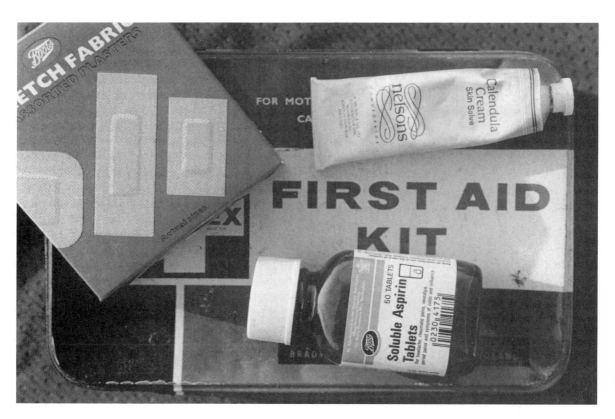

It's always advisable to take a first aid kit when fishing abroad. You could be miles from anywhere – a small cut could quickly turn septic if not treated immediately.

These E.T. fume coils will help keep a lot of the flying nasties that lurk on the shores of many foreign lakes away from you.

Nash Buzz Off – a good quality mosquito repellent that will help to make life more comfortable.

very difficult to obtain when you are fishing abroad, whereas it's often possible to hire an old car battery locally.

As well as the obvious advantage of using the echo-sounder to locate fish, almost more important is finding an area where there is a good chance of landing them. Many of these huge waters are valleys dammed and flooded for water-supply purposes. The bottom may be a jungle of obstacles, including swamped forests and even submerged villages. Can you imagine the nightmare of fishing such an area? I like to search out the flatter, more open areas – perhaps former grazing pastures or similar. The echo-sounder makes this possible and enables the angler to assess what swims give him realistic chances of extracting fish from them.

It's rarely the case of finding an ideal spot – a great shoal of carp over an old open field with not a fence, post or tree in sight. Carp love under water obstacles – even very naive fish that have never been fished for – so it's usually a matter of finding a compromise.

Take plenty of line, hooks and swivels with you. The chances of finding a tackle shop in parts of the world that aren't heavily fished are very

Where to next!

slim. Fortunately most of these items do not weigh very much so you can stock up on the essentials. A first-aid kit and mosquito repellent also get part of my valuable baggage allowance. There are some really nasty stinging, crawling, flying, biting beasties around some of these foreign waters, but I am sure that will not put you off! For those of you travelling throughout Europe the car can be loaded to the gunwales and it's really a matter of how far you want to drive.

CONTACTS

It always pays to try and get in contact with someone near your chosen location. This can be done via the letters page in The Carp Society magazines. With so many members someone usually knows a contact near most of the waters in Europe. Those who are tempted to travel a bit further afield will find things much more difficult. I had to make three exploratory trips to Bulgaria before I cracked it, and I'm sure the same will go for Romania, Russia and beyond as I spread my wings in search of new carp to catch. The information that I have found so far has been put to good use and already back-up trips have been professionally organised for anglers seeking a chance of immediate success. Barnsley-based Anglers Abroad are specialists in organising angling holidays.

For carp fishers with the true pioneering attitude, who knows where we may next bump into each other? I have heard that one of the Indonesian islands has some good carp, and the weather is marvellous. Fancy a trip.

14 WHAT DOES THE FUTURE HOLD?

At the time of writing the British record carp stands at 51½ lb, caught by Chris Yates from Redmire Pool in 1980. This record has now stood unchallenged for over a decade. Before Chris's magnificent fish, the late father of carp angling, Richard Walker, held the record for three decades with the most famous of all carp – the 44lb common again caught from Redmire Pool. For about the last five years of the reign of Walker's 44-pounder many of us thought that his record would be toppled. But no one even in their wildest dreams thought that it would be a fish of such magnitude as Yates's. About that time there were several captures of fish between 40 and 44lb, so it was not unreasonable to expect that one of those might at some stage have slipped over the magical 44lb mark. But I am sure no one reckoned on a sudden increase to more than 50lb.

Let's have a look at the current scene and perhaps do a bit of crystal-ball gazing. Four fish of more than 45lb have been caught in the 1991–2 season. None of these fish is particularly fat, spawn-bound or of an unnatural shape. They are just very large carp. I believe that any of those four fish in the right circumstances could topple Yates's fifty. When we are talking fish of this calibre another 5lb in weight is certainly not beyond the realms of possibility. What of any uncaught monsters out there? I am sure that on some of the very large, lightly stocked gravel pits there are fish swimming around of massive proportions that have never been caught. We are not talking about lots of fish, just a very small handful up and down the country.

One of the four fish over 45lb was a new fish this season – Pete Springate's Wraysbury 45lb 6oz mirror from Wraysbury. This was from a typical very rich, lightly stocked large pit, where the carp have grown to immense proportions with no influence from the carp angler. If the record is broken within the next five years, as I think it will be, I doubt whether there will be such a staggering increase as there was between Walker's fish and Yates's. It's more likely to be an odd couple of pounds or maybe just ounces. But it's certainly on the cards – more a question of when than if.

IMPORTED CARP

There is another situation in which the record could be broken tomorrow, and by a fish well in excess of 50lb. I hope this never happens as it will be a fish that has been imported from abroad. We are at present on the threshold of a situation that could change the face of carp fishing for ever in this country. I know I wax lyrical about foreign carp but I think that foreign carp should stay in foreign lands where they have grown to the proportions their environment allows. To start bringing fish into this country that have grown to, say, 60 or even 70lb and put them in a small environment unnatural to them, where they will probably be caught instantly, and would destroy our carping heritage.

Those who see an opportunity for making a quick buck argue that since the carp are not indigenous to the British Isles there is no harm in introducing giant carp from abroad. What these people fail to understand is that massive carp have never been introduced here; the big fish that are to be found have grown on and become as much a part of the modern angling scene in Britain as any other native fish.

The restrictions on the importation of foreign carp could be lifted at any moment and the floodgates would be open, allowing a stream of large carp to be transferred from across the Channel. I hope that anglers here will unite and boycott these imports in order to protect our heritage. One way to help is to join The Carp Society. Its members are fully committed to preventing the importation of fish. So help give weight to the cause. We really must stop any attempt to bring large, artificial record fish into British waters.

THE CARP SOCIETY

The Carp Society is the one body that is looking towards the future of carp fishing. With so many carp anglers, tighter controls are needed on fish movements even within the country itself, on the well-being of the carp, and on exactly what are the right and wrong methods and baits for catching them.

The society has issued a code of conduct which gives all would-be carp anglers firm guidelines on the proper attitude to our beloved fish. Furthermore, they have already secured waters for the exclusive fishing of their members, including the most famous water of all, Redmire Pool. For many years while it was under a tight syndicate regime I tried time after time to fish this famous water, without success. For those of us who have carp angling in our blood it has to be one of our dreams to fish this Mecca of British carp fishing. Since the Carp Society has secured rights to the water my dream has been fulfilled, and I am sure that goes for hundreds of others too. As well as Redmire they have Yew Tree Lake in Norfolk and look all set to purchase the famous Horseshoe Lake in Gloucestershire. They are a forward-thinking group, always on the lookout for new ventures, and I am proud to be part of the organisation. Magazines and conferences provide a forum where major issues can be discussed, catches reminisced on, and up-and-coming newcomers can be entertained by the top carpers in the country.

The Carp Society, a marvellous organisation that every serious carp angler should be proud to belong to.

EVERYDAY CARPING

Apart from monster record carp, what is the future for more everyday carping? Quite honestly, I believe we have never had it so good and save for some unforeseen disaster it can only get better. More and more carp waters open every year and they are spreading throughout the whole of the country. Good carp waters now exist even in the far north of England and into Scotland.

THE MATCH SCENE

Carp anglers are also enjoying a spin-off from the match-angling fraternity, for there is a current trend to match-fish for small carp. The attraction is that our quite hardy creatures will feed on most baits and are probably the least affected by changing climatic conditions, which makes them a desirable fish to stock into match waters. Most of the fish introduced are of a young, fast-growing strain, usually between 4 ounces and a couple of pounds in weight. These are quite manageable on the light lines and small hooks used by our match-fishing friends.

On many lakes they don't stay that size for ever, often growing on quite quickly. On waters which are regularly match-fished, in addition to the natural food supply the matchmen's bait gives an enormous boost to the larder. Soon these fast-growing fish become a little too unmanageable for the matchman's light-line tactics and then either they are moved to other waters where the specialist carp angler can catch them or further smaller stocks are introduced.

There are several waters around the country where both the matchman and the carp angler can fish side by side on heavily stocked waters. On my own patch, the famous Willow Park is a premier match venue with a lot of major competitions held there every year. Most winning match weights, feature several of the smaller carp, but on that same water upper doubles are in abundance with quite a few twenty-pounders. The best of these larger fish is now about 26lb, which makes the fishery desirable for both the match angler and specialist carper alike. Similar venues are Layer Pits, near Colchester, and Broadwater Lake, near Godalming. Both are regularly match-fished and both produce specimen carp to over 20lb. These are just three of many examples and, provided that a balance can be achieved so that stock levels do not become too demanding for the water, they make very attractive fisheries and I can see many, many more of them springing up all over the country in the foreseeable future.

RESERVOIRS

One type of water that I am surprised hasn't been capitalised on is our vast network of reservoirs. The few that have been stocked with carp have been amazingly successful and there are one or two around the Walthamstow area where thirty-pounders are now being caught regularly. These vast concrete bowls are ideal for stocking with fast-growing carp – the wide open spaces let the light in and allow a rich food chain to develop very quickly. The carp can graze on this and grow very fast. I am sure that many more reservoirs could be stocked. Not only are they capable of accommodating many hundreds of anglers; they could well take the pressure off some of the more overfished known waters around the country.

The environment in these reservoirs is obviously ideal: the few carp that have found their way into one or two of the trout reservoirs have grown on to large proportions in a relatively short period. So, who knows? Perhaps there is a giant living the life of Riley in one of these massive trout reservoirs.

RIVERS

Rivers, for the most part either forgotten or largely neglected, present almost the final frontier for the exploring carp angler in the United Kingdom. Many British rivers hold good stocks of good-size carp, yet in the main they are ignored. In some respects I can understand this, as carp fishing here is all but synonymous with still waters and bivvying up behind multiple rods. Running water is more problematic and just doesn't lend itself to the session-type fishing that has almost become a custom. Some anglers, of course, are already having a crack at rivers, but they are so far in the minority. The full potential of carp in our river systems has by no means been completely realised. The River Trent has probably seen the most attention and has already produced fish of more than thirty pounds. Anglers in the know are convinced that a forty-pounder is only just round the corner.

Each river and almost each section of any river appears to fish completely differently. There are very few set rules with river carp, and they are amazingly nomadic. It seems that no amount of baiting will hold them in one spot; when they have an urge to move they will do so regardless, often several miles at a time. Until recently I firmly believed that carp stayed between locks and weirs, and what appeared to be localised populations seemed to endorse that opinion, but a season or so ago while fishing my local River

Not your normal carp venue and you certainly won't find many bivvys here. Although the largest carp I have taken from this insignificant little stretch of water is only 16½ lb it does offer the ultimate in peace and quiet. This is one of the best opportunities for the angler to get away from it all.

Thames I caught a carp two sections away from where I had caught it the previous season. That fish had to negotiate two locks or two weirs to move to the new area.

How often that happens I have no idea and what might make them want to confront the hazards of such a journey only they know. But what I can tell you is that that was not an isolated case: a couple of my friends have experienced the same thing. Like the Trent, the Thames has already produced thirty-pounders. In fact the largest that has been authenticated was not far short of 40lb, so its pedigree speaks for itself.

On these larger-type rivers – such as the Thames, the Trent and the Medway, which all contain a good head of carp – there are many other problems. Boat traffic can be a real nightmare. In the height of the summer it can be almost non-stop, and even through the night boats will still be passing to and fro, especially at weekends.

Location

Virtually any out-of-the-ordinary obstruction – bridges, weirs and locks – are the first spots that should be investigated. The confluences of smaller rivers and outfall pipes from factories are all worth looking for. Don't think just because carp are normally associated with still, quiet waters that they will not be found in the faster, more turbulent parts of the river. I have caught carp right under the sill of large weirs, areas that you might think more suitable for barbel.

Visual location during the daytime, unless you are on a very quiet part of the river, is very difficult. On the bigger rivers I like to walk the banks between midnight and first light. This is often the quietest period from the point of boat traffic, and carp can easily be heard heaving themselves from the water. Once I have located carp I fish for them until the action peters out, and then the process starts over again. Sometimes it may take several weeks to relocate a shoal of moving fish so it's something you really have to work hard on to ensure success.

Baits

Baits for river carp are another peculiar thing. On some waters they accept boilies instantly while on others even after months of prebaiting they still take them only reluctantly. The two extremes are best illustrated by the Thames and the Trent. Trent carp seem to respond almost immediately to boilies, and at the moment it seems the more the better – they just can't get enough of them. But on the Thames of all the carp I have caught over the years less than five per cent have fallen to boilies, and not for the want of trying. Sweetcorn, hemp and casters have accounted for most of the fish in the Thames, with the odd few fish taken on surface-fished crust when I've occasionally found them cruising near the top.

Set-Ups

The rod-end set-up can also look a little alien compared with the more traditional stillwater methods. On both the Thames and the Trent and to some degree, but not quite so much, on the Medway, many of the lightly fished swims are on the far bank or against bridge pillars in the middle of the river. Here the angler is confronted with faster, streamier water between him and his quarry. Obviously, the normal carping methods, with rods fished low hand bail arms open, are useless. Rods are held high in the air, sometimes in an almost vertical position, with the line held tight in a clip or with a heavy-tension free spool or baitrunner system. It may well take 4oz of lead to make sure that the bait is presented correctly – all very different from fishing for their stillwater cousins.

On the Trent and the Medway it seems that carp can be caught through most hours of the day and night (where night fishing is allowed) but on the Thames, except the odd fish taken in daylight hours on the top, all of my fish have come at night. This applies even on the quietest parts of the river. I can't find any rhyme or reason for this but it is a fact.

Smaller Streams

It's not just in the big river systems that carp can be found. Lots of tiny, insignificant pieces of water, resembling brooks more than rivers, also contain carp. Many of these small streams and backwaters contain carp only at certain times of the year. These tend to be the most nomadic fish of all, and return to a larger river as water levels rise and fall.

The best thing of all about these very small venues is that I have found that the carp in them can be caught more easily. Generally speaking, I would approach them in chub-fishing style, with stalking rod, landing net and a pocket of bits. Baits are also kept very simple: a few lobworms and a loaf of bread are the order of the day. Miles of river can be covered by this stalking, wandering method. Odd fish can be picked up here and there and when you find them it is usually in small groups up to about half a dozen. With a bit of stealth the largest member of the group can be targeted. It's quite amazing just where these small-stream carp can be found: sections of river no more than 4 or 5 feet wide, with only just enough water to cover their backs, often contain fish. But it's very much a case of here today and

gone tomorrow, so there is definitely no bivvying up in your favourite swim.

I have yet to catch a twenty in a small stream. Generally speaking, I would expect to find singles and doubles. They are good fun and hard-fighting. I am sure a twenty will turn up one day on an insignificant little stretch of water but until then it is enough just to wander up and down catching the odd fish on banks that are not packed out.

River fishing might not suit everyone. In fact I'm sure it won't. But if you are looking for a new challenge I don't think you will be disappointed.

CANALS

The only other waters that may have been overlooked are canals, though I get a feeling that even these are gaining in popularity. Clubs have now stocked many canals with carp (in some respects this is a similar situation to the specialist match venues mentioned above). Small carp up to a couple of pounds have been introduced to boost match weights. These have now grown on and are being targeted by a few specialist carpers. Fish of more than thirty pounds have already been taken, so who knows what the upper limit is for these canal fish?

I only hope that the matchmen don't get too fed up of being continually smashed by these heavyweights and that they are subsequently removed. At present they offer yet another alternative to what is considered the normal type of carp water.

So there we have it – the future looks rosy for the ever-growing band of carp anglers. Those who want to fish traditional waters – other than small syndicates or exclusive clubs – will be sharing their fishing. For others who want to get away from it all rivers and canals could well be the answer. The main thing is to enjoy what you are doing and look after our carp-fishing heritage. At times it has teetered on a knife edge.

And, as they say, 'take only memories and leave only footsteps'. Good carping!

FURTHER READING

Angler's Mail, King's Reach Tower, Stamford Street, London SE1 9LS.

Angling Times, Bretton Court, Peterborough PE3 8DZ.

Big Carp, 65 The Quantocks, Flitwick, Bedfordshire.

Big Fish World, Sandholme Grange, Newport, Nr. Brough, North Humberside HU15 2QE.

Carp Fisher, The Carp Society, 33 Hainault Road, Ilford, Essex IG6 3AZ.

Carp World, Angling Publications, 1 Grosvenor Square, Sheffield S2 4MS.

Coarse Fisherman Metrocrest Ltd., 67 Tyrell Street, Leicestershire LE3 5SB.

David Hall's Coarse Fishing, 60 Hillmorton Road, Rugby, Warwickshire CV22 5AF.

BOOKS

Bailey, John, *Carp—The Quest for the Queen* (Crowood).

Batten, Dave, *An Introduction to Carp Fishing* (Crowood).

Cottam, Bill, and Paisley, Tim, *Carp In Depth Series: Carp Baits* (Angling Publications).

Cundiff, Julian, *Carp In Depth Series: Carp Waters* (Angling Publications).

Davies-Patrick, Tony, *Big Fish in Foreign Waters* (Angling Publications).

Harry, John, *Savay* (Harry/Hawkins/Hucksters).

Hilton, Jack, *Quest For Carp* (Pelham Books).

Gibbinson, Jim, *Big Water Carp* (Beekay).

Hutchinson, Rod, *Carp Now and Then* (Beekay).

Hutchinson, Rod, *The Carp Strikes Back* (Wonderdog Publications).

Hutchinson, Rod, *Rod Hutchinson's Carp Book* (Hudson–Chadwick Publishing).

Little, Andy, *Angler's Mail Guide to Big Carp Fishing* (Hamlyn).

Little, Andy, *My Passion for Carp* (Beekay).

Maddocks, Kevin, *Carp Fever* (Beekay).

Maddocks, Kevin, *The Beekay Guide to 1000 Carp Waters* (Beekay).

Maylin, Rob, *Tiger Bay* (Beekay).

Maylin, Rob, *Carp* (Beekay).

Paisley, Tim, *Big Carp* (Crowood).

Paisley, Tim, *Carp Season* (Angling Publications).

Paisley, Tim, *Carp Fishing* (Crowood).

Skoyles, Brian, *Carp In Depth Series: Floater Fishing* (Angling Publications).

Stritton, Derek, *Carp In Depth Series Carp Waters* (Angling Publications).

Tomkins, Alan, *Carp In Depth Series Rigs and End Tackle* (Angling Publications).

Townley, Ken, *Carp In Depth Series Tackle and Tactics* (Angling Publications).

Various Authors, *For the Love of Carp* (The Carp Society).

Yates, Chris, *Casting at the Sun* (Pelham Books).

USEFUL ADDRESSES

NATIONAL RIVER AUTHORITIES

Anglian Region

Kingfisher House
Goldhay Way
Goldhay
Peterborough PE2 OZR
Tel: 0733 371811.

Northumbria Region

Eldon House
PO Box 4
Regent Centre
Gosforth
Newcastle-Upon-Tyne NE3 3UD
Tel: 091 213 0266.

North-West Region

PO Box 12
Richard Fairclough House
Knutsford Road
Latchford
Warrington WA4 1HG
Tel: 0925 53999.

Severn Trent Region

Sapphire East
550 Streetsbrook Road
Solihull
B91 1QT
Tel: 021 711 2324.

Southern Region

Guildbourne House
Chatsworth Road
Worthing
West Sussex BN11 1LD
Tel: 0903 820692.

South-West Region

Manley House
Kestrel Way
Exeter EX2 7LQ
Tel: 0392 444000.

Thames Region

2nd Floor, Kings Meadow House
Kings Meadow Road
Reading RG1 8DQ
Tel: 0734 535515.

Welsh Region

Rivers House
St. Mellons Business Park
St. Mellons
Cardiff CF3 0LT
Tel: 0222 770088.

Wessex Region

Rivers House
East Quay
Bridgwater
Somerset TA6 4YS
Tel: 0278 457333.

Yorkshire Region

21 Park Square South
Leeds LS1 2QG
Tel: 0532 440191.

OTHER ADDRESSES

Dr Bruno Broughton
(Fishery Management)
27 Ashworth Avenue
Ruddington
Nottingham NG11 6GD
Tel: 0602 841703.

The Carp Society
33 Covert Road
Hainault
Ilford
Essex IG6 3AZ.

Publicity
Maurice Steeles
PO Box 54
Northolt
Middlesex.

Publications
Dennis Johncock
PO Box 153
52 Station Road
West Drayton
Middlesex.

Redmire Pool
Les Bamford
PO Box 1805
London.

A.C.A. (Angler's Co-operative
Association)
23 Castegate
Grantham
Lincolnshire.

Anglers Abroad
Tim Meadows
6 Park Street
Wombwell
Barnsley
South Yorkshire S73 0DJ
Tel: 0226 751704.

Geoff Shaw's French Carp Trips
Tel: 0268 690844.

BAIT AND TACKLE DEALERS

Hinders of Swindon (Particles)
Ermin Street
Stratton St Margaret
Swindon
Wiltshire SN3 4NJ
Tel: 0793 825372.

John E. Haith (Particles)
Park Street
Cleethorpes
South Humberside DN35 7NF.

Streamselect Ltd. (Richworth
    Boilies)
Island Farm Avenue
West Molesey
Surrey
KT8 OU2.

Crafty Catcher Products (Boilies)
28 The Cotes
Soham
Cambridgeshire CB7 STU.

Carpbuster Baits (Ingredients)
25 Fox Lane
Keston
Kent BR2 6AL.

Nutrabaits (Ingredients)
25–27 Fife Street
Wincobank
Sheffield S9 1NN.

Premier Baits (Ingredients)
15 Blenheim Close
Pysons Industrial Estate
Broadstairs
Kent CT10 2YF.

Rod Hutchinson's Fishing
    Developments
Redburne Road
Louth
Lincs.

DAM (UK) Ltd.
29 Dunlop Road
Hunt End
Redditch
Worcestershire B97 5XP.

Cobra Products
73 Paines Lane
Pinner
Middlesex HA5 3BX.

Daiwa Sports Ltd.
Netherton Industrial Estate
Wishaw
Lanarks ML2 0EY.

Drennan International Ltd.
Leopold Street Works
Oxford
Oxon OX4 1PJ.

E.T. Fishing Products
Unit 72, French & Jupps Maltins
    Industrial Estate
Stanstead Abbotts
Ware
Hertfordshire SG12 6HG.

Fox International
Fowler Road
Hainault Industrial Estate
Hainault
Essex 1G6 3UT.

Gold Label Tackle (Terry
    Eustace)
2c Beech Road
Erdington
Birmingham B23 5QN.

Kryston Advanced Angling
    Products
Bolton Enterprise Centre
Washington Street
Bolton BL3 5EY.

Magnum Stainless
14 Lyndhurst
Blackwater
Camberley
Surrey.

Middy Tackle International Ltd.
34 Brook Road
Rayleigh
Essex SS6 7XN.

Partridge of Redditch
Mount Pleasant
Redditch
Worcestershire BN7 4JE.

Roberts Fishing Tackle
    Developments (John Roberts)
102 Minster Road
Westgate On Sea
Kent CT8 8DG.

Shimano UK Ltd.
Unit B2, Lakeside Technology
Park, Phoenix Way
Swansea Enterprise Park
Llansamlet
Swansea SA7 9EH.

Solar Tackle
35 Sutherland Road
Belverdere
Kent DA17 6JR.

EUROPEAN TOURIST OFFICES

FRANCE
French Government Tourist
    Office
178 Piccadilly
London W1V 0AL
Tel: 071 491 7622.

HOLLAND
Netherland Board of Tourism
25–28 Buckingham Gate
London SW1E 6LD
Tel: 071 630 0451.

BELGIUM
Belgium Tourist Office
Premier House
2 Gayton Road
Harrow
Middlesex
Tel: 081 861 3300

GERMANY
German Tourist Office
Nightingale House
65 Curzon Street
London W1Y 7PE
Tel: 071 495 3990

SPAIN
Spanish Tourist Office
57–58 St James Street
London SW1A 1LD
Tel: 071 499 0901.

INDEX